Ellery Queen's
LOST LADIES

Edited by Ellery Queen
and Eleanor Sullivan

In this intriguing anthology of stories by some of our best writers – Stanley Ellin, Isaac Asimov, Ursula Curtiss, Shirley Jackson, and many others – the central characters are women ... women who are lost literally or figuratively. Some disappear, some just become disillusioned, some are hurt by love while others are saved by love. The stories are sometimes amusing, sometimes scary, but always fascinating.

Ellery Queen's

Lost

Ladies

Edited by
ELLERY QUEEN and
ELEANOR SULLIVAN

John Curley & Associates, Inc.
South Yarmouth, Ma.

Library of Congress Cataloging in Publication Data

Main entry under title:
Ellery Queen's lost ladies.

   Orginally published: New York, N.Y.: Dial Press:
Davis Publications, 1983.
    1. Detective and mystery stories, American.
2. Detective and mystery stories, English.
3. Women—Fiction.   4. Large type books.
I. Queen, Ellery.   II. Sullivan, Eleanor.
III. Title: Lost ladies.
[PS648.D4E3857 1985]   813′.0872′08   84–20014
ISBN 0–89340–878–6 (lg. print)

Published in Large Print by arrangement with Davis
Publications, Inc.

Distributed in the U.K. and Commonwealth by Magna
Print Books.

Printed in Great Britain

COPYRIGHT NOTICES AND ACKNOWLEDGMENTS

v

vi

The Way Out by Edward D. Hoch; © 1971 by Edward D. Hoch; reprinted by permission of the author.

Just Like the Old Days by Anthony Bloomfield; © 1977 by Anthony Bloomfield; reprinted by permission of Harold Ober Associates, Inc.

The Tomato Man's Daughter by Joyce Harrington; © 1975 by Joyce Harrington; reprinted by permission of the author.

Contents

Ellery Queen's
Lost Ladies

Introduction

In their separate battles for survival, women and men often find themselves defining the differences between the sexes – sometimes after it's too late. This latest anthology from Ellery Queen consists of 23 moving, sometimes amusing, sometimes horrifying stories about women who are lost, literally or figuratively, in worlds they have chosen or been trapped into.

You will find a surprising number of variations on the theme of this collection. Absences that make the heart grow fonder, others that make the heart grow fearful. Women scorned, disillusioned, bitter, victimized. Naive women and sophisticated women, women suddenly in trouble and women with a death wish. Women who are hurt by love as well as women who are saved by love – for what is lost can, as we know, be found, just as what is seemingly lost may not be lost at all.

In reading about these various lost ladies, note how their surroundings, attitudes, and problems reflect the times in which their stories were written (the copyright dates on pages v and vii will help verify your guesses). Read and discover. Detect, learn, and uncover. And be assured that women are not alone in occasionally vanishing without a trace. The next Ellery Queen anthology will be entitled *Ellery Queen's Lost Men*.

ROBERT TWOHY

Goodbye to Francie

Francie would like a picture of him, with a dashing little beard, to put on the mantel in her apartment – with an inscription: *All love to Francie from John.* John Wendle smiled.

He said at dinner to Leona, his leathery, rawboned wife, "I've been thinking of growing a beard."

She squinted her small, pale-blue eyes and considered him. "Turn your head. Hmm. Yes, it might be quite artistic. Fitting, too, for a young playwright. Well-groomed beards are in fashion now."

He spent the next three weeks growing a beard. That was about all he did – lie on the couch in his downstairs study and let his beard grow.

He neglected to work on his play. But that was all right, he hadn't worked on his play for months – in fact, since he had married Leona a year and a half ago. There wasn't any particular need to, and Leona didn't mind. She could still haul him around to her

3

friends' parties and show him off as her husband, the playwright. He had had a play produced once. He could write or not, as he pleased; his main duty, as far as Leona was concerned, was to be witty and charming at social functions so that she would be the envy of the ladies of her social set who had lost husbands, never snagged them, or become bored with the ones they had.

So long as he was punctilious about this duty his time was his own, and Leona would continue to replenish the fairly sizable sum she had deposited in his bank account at the time of their marriage.

So John lay around, letting his beard grow and thinking of Francie – and the month of April passed.

The costume-maker knew John professionally – he had become acquainted with him during the years before his marriage when John was doing little-theater writing and acting in San Francisco. The costume-maker worked from his fusty old flat on Fulton street, near the Park. He was over seventy, retired, cantankerous, solitary, and he hated radio, TV, and newspapers.

He had John sit on a chair that had been old when John was born, then he turned a bright light on him and with thumb and forefinger twisted John's bearded face this way and that. "Yes, I can duplicate it."

"Exact shade and everything?"

"I said so, didn't I?"

"And no danger it would fall off? I mean if, say, a woman should stroke it?"

"If a woman yanked at it she could pull it off. Not otherwise."

John had three modeling sittings, and then he had his false beard, an exact duplicate of the one that sprouted naturally from his chin and cheeks, with plenty of adhesive material and clear instructions as to how to put it on and take it off.

He drove back to Marlborough, which was the town in which Leona had lived for more than twenty years, since her first marriage – which had ended five years ago with the death of her first husband, whose heart had not been able to take the excitement of several million dollars. The house was a reasonably tasteful pink stone one, two stories, on a good street of widely scattered demi-estates. There were no servants. Leona enjoyed doing her own housework, charging about with vacuum cleaner and mop, slashing rosebushes in the back yard, and preparing large and uneventful meals in the modern electric kitchen.

John parked the foreign sports car she had

given him as a wedding present next to her three-year-old convertible. She was hosing the walk. She greeted him amiably, not suspicious or even much interested as to where he had spent the day. His time was his own – except for duty time. She wasn't worried about him. She knew that he was too aware of the good things that had come into his life to jeopardize them by uncircumspect behavior. A little hanky-panky on the side – she could tolerate it, if it came to that. But nothing serious – no scandal, nothing for her friends to giggle about behind her back. She trusted John; she knew that whatever he did would be done with discretion.

She watched him go into the house, a small light-boned man, brown-eyed, graceful in his impeccable jacket and slacks, with his soft brown hair and beard. She smiled, considering her good fortune. Who would have imagined that at forty-five she could have run down such a good-looking young one?

On May fourth John drove to a two-story modern apartment building in Pine City, fifteen miles south of Marlborough on the San Francisco peninsula. There was a swimming pool, and some lithe brown

6

bodies, male and female, were attractively arranged around it.

John looked approvingly and some of the females looked approvingly back at this slim, neat, attractively bearded young man who had appeared at the entrance to the enclosed court area.

John found the door marked Manager and knocked. A fiftyish man in khaki shorts, with lean muscular arms and legs and a pot-belly, appeared.

John said, "You have an apartment for rent?"

"I do. Number Twenty-nine."

It was on the upper floor, off an open balcony that looked over the court area and pool. Furnished, one bedroom, modern kitchen – no children or pets, said the manager.

John asked the rent. They returned to the manager's apartment to complete the deal.

The manager said, "Just you and the wife, huh?" He had noted John's wedding ring.

"That's right. She's a TV actress, on location in Los Angeles."

"Really? That's interesting. We have all kinds of interesting young people here. Airline stewardesses, nurses, a few medical students, advertising men, salesmen – we're a real lively bunch." He winked.

7

John made an appreciative sound and took cash from his wallet.

The manager, potbelly resting against his desk, peered at his receipt pad, pen poised. "Name?"

"John Watson."

"And your wife's name? That's for the label on the mailbox."

John hesitated. "She goes under the name of Francie Scott."

"Scott?"

"Yes. That's her stage name." John put a cigarette in his lips, frowning down at the match he held to it.

The manager eyed him. "Does she use the name Watson at all?"

"Well, not very often."

"I see." The ballpoint tapped the desk. "It's just that it might look a little funny on the mailbox – John Watson and Francie Scott, in the same apartment. Couldn't we call you John and Francie Watson?"

"Well – she might miss some mail that way."

"Then how about John Watson and Francie Scott Watson?"

John shrugged. "All right. If you want it that way."

The problem solved, the manger got up and gave John keys. He was now expansive,

8

the genial host. "Have a shot." He got a bottle and glasses.

"What do *you* do, Mr. Watson? You in TV, too?"

"No, I sell dental supplies. I'm on the road quite a lot."

They finished their drinks. The manager said, "Come on out. I'll introduce you around."

John looked at his watch. "Thanks, but I've got to run. I have an appointment."

The manager stood at his door, looking after John. One of the men by the pool drifted over. "New tenant, Burt?"

"Yeah. Nice clothes, huh? That lad's got loot."

"What's his name?"

"Says its Watson, so it's Watson as far as I'm concerned. Says he's a salesman. Moving in with his wife, only she isn't."

"How do you know?"

"I know." He winked. "I've been in this business too long. She's some chick he has on the side. It's all right with me as long as he keeps it quiet. That's all I ask of all you sharpshooters. Just don't embarrass me and I won't embarrass you. Okay?"

The young man, laughing loudly, clapped Burt on the back. "You're all right, Burt, you know it?"

Francie moved in during the next week. A cab brought her toward evening. The cabman helped her up with her several bags. Burt, the manager, emerged from his apartment to greet her. Her gloved hand accepted his, but was removed immediately. Her voice, her looks, were, he thought, pleasant but cool. She was nicely dressed, wearing a light gray coat. Her shoes were also gray. She wore dark sunglasses. Her auburn hair had a reddish tinge. The luggage handled by the cabman looked expensive. Plainly, Francie Scott or Francie Watson or whatever her name was had money behind her.

Burt's initial impression of her was Class; he was anxious to see her in a swim suit. She could be, he thought, one of the apartment house's brightest lights.

The following day, as the tribe began to gather at the water's edge, Burt padded up to Number Twenty-nine in his habitual shorts and rope sandals and knocked.

"Come in."

The record player was on – something, Burt noted with dismay, jangling and electronic. She sat with a book. He couldn't see the title, but the bulk was formidable. She wore flowing, long-sleeved green

10

pajamas that had come from no bargain counter. The reddish-tinged hair was arranged just so. What was that in the cup beside her on the low table? Tea?

Her gaze was cool. He realized that her lightly mascaraed eyes were green.

He said, "The gang's down by the pool. They'd like to meet you."

"Thank you, but it's impossible for me to take much sun." The shades were adjusted to cut most of it out of the apartment.

"Really?"

"Yes." She did not elaborate.

Burt knew a cold shoulder when he encountered one. "Well, maybe another time, okay?"

At the pool he hunched his shoulders, rubbed his hands together, and said, "Brrr!"

Jackie, the sharpshooter, said, "What's the matter, Burt?"

"Got a chill from Number Twenty-nine. Pour me some medication."

He downed the medication, licked his lips, and said, "I guess we can scratch that chick from our fun-and-games. She's what they call the aloof type."

Jackie winked. "Maybe I can thaw her."

" Leave her alone," said a blonde girl, who loved Jackie with a purple passion that was

11

occasionally and casually requited. "If she doesn't want us we don't want her."

Burt nodded. "Them's my sentiments. The guy seems decent, but she's a cold fish. And who needs cold fish? We got plenty of warm fish around here!" And he beamed at them – he, Burt, grand sachem of this tribe of enlightened Good Guys.

The following Sunday morning, Jackie, a little boiled on Bloody Marys, took it into his head to pay the new tenant a call. Francie's aloofness intrigued him. Don't judge a book by its cover, and all that.

He knocked. The door opened. The nude upper half of John came around it.

Jackie blinked at the brown-bearded face. "Oh. 'Scuse me. You must be the husband."

John nodded pleasantly.

"I'm Jackie." Hands met. John's grip was cordial.

"Sorry to disturb you. I wonder if you have any – any coffee."

"One second." John disappeared, calling, "Francie?"

"What?"

"Where do we keep the coffee?"

"First cupboard left, top shelf."

John appeared, again the top half of him, a slice of bare hip showing around the edge of the door. Jackie accepted the coffee. "I only need a little."

"Take the whole thing, it's almost empty. We have more."

"Well – thanks."

Jackie said later to Burt, in the manager's office, over more Bloody Marys, "He's an all-right guy. I broke up a bit of love-making –"

"Really?"

"Well, I assume so. He didn't have any clothes on. But he was okay. Really, a very cordial guy."

That became the general opinion of John, who would be seen infrequently, coming and going. He didn't join the poolside revelry, but he was always pleasant. His chilled wife – if she *was* his wife, which no one believed for a moment – seemed to have no effect on his own temperature.

Had Francie been a regular daily tenant, Jackie and the others might have tried to break through the chill. But she came and went. Three or four days might elapse before she would be seen again. A cab would come, and she, with one light bag, would enter, or leave. Whether or not she was a TV actress, it was obvious that she had some occupation. She was not a bored young mistress, potentially vulnerable. She had no need or even any desire, obviously, for the bronzed young male cupcakes who decorated the environs of what they themselves jovially referred to as Burt Wozzen's Stud Farm.

So the month of May and most of June passed.

On June twenty-seventh John parked his foreign sports car and climbed up to Apartment Twenty-nine. He took off his jacket, got a broom and a vacuum cleaner from the closet, and set to work.

After vacuuming, he took books, records, and magazines from their various racks, piled them on the floor, and began to dust them with a damp cloth.

The door was open. Burt appeared. "Cleaning up, hey?" he said perceptively.

John admitted it.

"You do a real housecleaning when you do it."

Burt watched a bit, then asked, "Why the big surge of activity?"

John shrugged, then smiled tightly. "It may be that we won't be here much longer."

"Oh?"

"Yes . . . I hate to leave a place in a mess."

"Well, I'll be sorry to see you leave." He wouldn't, really. John was all right, but

14

Francie – he wouldn't be sorry to see *her* leave. It would make room for a live one.

John said, "We're paid up, aren't we?"

"The place is yours for another week. Look, most people don't go to this much trouble. Let me give you a hand."

John smiled. "I'd be grateful."

For the next hour they did a thorough cleaning of the entire apartment. Burt talked. He slid questions into his chatter. John, always courteous, answered obliquely or vaguely. But Burt was able to tell Jackie later that afternoon, "They're splitting. They aren't married – I knew that all along, of course. She may be in TV or she may not – he doesn't really know. Apparently he met her in a bar in San Francisco. He's beginning to wonder a lot of things about her. He says that lately she's been talking about something that scares him – he wonders if she might be a little nuts. He wouldn't tell me what it was but he indicated pretty clearly he's ready to wind the whole thing up."

Jackie drew a breath, glancing down with satisfaction at the bulge of his golden-brown pectoral muscles. "Well, I don't know. I think there's hidden fire there. I'd like to have struck a match."

Jackie considered that he knew just about all there was to know about women.

15

San Vicente is a town eight miles north of Marlborough. The southbound train stops there at 11:15 P.M. That evening as it came clanging up, Francie, carrying one light bag, boarded it. She took a rear seat in a nearly empty car. She smoked three cigarettes, gazing out the window; then the Pine City depot came into view. She got off.

A cab was hovering. She flagged it. The driver said, "Hi, Miss."

She nodded briefly.

"Usual place?"

"Yes."

He took her to the apartment.

She said, "Wait for me. I think I'll go out for a snack."

The cabman idled the motor for ten minutes, while the meter clicked off dime after dime. Then he heard the slam of a door and a swift clatter of heels. She came into sight, carrying the bag.

He opened the door from the inside. The girl was breathing heavily. She crouched in a corner of the rear seat, staring ahead.

"Where to now, Miss?"

"What? Oh. Marlborough."

"Marlborough?"

"Yes." She jabbed a cigarette into her lips

16

and murmured, "All over, is it? Well, it'll be all over, all right."

"Miss?"

"Nothing. Just drive, will you?"

He gave her a peculiar look, then slipped into gear and headed for the freeway.

John Wendle came out of his study. He wore shirt and slacks; his face was pallid.

He went to the front door, opened it, and reached around the edge of it to ring the doorbell.

There was no sound from upstairs.

He rang again.

Leona's voice came from upstairs. "John? Are you answering the door?"

He waited, silent.

Her voice again, booming: "John! Are you home?"

He heard her slippered feet padding toward the stairs.

He stood there, his right hand slightly behind him, as first her slippers, then her ankles, then her bathrobe appeared – and finally her shoulders and face. Her sleep-rumpled face, the small blue eyes peering –

"John! Is that you?"

He moved toward her, hand still behind his hip.

17

"Now why in the world did you start ringing the bell –"

He was at the bottom of the stairs now. She was six stairs up. Now he raised his right hand. Her eyes darted to the gleaming .22 pistol in his hand, but before her mind could register what it was he squeezed the trigger.

Her face seemed to empty. She was falling slowly, heavily, twisting. He fired again.

Then, for a long time, he stood at the front door, listening. There was a house across the street – the only house nearby. Mr. Holman, a retired attorney and widower – a man who was regular in his habits, lived in it. He was always asleep by 11:00, in his bedroom at the rear of the house.

There was no light, no sound from across the street. Mr. Holman slept.

John looked at his watch. 1:57.

He went into his study and took from the desk a cardboard box in which he put a number of items, including some cosmetics. He carried this box through the house to the back yard, then spent some time digging in various places in the soft earth around the rosebushes, burying the items separately. When he finally returned to the house and carefully washed the earth from his hands his watch showed 2:28.

Stepping over the body of his dead wife,

18

John Wendle went upstairs to his bedroom, put on his pajamas, and went to bed.

He lay there, staring at the window, until it became light.

At 7:30 John got up, put on a bathrobe and slippers, and went into the study. He came out with the .22. He went to the front door and opened it partly. Turning, he leveled the .22 and fired two shots into the body of Leona.

He stood there a few moments. Then, the gun hanging from his hand, he went out the front door.

Mr. Holman, a piece of toast in his hand, was peering out of his front window.

John walked steadily up the steps to the Holman door and rang.

Mr. Holman said sharply through the door. "What is it, Wendle? Why do you have a gun in your hand?"

"I just shot my wife."

"What!"

"Call the police, please. I just shot my wife."

"Wait there, now! Wait there!"

"I'll wait," John said. "I just shot Leona."

He heard Mr. Holman rush away from the door. Then he heard the dialing of the phone. John sat down on the steps, the gun in his

19

lap. He was sitting there when the police arrived.

At the police station, Detective Captain Mills conducted the interrogation.

"Why'd you do it, Mr. Wendle? What was your motive?"

"Well, she had the money, you see, and there were always quarrels about it. I just had enough of it. It started this morning again when she called me a worthless deadbeat. I couldn't stand any more of it. I ran to my study and got the gun and shot her."

"How many times?"

"Oh, three or four, I don't know."

"We don't have the medical report yet, but apparently there were a number of wounds. But Mr. Holman across the street says he heard only two shots."

"Really?" John frowned. "I – I don't know. I was in a daze."

The detective rubbed his mouth speculatively, then shrugged. "Okay. Now – how long have you had the gun?"

"A couple of months."

"Why did you buy it?"

"Why? Well, I suppose I had it in my mind to kill her."

20

The detective said confidentially, "She's a lot older than you."

"Yes."

"Was there another woman involved, Wendle? Another woman?"

"No."

"Sure?"

"Of course." His eyes met the detective's momentarily, then flickered away.

Mills said, "Well – we'll leave that for the moment. You realize you've just made a confession of murder?"

"Yes."

"You'll sign it?"

"Yes, I'll sign it."

Mills went to the front office of the modernistic station where photographers from all the Bay Area newspapers and TV studios were waiting. Murder in Marlborough, where so much of San Francisco's high society lives, is always big news.

The captain said, "Okay, boys. Please keep it orderly and no standing on the furniture. I'll bring him out."

Which he did. John, somewhat withdrawn, but composed and courteous, allowed himself to be photographed from numerous angles.

Then he was led off to a cell, under the station.

He lay down on the cot and fell sound asleep.

Mills came down to his cell. He looked grim. "Wendle, you're lying."

John stared at him.

"Your wife wasn't killed this morning. She was killed last night."

"No," John said. "You heard Holman's testimony. I killed her this morning."

"Autopsy shows that your wife died no later than three o'clock last night. She died either of a bullet in the abdomen or in the heart – either wound could have been fatal. She had two other wounds in her body – both of them fired long after she was dead."

He gazed steadily at John. "Those last two wounds were the ones you made this morning. They were the ones Holman heard."

John, after a long silence, said, "All right. It's true. I killed her last night, at about two o'clock. Then I fired the two shots this morning."

"Why?"

"To be sure she was dead."

The captain scowled. "Come off it, Wendle! Do you expect me to believe that?"

John spread his hands. "What do you want me to say?"

"The truth."

"I'm telling you the truth."

The captain said harshly, "Who's the woman, Wendle?"

"What woman?"

"We found a woman's suitcase in your study. Full of clothes."

"My wife's," John said quickly.

"Not those clothes. Your wife could never begin to fit into them. Whose are they, Wendle?"

John didn't answer. Mills said, "You're protecting some woman. Your car was found in the parking lot at the San Vicente depot. Who drove it there?"

John, after a few moments, said, "I did."

"When?"

"Yesterday. Last night."

"How'd you get home?"

"I took a cab – no, I walked."

"Drove your car eight miles to the depot, parked it there, then walked home, hey?" The detective shook his head. "You're just being silly, Wendle."

John stood up. He said loudly, "Damn it, Captain, what do you want of me? I've confessed, haven't I? You've got your case."

23

"I thought so this morning." He leaned forward. "Who's the other woman?"

"There isn't any other woman."

"All right." Mills stood up. "We'll find her. And when we do I think it'll add up."

He went upstairs to his office. The sergeant who shared it with him was on the phone, writing on a pad. "Yeah – yeah – Okay."

He looked at the captaion with snapping eyes. "A break. A guy down in Pine City, an apartment-house manager named Burt Wozzen, recognized the picture of Wendle on TV."

"So?"

"So Wendle has been shacking up in that apartment house with a broad named Francie Scott."

The captain sucked in his breath, then let it out. "You don't say? Well, let's go, Sergeant. Let's go see Mr. Wozzen."

Burt Wozzen said, as he unlocked the door to Apartment Twenty-nine, "I saw his picture on TV and I had to call you. I sure as hell don't like the bad publicity for the apartment house, but I know he didn't do it. He's not the type. Then there's the fact that *she* came in late last night. I heard

24

something smash and then she slammed right out."

"Really? What time?"

"About midnight?"

"Came in and went out, hey? And never came back?"

"Not to my knowledge."

The sergeant pointed. "There's a busted floor lamp. That's what you must have heard smash."

"Right," said Mills. "And there's something else – some torn-up paper."

He stooped, picked up fragments of paper, and spread them on a low table. "Hmm." He made adjustments. The other two watched him as he worked out the jigsaw.

"Hah. Here it is." And slowly he began to read:

"Francie: Don't think of it. It's too appalling. What gave you that idea? *Of course*, I don't love Leona; she knows that as well as you do. But we made a bargain when we got married and she's kept up her end. I intend to keep up mine. When you speak of the possibility of *getting rid* of her, my mind just goes numb. I wonder what might be happening inside *your* mind.

"I think it might be good if you went away for a while – perhaps back East. Where is it you're from – Philadelphia? Why not go back

25

there? Perhaps the excitement, the easy living, has been too much for you. I think if you get out of this atmosphere for a while you'll be able to think clearly again.

"Think it over. I'll come down to the apartment this weekend as usual, and we'll talk then. I'll have money, all you'll need for the trip back East. Please be reasonable and constructive in your thinking. Believe me, everything has to end sometime.

"John"

The sergeant whistled. "That's evidence, Captain."

"It sure is. He left it for her, she read it, blew her cork, threw down the lamp, tore up the note, rushed out... Okay, Wozzen." He took out his notebook.

The manager said, "Call me Burt. Everybody does."

"Okay, Burt. Tell us about John and Francie."

"What do you want to know?"

"Everything – everything you can tell us."

The captain worked hard that afternoon, talked to a number of tenants of the apartment house and some cabdrivers, and got more and more cheerful.

At about 7:00 P.M. he arrived in John's cell,

26

holding something behind his back. "Okay, Wendle. Let's talk about Francie Scott."

John looked at him stonily.

The captain revealed what he had behind his back – a framed picture of John inscribed: *All love to Francie from John.*

"It was in the bedroom of the apartment in Pine City. Nothing to say?"

John shook his head.

"We found the note you left her... This is how we reconstructed it. she read the note, blew her top, got a cab to drive her to Marlborough – we've got the driver's story – and he dropped her off at Raven Road at about 1:00 A.M. Raven Road – not more than a hundred yards from your house."

John sat motionless, his eyes fixed on him.

"She walked up to the house. She had your gun –"

"How?" John's voice was stiff. "How would she get it?"

"I don't know, you tell me. I have a hunch the gun was for her, anyway. We have the picture of an attractive, kind of peculiar woman who traveled around a lot. I think that was why you bought the gun – to give to her for protection. Anyway, let me go on. She rang the bell, your wife answered. They argued. Francie pulled the gun and shot her.

Then shot her again as your wife was falling. Isn't that the way it was?"

John said, "How would I know? I was –"

The captain pounced. "Asleep? You were asleep? Yes, but you heard the shots, jumped up, ran to the stairs, and saw what had happened."

Mills paced. "I can see it clearly. You knew they'd arrest her, put her away – but there was still a chance to save her. If you could buy some time, give her some running room – you'd take the heat until she got away."

"Noble of me," John said sarcastically. "If you really *did* read that note you'd know I didn't love her that much."

"I've considered that. You're noble – up to a point. The thing is, if the heat gets *too* strong you can always tell the real story, tell all about Francie. What you were after was time – time for her to get away. Well, I'll hand it to you – you accomplished it."

John sighed. "It's wonderful to have an imagination. You really ought to write fiction."

"No, I'm happy as a detective." The captain smiled. "The two shots you fired this morning, heard by a witness, were masterful – they eliminated right then and there the thought of *anyone else* being involved. Until

28

we got the medical report, of course. By that time Francie was long gone. You'd given her the keys to your car and she drove it to San Vicente and caught the 2:37 train to San Francisco."

"Really. Are there witnesses who saw her?"

"Not yet. But it's the only explanation for the car left at the depot... Then there's something else. The suitcase in your study contained a gray dress, gray coat, gray shoes – that's the outfit the cab driver described her as wearing."

John, after a pause, said, "You mystify me. What's your deduction?"

"She knew that if we got on her trail early, she might be recognized in those duds. She had another outfit in the suitcase, of course."

"Why didn't she take the suitcase with her?"

"Same reason. It might be remembered and cause her to be recognized."

John shook his head. "Captain, it's beautiful – a beautiful reconstruction. But the plain fact is that I'm the one who murdered Leona. Francie *did* appear at the house last night, yes – but I killed Leona."

"And why did Francie run away?"

"What?"

"And why did she come to your house at all?"

John shook his head stubbornly. "I killed Leona."

"Would you take a lie detector test?"

"I don't believe I have to, do I?"

"No, you don't." The captain patted his shoulder. "Okay, Wendle, stick to your story. We'll see which one the Coroner's Jury believes."

An all-points bulletin went out on Francie Scott, who could be accurately described by numerous residents of Burt Wozzen's apartment house. Unfortunately there were no photos of her. It was surmised that John had probably destroyed whatever photos he may have had.

Unfortunately also, no information as to her background could be gleaned. John steadfastly refused to discuss, with the police or the press, any aspect of his relationship with her – where they had met, what she claimed to have done in her past, how she supported herself, how *he* supported her, what her interests were. All he would say was, "You're on a wild goose chase. There's no need to involve Francie. *I* killed Leona."

The police tried to locate fingerprints of Francie, but found none in the apartment or in the car. As far as the car went, that was understandable – she must have been wearing the gray gloves when she drove to the San Vicente station. But the lack of prints in the apartment was singular – until Burt Wozzen recalled how John and he had cleaned the place from stem to stern the day before the murder.

The search centered, in time, on the Philadelphia area, but no information turned up.

The girl had vanished from the face of the earth.

After the Coroner's Jury, which met three days after the killing, had brought in a verdict against one Francie Scott, the District Attorney considered charging John Wendle with having been an accessory after the fact.

Captain Mills said, "Sure he is. But we could never make it stick. There's no hard evidence. Besides, the papers have made him a kind of hero."

"True."

"Another thing. If we turn him loose, Francie may contact him – she may need money."

So, the third evening after his arrest, John was released – and just in time, he thought, as he retired to his bathroom to detach his false beard and shave. Real hair sprouting under the false hair had caused an itch that was almost unbearable.

He would remain in seclusion, and in a week have the beginning of a real beard – different shape, but enough to cover the soft, almost feminine curve of his lower cheeks.

That night he went out in the back yard, dug up the various items he had planted, and carried them into the house in the cardboard box. He carefully smashed the two tiny bits of green glass to powder on the kitchen sink and flushed the powder down the drain. The unlabeled tube of adhesive material was no special danger; he merely poked it down among empty cans and coffee grounds in the garbage. The cosmetics he carried upstairs and put in among other things in his late wife's bathroom. The auburn wig he sliced into strips with a sharp kitchen knife, cut the strips into small bits, and flushed them down the toilet.

He stood at his desk and gazed down at the manuscript of his play. Perhaps he would start work on it soon. If it were produced, if it made him famous, people would ask him if it was his first. Yes, he would say. He would make no mention of the previous play, which had run only two weekends to no particular acclaim in a little theater in San Francisco five years before.

Not that he was ashamed of it. In fact, he thought it was excellent. A comedy of the theater of the Absurd school, with helter-skelter characters, black humor, random comings and goings.

Fortunately, the play was long forgotten, and in any case no one would connect it with him, John Wendle. It had been written under a nom de plume. And under the same pseudonym he had acted the title role.

One San Francisco critic had given it a brief review:

"As a play, *The Transvestite* is quite boring and derivative, but whether he is playing Jo-Jo or Jo-Jo's sister, Frank Scott is totally convincing."

FLORENCE V. MAYBERRY
A Goodbye Sound

"Shut up, Joe," I said. "You bore me."

Joe looked as if he would cry. I can't stand a man who goes around all the time looking as if he could cry. Joe's that kind."

"Well –" He cleared his throat, a nasty, fluttering sound. It was too bad, I knew it was wrong, but Joe couldn't take a deep breath without irritating me. "Why can't you look at me like you do at everybody else? Like just smile nice at me sometimes. Like for instance you don't even know those guys standing over there, they're just waiting for a table and you never saw them before, just happened to look their way. And you give 'em a big smile like you were the hostess out here." A hesitation. "Or maybe you do know them."

"Whether I do or not is not your affair. Now listen, Joe, you've been after me to go out with you for months. So I'm out. With you. So why not cool it, lay off the witness-box stuff."

"Sure, okay, Lolly."

"Laura!"

"Okay, Laura."

What's a woman to do with a man like that? *Roll over and play dead, Joe, sit up and beg, Joe, fetch me my slippers, Joe.*

"Order anything you like, hon, the world's yours tonight."

"The prime ribs, please."

"Yeah, that's good, that's the ticket, best thing on the menu. Hon, you can have prime ribs every day, every night, if you'd only want it that way. I just finished a quarter-million-dollar contract, Lol – Laura. Your old man –" He choked it off, trying to laugh. "I mean your old ex-husband is in the bigtime contracting now. Kept slogging along until I made it."

"Maybe I ought to go back in court and try for alimony this time. First time, it would have been like suing a four-year-old kid for his nickels." *That's right, ruin his fun, be mean, you shrew.*

"I told you, if you'd only hang on a little while, maybe make me feel like I was something, I'd make it." He tried to laugh again, but it was like the laugh was hiding behind a door, afraid to come out. "I'm slow, hon. But right along with that, I'm too dumb to know how to give up."

That was for sure. He's telling me?

Divorced two years and every week, regular as clockwork Joe telephoned. *Hon, let's try it again, willya, Lolly, willya just go out to dinner with me and talk a while? I get terrible lonesome, you gotta eat anyway. Hon, do you need any money, I gotta few bucks ahead, construction's picking up.* Hon, hon, over and over. So once in a while I gave in, like throwing a dog a bone. Damn a man like that. Who needs his money? I make plenty doing beauty work.

"Prime ribs for the lady. Medium-rare, same as usual, hon? Baked potatoes, all the fixings. Same for me. Don't give the lady no coffee till later, she drinks it with dessert. That still right, hon?"

A crawly feeling shivered my back, crept into my jaw. My teeth started to chatter. Nerves, I mean, like before a fit.

The food came, beautiful stuff because we were at Eugene's, where it's maybe the best in Reno, but I looked at it like it was poison. Joe did that to me, always. He didn't mean to, but he did. Slender I always was, but by the time Joe and I broke up I was nothing but skinny. Chemical reaction, maybe. Or maybe I'm just mean. But I think it's more than that. I'm a one-man woman.

I never should have married Joe. My fault, of course, because I knew I shouldn't and he

36

didn't. That's why I stuck it out with him for three years and then let him hang around these past two years. No woman ought to marry a man when she loves someone else she can't have.

"Joe, are you still smacking your mouth after every swallow? You come to a swell place like this and still eat like you're in a truck-stop diner."

"Sorry, Lol – Laura. Hon, I keep telling you. I need a nice woman to shape me up, make something out of me. All I do any more is hang around with guys. Honest, Laura, you're the only one. I tried going out with other women but it's no use. Not after you."

See what I mean? What he should have done was reach that big paw of his across the table, smack me hard, and walk out. Never phone again. And I tell you, that would have been a big relief, no more anticipating that call every week, trying to think up new ways to say no.

"Eat up, hon, come on, tear into that meat. Or you'll get skinny again, like you were after –"

"I don't want to talk about it, Joe."

"You should of kept the baby, Laura, maybe that's what turned you bitter. I wouldn't of cared it wasn't mine, anything

37

yours is mine far as I'm concerned. You should never have –"

"Damn you to hell!" Whispered, so the tables around couldn't hear. "You dumb stubborn ox, you still believe I'm a murderer! That I deliberately killed my darling baby, my poor lost baby! How many times do I need to tell you I *wanted* that baby?"

"Well, hon, I wouldn't of cared it wasn't mine. I told you that when you told me about it, right from the start. You were honest with me, and I said if it's yours I'd love it no matter who it looked like."

Maybe now you won't keep thinking I'm the witch you started out thinking I was. Who wouldn't act like a witch, getting reminded every day that I loved someone I couldn't have? Besides hanging onto the conviction I had murdered my unborn baby. It was a miscarriage, not an abortion. Joe was determined not to believe that, perhaps in the hope that I had deliberately rid myself of my last attachment to Chris. Well, he was wrong. It was a miscarriage. My baby's silly mother cried too much.

"I like Chris myself, Laura. I wouldn't of cared. Because I understood why you went for the guy, you just a green kid and him knowing how to handle women. Only when you found out he was married you should of broke it off. But that's the trouble, women get took in by a good line, him throwing money around, regular guys don't have a chance."

"Joe, I have to go. I don't feel well."

"Aw, hon, we barely started eating –"

"You stay, Joe. Eat yours and mine, too. And don't call me again. Ever. Just leave me alone." I got up, skimmed past the tables and waiters, fast.

It felt good in the open air, a nice warm night, the moon big and bright. The white clean moonshine seemed to shower me off, wipe away what Joe stirred up, and I stopped wanting to cry. Nevada's moon, I think, must be the most beautiful on earth, so brilliant, so white. I felt like diving into its glow, swimming in it.

"You're moon mad," Chris used to tell me. Then he would say in his soft, gentle voice, slurred by a Danish accent, "So am I, little Laura, when I see you in the moonlight and hold you in my arms." How many millions of men have said those same dumb words to how many millions of dumb girls? So it wasn't the words, it was the way Chris said it.

A taxi moved up to me, ready for a passenger. I opened the door and got in. But

I couldn't close the door because Joe was holding it, all two hundred pounds of him. "Hon, why take a cab when I gotta car? I'll pay the guy his fare, he won't lose nothing. Listen, hon, you gotta eat something – Listen, fella, I'm not taking your fare, here's a couple bucks. Come on, Lol – Laura."

Two couples going inside the restaurant stared at us. One of the women looked like a customer of the beauty salon where I worked. And it was so dumb, squabbling in front of Eugene's. So I got out and let Joe lead me to his big car. A good one but all dusty, with rope and a can of oil in the back, and papers, chewing-gum wrappers, and gravel on the floor in front.

"I know what you're thinking, Laura, didn't wash his car before he picked me up. Well, hon, I been out on the job, way off the paved roads, in soft dirt. So I got to carry extra oil and a rope in case. And I barely got back tonight, tore back like crazy, didn't want to disappoint you, hahaha!"

The poor guy. Oh, God, the poor guy.

"How about a little run up to Virginia City, hon? It's warm down here tonight, be cooler up there. Those old ghosts chill the place off, huh, hahaha!"

"Okay."

Might as well. I wasn't going to get rid of

Joe any more than you can break a bulldog's hold on something he's locked his jaws on by smacking his rump. I switched on the car radio, the knobs gritty under my fingers, put it on loud so Joe would need to shout to be heard; a man can't shout forever.

Lovely music, a great "mood" program, bittersweet, haunting. It drowned out Joe and I spun out with it, far out. It was easy to forget it was Joe beside me, he was merely a broad-shouldered male figure. But pretty soon, dreaming with the music, he was more than that. He was Chris.

Chris beside me while we zoomed along, not toward Virginia City but toward Carson City and Lake Tahoe. Five years ago. A time when I barely knew Joe – he was only one of the men who worked for Chris. Once in a while we would bump into him and other employees of Chris in some night spot. And they would all cluster around Chris as if he were a magnet and they were iron filings. The same way I did.

I try and try to figure out why Chris was so attractive to everyone. But I never can put it in words. He simply was. Sitting beside him could put me on a cloud, soft and gentle, yet somehow firm and secure at the same time. His voice was so tender. Once I heard him speak when he was angry, not to me but to a stranger who tried to dance with me. Even then his voice was tender, a velvet-covered steel trap closing gently, but unstopably, around the man.

In size he wasn't as big as Joe. But he exuded a mountain feeling, a mountain covered with grass and the sun streaming over it. A dopey woman in love? True. Absolutely true.

Joe shouted over the music and drove away Chris and my dream. "How about you and me trying it again, Laura, whaddaya say? You're acting like you're a million miles away. Put your mind on me a little bit, hon."

"Joe, turn around. I don't want to go up to Virginia City. Tomorrow's a big day at the beauty shop and we're short-handed. Turn back to Reno at Steamboat Springs."

"Awwww, hon! Just when I'm feeling good, you back beside me. Listen, take tomorrow off. I'll give you whatever it takes to make up your lost pay."

"I don't need your money, Joe."

"Please." His voice was uneven, shaky. "I need to be a little happy once in a while."

So I said okay, okay, and we went up the steep climb from the valley, around the last bend, into Virginia City. Tourists ambled up and down the long main street, gawking at the store windows, going in and out of the

42

fake oldtime saloons, laughing as if it was a ball, you know, gay like fun. And all the time it was nothing but an old dead town, faked up for dollars. It gave me the creeps. Like watching people laugh in a funeral parlor while they ogled a fancy old-fashioned coffin.

We got out of the car and drifted with the crowd, Joe hanging onto my arm. But even with the crowd, with the tinpanny piano music coming out of a bar and Joe trying to make talk, I couldn't stop being back with Chris. The thought of him simply wouldn't go away. It wiped out Virginia City, Joe, everything.

Chris, darling, are we going to be married? Someday, I mean.

Little girl, don't worry, let me take care of that. Don't you worry your pretty head about that. I have problems. I need to handle those problems first.

I'm sorry to bother you, Chris, it's just I love you so. I suppose a girl shouldn't keep telling a man how much she loves him but it's the way I feel. I'm no good at pretending.

He had patted my hand then, tenderly, almost as a father would pat his daughter, and said that was why he loved me, my eyes so deep and true, they couldn't lie, nor those sweet lips –

43

"Wanta go inside one of the joints, Lol – hon? Have us a little fun?"

"Damn!" I said. "I'd as soon dance on somebody's grave."

Joe's jaw dropped and his eyes turned moist. Poor guy, poor guy. Why couldn't he just fade away, leave me alone?

"It's Chris," he finally said. "I can tell. You're thinking of Chris again. When you gonna get him out of your system? After the way he done you dirt."

"He didn't! I was twenty-one. I can take my own blame."

"Hon, you were nothing but a dumb little kid, barely twenty-one. What's twenty-one mean, it ain't magic. And Chris close to forty, smart, wheeling and dealing with Nevada's big shots, knowing all the angles."

"Take me home!"

"Okay, hon, have it your way. But I still think it was a damn shame, leaving you so mixed up you can't love nobody but him."

"Shut up, Joe!" *Shut up, shut up, shut up, why tell me what I know too well?* I'm like my great-grandmother and she was Indian, full-blooded. Outside I'm blonde as a Scandinavian, but inside of me I'm Indian. And Indians don't change loyalties easily; when they get set on an idea, that's it. Forever. At least that's what I've heard.

Anyway, that's how I am. For me, Chris is it and always will be.

Joe did what I said, shut up, led me back to the car and we headed for Reno. The moonlight turned the night into a twilight, only more shimmering, just as it was the night Chris and I drove to Tahoe. Our last night together. I remembered I had leaned close to the windshield, let the moonlight bathe my face, smiled at Chris. So he drove off on a side road and took my face in his hands. "My beautiful little girl," he said.

"Yes, Chris."

He kissed me, then drew my face back to the windshield, into the moonlight. "No wonder you love moonlight, little Laura, you're moonbeams made flesh. This is how I want to remember you. Always."

Something was wrong about the way Chris said that. A strange inflection, a goodbye sound. As though he had dropped a pebble into a well that I had expected to be full, but there was no splash. Lost. Gone. A goodbye sound.

I swallowed hard to keep back a question about that, because something told me I didn't want the answer. I've heard, too, that Indians are psychic. Anyway, I didn't ask. I smiled instead. If some crazy thing was going to happen, if I was going to lose Chris, I didn't want him to remember ugliness.

Chris drove back to the highway, and that night I think we dropped into every nightspot around the lake. Joe showed up in one of the clubs and then kept following us from place to place, hanging onto us like a burr. Truth is, Chris seemed to encourage him. He would have had to, otherwise Joe wouldn't have stayed. Chris knew how to get rid of people he didn't want around.

Once I whispered, "Tell Joe to get lost." But Chris only patted my hand and said, "Who can blame the man? He's in love with you. Who wouldn't be in love with you?"

Without any thought it popped out. "Maybe you wouldn't, Chris." Was that my Indian great-grandmother coming out in me, knowing the way all primitive people know.

We kept dancing, Chris silent. Finally he said, "Little girl, you've picked up the feeling of what I have to tell you tonight. Not all, but part. I do love you. But tonight is goodbye for us. Our last time together. That's why I want to remember your face, everything about you. Darling, it has to be. The end, I mean."

"Why?" It was a weak, strangled sound.

"I've learned in business, no use explaining. When the end comes, face it –

quick, sharp, no turning back. It's simply I have too many involvements, business, everything. It won't work out." He bent and kissed my forehead.

My head floated up among the colored, spangly lights, my body a numbed automaton on the dance floor below. Then my head fell back on my body, and all of me was numb, too numb to be surprised that a smile had frozen on my face. Who wants to remember a tear-streaked face?

"Dance with Joe, little sweetheart, he's been waiting for that all evening," Chris said, when we went back to our table.

Joe stood up and looked at Chris as if he was going to lick his hand. My smile was still frozen as Joe led me back to the dance floor. Over his shoulder I watched Chris call the waiter, speak to him. Then he looked toward me, smiled, nodded his head approvingly, turned and left. Just left. That's all.

The numbness suddenly went away and I started falling into a black pit. I clung hard to Joe while I was doing it, and he squeezed back. "Aw, honey, what's this? Huh? You go for me a little bit?"

I shook my head.

"I sure wish you would, baby. Just a little, you know, like at least be friendly."

"Chris has left me," I said. "So I'm dead.

Mind playing hearse and taking me home?"
My voice sounded flat and far off, like
someone else talking.

Joe's head swung toward our table. "You
mean he's gone?" I nodded. A wide happy
grin spread over his face. "Gone," he said
with satisfaction. "Well, now let's you and
me have some fun for ourselves. We don't
care if –"

"I care," I said. "Please take me home."

Joe led me back to our table. The waiter
came over and said, "The gentleman with
you said to bring you anything you want, it's
his party, all paid for."

"Laura, honey, the night's young. And the
first time, me with you, Chris doing this for
us. It's like a dream, lemme dream a while."

"Take me home, Joe. Otherwise I'll call
a cab."

Now, all these years later, I was telling him
again, *Take me home, Joe*. Time hadn't
changed anything.

We curved down the mountain from
Virginia City, saw the valley spangled with
lights, and Reno a shimmer of neon toward
the north.

"Hon, didja hear what happened today?
You musta, the way you're all sunk into
yourself tonight.

"Hear what?"

48

"Chris got divorced today."

It couldn't be true. It was a crazy made-up daydream, an idiot fantasy that fairy tales come true.

"His wife finally got onto him. Took him for a bundle."

Good. Take every dime. That way I can prove it's Chris I want, not money.

"I'm really sorry, Lol – Laura. Honest. You may of always thought I only cared about what I wanted. Like, only wanting to hang onto you. But honest, all along I felt bad for you, the way you were hook, line, and sinker for Chris. He wasn't worth all that, not that he ain't a great guy. That is, with guys. But not worth all that grief. From you."

"Well, you don't have to be sorry for me any longer, Joe." All the sad five years of waiting for something I never expected to get wiped out! Because here it was, the pot of gold at the end of the rainbow. Laughter bubbled out of me – the first time I had laughed like that since Chris went away. "Not any more, Joe!"

"Gee, hon, that's great. Really great." I looked at Joe affectionately. He was kind, actually sweet, to be glad just because I was glad.

" You see, I was afraid you'd be all broke

up. I mean, I figured you'd been holding onto the hope that someday you and Chris would finally make it. Then when he got his divorce today and right off married that kooky kid from New York. I mean, right today, I figured you'd take it hard."

The valley's lights went out. Blown out the way one blows out an oil lamp. When they came back on, they were blurred and my head was dizzy.

"But since you're taking it good like this, maybe I got a chance with you after all."

Keep talking, Joe, so I don't have to.

"Hon, I'll never stop loving you. You're so beautiful. I mean, looking at you sideways like now, you're like a beautiful statue or something. Honest, when I first saw you with Chris, it kinda made me sick, you so young and little and pretty."

To disinfect a wound, split it wide and rub salt in it. I may die from it, but the wound will be clean.

"Joe, is this true? Or are you making it up to try to make me forget Chris?"

He looked stunned. "Why would I make up a thing like that? Anyways, you could check, couldn't you? Oh, Lord, you're not taking it cool after all. But you'd have to find out sometime. Honest, I thought maybe you'd already heard."

50

"How did you find out?"

"Hell, I do business with Chris. See him all the time. So today late, when I first got in from the job, I went to his office about something. And Chris invited me to the party he's throwing tonight, even introduced me to the kid he just married, she was there, that's how I know she's kooky, giggling and crawling all over Chris."

"Where's the party?"

"I'm not going. Gee, hon, think I'd take you home and run off to that party?"

"I'm going to the party. Take me, Joe."

"Now, listen, that's no good, you got a bad sound in your voice, you don't want –"

"Take me to the party, Joe."

"Hell!" Joe said.

The party was at the Mapes Hotel in a private suite, the door wide open, come-one-come-all, so we walked right in. Flowers were everywhere, in baskets, in vases, gift cards thrusting from them. The room smelled like a funeral. When my father died, the funeral parlor smelled exactly like this wedding party.

The guests, laughing, milling around, were only a moving color-dotted blur. And in the center of the blur was Chris, sharp and clear, with a small blur beside him that bounced and jiggled and swung on his arm. Chris looked just the same. Smiling, eyes blue as the sky after a good clean rain. Stocky, strong, And he saw me. As Joe and I came in, he was looking toward the door.

Chris dropped the bouncing blur off his arm and walked to us. He kept smiling. Smiles, I knew from five years before, don't really mean anything. "Hello, little girl," he said. "It's been a long time." Tender, loving voice. I had to bite my lips to keep them from trembling. "I hoped you would come to wish me happiness."

The small blur skipped over to us and caught hold of Chris. It shook its shaggy curls from its little heart-shaped face, came out of the blur, pursed its mouth into a pout, and asked, "Aren't you going to introduce wifey, hubby-doll-boy?"

Hubby-doll-boy introduced us us. "Valerie, these are special friends, Laura and Joe Walker. You've already met Joe, remember? At the office. Joe used to work for me but now he's my competitor, a real great guy."

Joe stepped forward, grinning, pleased. "Congratulations, you two. Yeah. May you look as good on your fiftieth anniversary."

"Oooo, super, isn't that darling, Chrissy, just super darling!" Valerie cooed.

Chris took my hand. It shouldn't have sent an electric shock through me. But it did. "And little Laura is a very special lady I've known a long time. A lovely *lady*." Emphasis on *lady*.

Valerie's big brown eyes narrowed as she looked me over. "Oooo, lovely, just simply lovely-lovely. Chrissy angel, kiss me, I've not been kissed for five whole minutes, mmm!" She stood on tiptoe, holding up her face, nuzzling the air. Chris bent and kissed her, red creeping over his face. "Mm-mm-mm, not that way, Daddy, big-*big* kiss!"

He kissed her again and she snuggled against him. Then he did it another time, on his own, a long hard kiss. He didn't have to do that. He could have waited until I couldn't see him.

I began to hear the voice. Not a real voice. Not mine or anybody's. Just a voice in my mind. It said, *I'm going to kill Chris, then I'll kill myself*. Flat, no anger, simply a fact.

I didn't argue with the voice. Why argue with what had to be? But I began to think, how? Should I use fingernails? The heel of my shoe? Hit him with a compact, stab him with a lipstick, choke him with a five-dollar bill? Those were my weapons.

Joe grabbed my arm and led me to the buffet spread. "Eat something, hon, you're kinda sick-looking, you oughta eat something."

"Maybe some water."

"It ain't healthy not to eat."

No knives, on the buffet table. Forks, but can a fork stab deep enough to kill? The cake cutter? Nothing but dull prongs.

My knees started to tremble and I went to a chair and sat down. A standup ashtray was beside the chair. I tried to think what my Indian great-grandmother would have done. Latched onto some brave's bow and arrow, or a tomahawk. A shotgun, if one was around. But her great-granddaughter wouldn't know how to pull the trigger on a gun if one was in her lap.

Chris was watching me over the top of Valerie's shaggy little head. Still smiling, but not comfortable. Uneasy. I never saw Chris uneasy before. He turned his eyes away, too quickly. Guilty.

Joe touched my shoulder, leaned down and whispered. "Hon, don't keep staring at Chris that way, you're giving the guy the creeps. After all, it's his wedding night, he ought to be let to be happy."

Why, I wanted to ask, just why? But that would have taken strength. I wanted to save all my strength to do what I had to do, before Chris left. Already he and Valerie were going around to their guests, bidding good night. Valerie giggling, snuggling, Chris moving quickly, in a hurry, people making cracks about that. Finally they headed in my direction.

"Go away, Joe," I said. "This is between Chris and me."

"Now, Lol – Laura –"

"Go away."

He shuffled off miserably. then the bridal couple came to me, the last one in the room. I stood up, my weapon ready. Say it loud, scream it. *Chris, you never saw our son. I grieved about losing him as well as his father. He never drew breath, but do you suppose in some other world he wonders what happened to his father and what made his mother cry so much?*

"Good night, Laura. Please wish us well."

I opened my mouth. "How –" *How does our son feel about us?* I swallowed. "How – how nice to see you again, Chris."

It wasn't easy, but I smiled. Smiles don't mean anything but they're not ugly. It's better not to remember ugliness. " I wish you well."

They turned, walked away, out of the room, out of my life. Gone. Would that be the same as dead?

Joe shuffled back. "Come on, hon, let's

go, you look all in. Hey, maybe you could eat a hamburger or something now. You know I worry about you, Lol – Laura."

"Joe, don't waste your time and feelings on me."

His face screwed up like an ugly baby's who isn't sure whether to cry or not. "I wish I could stop. But some things you can't help."

I knew about that. That I understood.

"Okay, Joe. Buy me a hamburger."

So Joe and I went downstairs to the coffee shop and had hamburgers. Like maybe a funeral feast?

JEFFRY SCOTT
The Good Neighbor

Miss Lidgett wrestled with the problem for days on end, before seeking George Abbey's advice.

"Really, it's like a parable," she explained fretfully. "The promised land awaits me – but only if I forfeit all my wordly goods! Too provoking. Nobody's rich any more, under this dreadful Socialism, but I do treasure my little bits and pieces."

"You'd better step into my office, then, Miss L." Grave and courteous as a foreign minister attending to an influential ambassador, Abbey led her along the side of his house and into what she thought of as the potting shed.

It was a beautifully constructed and cleanly little building, for George Abbey never set his hand to anything shoddy. In there, with the smell of sedge peat, and the sight of scrubbed earthenware flowerpots standing in obedient ranks according to size, some of the tension drained out of Minnie Lidgett. Hanks of raffia, hanging from the

57

crossbeams, brushed her hair; through the single sparkly clean window, she was further soothed by a view of the garden – velvet lawns, weedless colorful borders.

George sat her down on a bentwood chair. "Now then, what's it all about?"

Miss Lidgett forgot what was on her mind, for a moment. George Abbey was her very favorite man – oh, not in *that* way, you understand, for she was sixty years old, a spinster from a generation brought up to believe that if carnality had any place at all in the scheme of things, it must be restricted to married people under the age of forty.

But she liked and admired him. Windermere Crescent had gone down in the world since she had moved into the newly built bungalow in 1948, after the death of her father, the Canon. These days, little Japanese motorcycles made the nights full of noise, there was a woman who wore a bathing suit to water her front lawn, standards were flouted, and respectability set at naught.

Abbey was the rock, the reassuring hint that the old ways had not entirely perished. His politeness was instinctive and he knew his place. With his round gray head and mild blue eyes, George put her in mind of an elderly schoolboy, working things out at a slower pace than the sharper rude folk in the neighborhood.

A shame about that wretched wife of his, she thought, and then winced because her musing was being conducted under the cuckolded husband's nose. All the same, it *was* a shame. Miss Lidgett had seen Gwen Abbey coming home late at night, each time in a different car driven by a different man.

"What's the matter?" Abbey inquired, his voice deepening with concern.

Miss Lidgett pulled herself together. Unbidden and unwelcome, a picture flashed in front of her inner eye: she had been looking for Chairman Mao, her Siamese cat, in the little cinder-topped alley behind Windermere Crescent some nights before. And there was Gwen Abbey, sprawled back across the hood of a car, half drunk and hysterical with merriment, while a man fumbled at her. Ugh!

She erased the vision and sat up straight. "My cousin lives in South Africa, George, and he wants me to visit him. He is a wealthy man and – well, there would be no problem over the – well, the expenses involved."

Abbey rubbed his jaw, a slow grin appearing above his blunt square-tipped finger. "What a bit of luck, my dear! We had a chap from Durban showing color slides at the Gardener's Club last year. Flowers straight out of Paradise, and shrubs to beat the band. You'll love it, Miss L."

Miss Lidgett nodded dubiously. "I'm sure it would be most pleasant, George. But I would be away for at least three months. Chairman Mao can go to a cattery, of course – he'd be well looked after. But the house would be empty and unattended. Now you know and I know that the majority of homes in Windermere Crescent have been burgled over the past five years. I'm convinced that the only reason my house has remained safe is that I never leave it for lengthy periods."

"Ah, I see your point." George upended his largest flowerpot and squatted on it, chin in palms, his brow creasing. "Personally I blame the window-cleaners. I'm sure they gossip about who's on holiday, who's got nice things. There's even a tale that they sell information to criminals."

"Decent society is under constant attack," Miss Lidgett said, hardly listening to him, her ears muffled by the steady hoofbeats of her hobby-horse. "At least once a week some unsolicited caller knocks at my door – opinion polls, circulars, jumble-sale collections, those dreadful ruffians hoping to buy antiques on the cheap or simply terrify silly women into parting with money.

Now, if they knock and there is no reply, a percentage of those callers promptly break a window and strip one's house."

She sniffed and shook her head. "I don't know why I'm burdening you with this, George. Except that you're a comfort. Wasn't it Somerset Maugham who said that the worst problems are those to which one knows the only possible solution? I must write to my cousin and decline his invitation."

"Hold on, Miss L.! Hold on, I'm thinking." And indeed he was. Miss Lidgett felt quite uncomfortable, for George Abbey's nondescript, pudgy face had drained of all expression, and his knuckles were yellowing under the tension of concentration.

A disloyal corner of her personality – the well bred, daughter-of-the-rectory corner – yearned to say sharply, "It isn't *that* important, you know." For the first time in some ten years of friendship she felt ashamed of having disclosed something of her life to a person who, for all his manifest worthiness, was rather common, tradesman class.

But then the strained emptiness vanished and George was twinkling at her. "Tell you what, nobody need know you're away. I mean, you don't mix with the rest of the Crescent, and your place lies back a bit from the road. If you don't advertise the fact that you're leaving, I doubt that anybody'll know."

Miss Lidgett stared at him. "But... no, what about the milk, and the letters?"

George chuckled and laid a finger alongside his squashy nose. "If you trust me with a key, Miss L., I can nip through the hedge at the back here, in through your kitchen, and take in the milk and the mail. You needn't cancel your milk, see; I'll just knock a pint a day off my order and take your bottle."

He was quite excited, and pleased with himself. "Yes, and I can draw the curtains every morning, and pull them across every night. It'll look as if you're still there."

Miss Lidgett considered the proposal. She had no qualms about giving Abbey a key. What little jewelry she had was at the bank, and he was one of nature's gentlemen, despite his class. She knew that he would never use her absence as an excuse to snoop and rummage among her possessions. That he was utterly honest went without question.

And yet...

"Is it practical, George?" Catching the spirit of his plan, she giggled. "I suppose it is."

"No trouble," Abbey claimed firmly.

"The neighbors are used to seeing me pruning your roses and running a mower over the front lawn – I've done that for years. So they're accustomed to seeing me being about your place."

"Well, if you wouldn't mind, George." Miss Lidgett clasped her dry, shapely old hands. "Oh, George! Am I really going to South Africa?"

"You're practically on the airplane," he assured her.

The scheme was polished and perfected over the next ten days. Abbey owned a hardware store and its revenue allowed him to live in semi-retirement. He persuaded Miss Lidgett that far from being a nuisance, keeping an eye on her bungalow would give him an interest.

"I suppose I'd better inform the police that I'm going away," she mentioned, during one of their conferences in the potting shed. "It would be dreadful if you were seen in my bungalow and somebody called the police, thinking you were an intruder, George."

Abbey mulled over the point. "I wouldn't, if I were you, Miss L. I'm not saying anything against the police, mind. But you hear funny stories. There was that case of the policemen breaking into places when they were on night duty, somewhere up Durham way. It was all in the papers.

"What I don't like is, they've got a special book where they put the names and addresses of people on holiday. Who's to know who sneaks a look at that book? No, it's a very long chance that anyone will see me in your place, and if they do – well, I'm a respectable man. And you can leave me a little letter of authority – To Whom It May Concern kind of thing."

He wagged a finger at her.

"A secret's not a secret if more than one person knows it. I'm not telling Gwen. But it's up to you."

"I expect you're right, George."

"I'll forward your mail once a week, as soon as you write to me with your Cape Town address," he continued. "By your leave, if there are any bills – telephone, utilities, and so forth, I'll pay them and we can settle up on your return, when you've had a look at the receipts."

No doubt about it, the episode was exciting as well as mildly embarrassing. The night before her departure – his wife was out, naturally – George carried Miss Lidgett's suitcases through the gap in the back-garden hedge and put them in his own car.

The following morning Miss Lidgett, far

too smartly dressed for a visit to the greengrocer, but otherwise unobtrusive, strolled out of the Crescent in the direction of the shops. George Abbey picked her up outside the supermarket and drove to London's Heathrow Airport. Three hours later she was heading across the globe.

The holiday swept Miss Lidgett off her feet.

The climate dazzled her and worked a change in her personality. She bought several swimsuits and once appeared, at a beach barbecue, with a naked midriff. Alfred, her cousin, and his wife Mildred were young in spirit, and somehow Miss Lidgett caught the trick of it.

Every week came a fat airmail package: George Abbey was punctilious, forwarding everything from personal letters to bargain-offer soap coupons. She was touched when, after a month, he sent a color photo of her front garden, with the roses in bloom.

And he wrote long covering letters, a quaint weekly mixture of steward-and-butler's report and local gossip. "You have a cracked rain-gutter at the back and I have taken the liberty of seeing to it. The one-legged blackbird is back and looks fit, I'm glad to say... Your Friend and Obdnt. Servant,. G. Abbey.

One morning Miss Lidgett found that the shallow drawer beneath her dressing table had jammed, and was taken aback when she counted the airmail packages stowed there. She had been away from England for four months.

"So? drawled Mildred. "You haven't seen half of the sights yet, darling. What's the rush? Your Good Samaritan is looking after everything."

"Yes, but... I'm outstaying my welcome."

"Rubbish, you're talking rubbish." Alfred squeezed her shoulder. "Once we've got the birthday party out of the way, then we'll *maybe* discuss your going back."

Margaret – Mildred and Alfred's daughter – celebrated her twenty-first birthday in three weeks' time, and was to become engaged on the same day. Sipping freshly squeezed orange juice, blooming in the sun, Miss Lidgett decided that it would be churlish to insist on leaving before the party.

A month later she began stirring herself for her return home. Several days were invested in selecting a very expensive present for George Abbey.

The taxi from Heathrow set Miss Lidgett down outside her bungalow.

A sense of anticlimax was inevitable, of course. She felt a pang – jealousy, perhaps, and knowledge of loneliness – to see the house unchanged. Not in the least neglected, but there was a change – in herself. The bungalow now looked mean and meager.

Sensibly she went straight indoors and to bed, unpacking only her nightclothes and washing gear. The next morning, having emptied the suitcases and set her wardrobe to rights, she went out on the patio.

Her heart lurched.

The man, burly and flashily dressed, was skulking behind the raspberry canes. Miss Lidgett whimpered and stepped back through the French windows, groping for the telephone. And then she replaced it after dialing only one digit.

The intruder, waving and calling, was George Abbey. Silently she watched him approaching. He was wearing flared trousers in a gaudily checked pattern, a crimson shirt, and a leather belt with a bright brass buckle almost the size of a saucer.

Equal to most challenges, Miss Lidgett was floundering. Abbey paused before the windows. "You're back then, Miss L.! Welcome home, welcome indeed!"

"Would you like a cup of coffee, George?"

"Wouldn't say no. Tell you what, I'll pop

back and fetch the paperwork. Won't be a mo'."

Miss Lidgett sniffed the air where George had been standing. Scent. After-shave, it was sold as, but she regarded it as scent. Dazedly she prepared the coffee. George returned with a buff-colored file under his arm, and she noticed that his shoes were white buckskin with gilt buckles.

It was a relief when he sat down and started explaining the contents of the file – phone bill, so much left in an envelope for the window cleaner ("So he'd never cotton to your being away"), so much given to the charity collections. ("I didn't return all the envelopes they pushed through the door, you understand, only the ones I was certain you supported").

"This figure, £108, is what I have receipts for, and this one, £15-25, is for payments to tradesmen and charity and so forth, where there aren't receipts."

Miss Lidgett opened her checkbook. "Thank you very much." She was absurdly embarrassed, for George Abbey had changed. It was more than the ridiculous clothes – he was full of himself, commanding, faintly impatient.

"The garden's a picture," she ventured, trying to discount her ambivalent feelings toward a man who had gone to much trouble on her account.

A shadow crossed his face. "Yes, well, I've spent more time over here lately than in my own garden. I didn't tell you about all the fuss when I wrote – no point in upsetting you.

"Gwen, my wife, upped and left me a couple of weeks after you went abroad. It had been in the cards for years, bound to happen. We both know she was flighty."

Miss Lidgett sputtered on her coffee. George gave her a straight look. "It was nice of you to look the other way for all those years, Miss L. Don't think I wasn't grateful for the way you ignored what was going on.

"Anyway, Gwen went off with one of her fancy men. Her sister cut up rough after a week or two, reckoned something must have happened to Gwen. The police came and I told them the whole thing – showed 'em all the clothes she'd taken. Her side of the wardrobe was damned near empty. Excuse the swearing, Miss L.

"Inspector Clough from the Borough Force, he was very nice, very understanding. But Gwen's sister was pestering him, so – well, they had to dig up my garden."

Miss Lidgett's ears were singing. "Dig up –"

69

"In case I'd buried Gwen's body there," Abbey explained. "It looks like a minefield now. I haven't had the heart to put it right – it would take years. I'm selling my house, moving down to the coast."

Folding the check in half, Abbey got to his feet. "Still, it's an ill wind and all that. I love my gardening, so I spent all my time on yours."

He paused, and she saw that his forehead glistened. "Up behind the raspberry canes, remember where you always wanted a garden shed? Well, that's what I was checking, just now. The concrete's hard, and I'll send a couple of men up from the shop this afternoon to erect the shed."

Miss Lidgett drew herself up. She reviewed the years in her mind – George Abbey's patience, his wife's deplorable and provocative conduct, and then, returning to the present, the matter of a new garden shed.

Calculations raced through her head. The police would have called on Abbey's next-door neighbors. So how had he – of course! Abbey had the key to her bungalow, and Miss Lidgett was not known to the police.

They had knocked at her door, and a woman had answered. There was a woman, all right: George Abbey's after-shave and flared trousers proved that. Yes, *a* Miss

Lidgett had assured the detectives that there was nothing she could tell them about Mr. Abbey. Apart from the fact that she never left the bungalow for more than an hour or two at a time, and therefore it was impossible for Abbey to have buried anything in *her* garden.

George asked humbly, "Anything else, Miss Lidgett, or are we all squared away now?"

"Nothing else, George. I wish you good fortune."

Abbey hung his head, the elderly schoolboy, the deceptive dunce. "Um ... I won't be seeing you again, then? Before I move?"

"No, George. I don't believe you will." Decision, not speculation.

Later that day Miss Lidgett inspected the neat square of concrete where the shed would stand. It lay in a pleasant corner, the privet hedge sheltering it. But it was not hallowed ground.

Then again, unlike the Almighty, Miss Lidgett was not all-seeing, all-knowing. There was at least a fifty-fifty chance that if she called the police and had the concrete broken up, had the earth beneath searched, nothing would be found.

And Gwen Abbey had been a terrible wife.

71

Was George Abbey to be persecuted when the only firm evidence against him was that of being an obsessively good neighbor?

Miss Lidgett shook her head, turned her back on the concrete, and walked back to the bungalow.

ISSAC ASIMOV

The Cross of Lorraine

Emmanuel Rubin did not, as a general rule, ever permit a look of relief to cross his face. Had one done so, it would have argued a prior feeling of uncertainty or aprehension, sensations he might feel but would certainly never admit to.

This time, however, the relief was unmistakable. It was monthly banquet time for the Black Widowers. Rubin was the host and it was he who was supplying the guest. And here it was twenty minutes after seven and only now – with but ten minutes left before dinner was to start – only now did his guest arrive.

Rubin bounded toward, him, careful, however, not to spill a drop of his second drink.

"Gentlemen," he said, clutching the arm of the newcomer, "my guest, The Amazing Larri – spelled L-A-R-R-I." And in a lowered voice, over the hum of pleased-to-meet-yous, "Where the hell were you?"

Larri muttered, "The subway train

stalled." Then he returned smiles and greetings.

"Pardon me," said Henry, the perennial – and nonpareil – waiter at the Black Widower banquets, "but there is not much time for the guest to have his drink before dinner begins. Would you state your preference, sir?"

"A good notion, that," said Larri gratefully. "Thank you, waiter, and let me have a dry martini, but not too darned dry – a little damp, so to speak."

"Certainly, sir," said Henry.

Rubin said, "I've told you, Larri, that we members all have our *ex officio* doctorates, so now let me introduce them in nauseating detail. This tall gentleman with the neat mustache, black eyebrows, and straight back is Dr. Geoffrey Avalon. He's a lawyer and he never smiles. The last time he tried, he was fined for contempt of court."

Avalon smiled as broadly as he could and said, "You undoubtedly know Manny well enough, sir, not to take him seriously."

"Undoubtedly," said Larri. As he and Rubin stood together, they looked remarkably alike. Both were the same height – about five feet five – both had active, inquisitive faces, both had straggly beards, though Larri's was longer and was ac-

74

companied by a fringe of hair down both sides of his face as well.

Rubin said, "And here, dressed fit to kill anyone with a *real* taste for clothing, is our artist-expert, Dr. Mario Gonzalo, who will insist on producing a caricature of you in which he will claim to see a resemblance. – Dr. Roger Halsted inflicts pain on junior high-school students under the guise of teaching them what little he knows of mathematics. – Dr. James Drake is a superannuated chemist who once conned someone into granting him a Ph.D. – And finally, Dr. Thomas Trumbull, who works for the government in an unnamed job as a code expert and who spends most of his time hoping Congress doesn't find out."

"Manny," said Trumbull wearily, "if it were possible to cast a retroactive blackball, I think you could count on five."

And Henry said, "Gentlemen, dinner is served."

It was one of those rare Black Widower occasions when lobster was served, rarer now than ever because of the increase in price.

Rubin, who as host bore the cost, shrugged it off. "I made a good paperback sale last month and we can call this a celebration."

"We can celebrate," said Avalon, "but

lobster tends to kill conversation. The cracking of claws and shells, the extraction of meat, the dipping in melted butter – all that takes one's full concentration." And he grimaced with the effort he was putting into the compression of a nutcracker.

"In that case," said the Amazing Larri, "I shall have a monopoly of the conversation," and he grinned with satisfaction as a large platter of prime rib-roast was dexterously placed before him by Henry.

"Larri is allergic to seafood," said Rubin.

Conversation was indeed subdued, as Avalon had predicted, until the various lobsters had been clearly worsted in culinary battle, and then, finally, Halsted asked, "What makes you Amazing, Larri?"

"Stage name," said Larri. "I am a prestidigitator, an escapist extraordinary, and the greatest living exposer."

Trumbull, who was sitting to Larri's right, formed ridges on his bronzed forehead. "What the devil do you mean by 'exposer'?"

Rubin beat a tattoo on his water glass at this point and said, "No grilling till we've had our coffee."

"For God's sake," said Trumbull, "I'm just asking for the definition of a word."

"Host's decision is final," said Rubin.

Trumbull scowled in Rubin's direction.

"Then I'll *guess* the answer. An exposer is one who exposes fakes – people who, using trickery of one sort or another, pretend to produce effects they attribute to supernatural or paranatural forces."

Larri thrust out his lower lip, raised his eyebrows and nodded. "Very good for a guess. I couldn't have put it better."

Gonzalo said, "You mean that whatever someone did by what he claimed was real magic, you could do by stage magic?"

"Exactly," said Larri. "For instance, suppose that some mystic claimed he had the capacity to bend spoons by means of unknown forces. I can do the same by using natural force, this way." He lifted his spoon and, holding it by its two ends, he bent it half an inch out of shape.

Trumbull said, "That scarcely counts. Anyone can do it that way."

"Ah," said Larri, "but this spoon you saw me bend is not the amazing effect at all. That spoon you were watching merely served to trap and focus the ethereal rays that did the real work. Those rays acted to bend *your* spoon, Dr. Trumbull."

Trumbull looked down and picked up his spoon, which was bent nearly at right angles. "How did you do this?"

Larri shrugged. "Would you believe ethereal forces?"

Drake laughed, and pushing his dismantled lobster toward the center of the table, lit a cigarette. He said, "Larri did it a few minutes ago, with his hands, when you weren't looking."

Larri seemed unperturbed by exposure. "When Manny banged his glass, Dr. Trumbull, you looked away. I had rather hoped you all would."

Drake said, "I know better than to pay attention to Manny."

"But," said Larri, "if no one had seen me do it, would you have accepted the ethereal forces?"

"Not a chance," said Trumbull.

"Even if there had been no other way in which you could explain the effect? – Here, let me show you something. Suppose you wanted to flip a coin –"

He fell silent for a moment while Henry passed out the strawberry shortcake, pushed his own serving out of the way, and said, "Suppose you wanted me to flip a coin without actually lifting it and turning it – this penny, for instance. There are a number of ways it could be done. The simplest would be merely to touch it quickly, because, as you all know, a finger is always slightly sticky, especially at meal time, so that the coin lifts up slightly as the finger is removed and can easily be made to flip over. It is tails now, you see. Touch it again and it is heads."

Gonzalo said, "No prestidigitation there, though. We see it flip."

"Exactly," said Larri, "and that's why I won't do it that way. Let's put something over it so that it can't be touched. Suppose we use a –" He looked around the table for a moment and seized a salt shaker. "Suppose we use this."

He placed the salt shaker over the coin and said, "Now it's showing heads –"

"Hold on," said Gonzalo. "How do we know it's showing heads? It could be tails and then, when you reveal it later, you'll say it flipped, when it was tails all along."

"You're perfectly right," said Larri, "and I'm glad you raised the point. – Dr. Drake, you have eyes that caught me before. Would you check this on behalf of the assembled company? I'll lift the salt shaker and you tell me what the coin shows."

Drake looked and said, "Heads," in his softly hoarse voice.

"You'll all take Dr. Drake's word, I hope, gentlemen?" – Please watch me place the salt shaker back on the coin and make sure it doesn't flip in the process."

79

"It didn't," said Drake.

"Now to keep my fingers from slipping while performing this trick, I will put this paper napkin over the salt shaker."

Larri folded the paper napkin neatly and carefully around the salt shaker, then said, "But, in manipulating this napkin, I caused you all to divert your attention from the penny and you may think I have flipped it in the process." He lifted the salt shaker with the napkin around it, and said, "Dr. Drake, will you check the coin again?"

Drake leaned toward it. "Still heads," he said.

Very carefully and gently Larri put back the salt shaker, the paper napkin still folded around it, and said, "The coin remained as is?"

"Still heads," said Drake.

"In that case, I now perform the magic." Larri pushed down on the salt shaker and the paper napkin collapsed. There was nothing inside.

There was a moment of shock, and then Gonzalo said, "Where's the salt shaker?"

"In another plane of existence," said Larri airily.

"But you said you were going to flip the coin."

"I lied."

80

Avalon said, "There's no mystery. He had us all concentrating on the coin as a diversion tactic. When he picked up the salt shaker with the napkin around it to let Jim look at the coin, he just dropped the salt shaker into his hand and placed the empty, folded napkin over the coin."

"Did you see me do that, Dr. Avalon?" asked Larri.

"No. I was looking at the coin, too."

"Then you're just guessing," said Larri.

Rubin, who had not participated in the demonstration at all, but who had eaten his strawberry shortcake, said, "The tendency is to argue these things out logically and that's impossible. Scientists and other rationalists are used to dealing with the universe, which fights fair. Faced with a mystic who does not, they find themselves maneuvered into believing nonsense and, in the end, making fools of themselves.

"Magicians, on the other hand," Rubin went on, "know what to watch for, are experienced enough not to be misdirected, and are not impressed by the apparently supernatural. That's why mystics generally won't perform if they know magicians are in the audience."

Coffee had been served and was being sipped, and Henry was quietly preparing the brandy, when Rubin sounded the water glass and said, "Gentlemen, it is time for the official grilling assuming you idiots have left anything to grill. Jeff, will you do the honors tonight?"

Avalon cleared his throat portentously and frowned down on The Amazing Larri from under his dark and luxuriant eyebrows. Using his voice in the deepest of its naturally deep register, he said, "It is customary to ask our guests to justify their existences, but if today's guest exposes phony mystics even occasionally, I, for one, consider his existence justified and will pass on to another question.

"The temptation is to ask you how you performed your little disappearing trick of a few moments ago, but I quite understand that the ethics of your profession preclude your telling us – even though everything said here is considered under the rose, and though nothing has ever leaked, I will refrain from that question.

"Let me instead ask about your failures – Sir, you describe yourself as an exposer. Have there been any supposedly mystical demonstrations you have not been able to account for by natural means?"

Larri said, "I have not attempted to explain all the effects I have ever encountered or heard of, but where I have studied an effect and made an attempt to duplicate it, I have succeeded in every case."

"No failures?"

"None."

Avalon considered that, but as he prepared for the next question, Gonzalo broke in. His head was leaning on one palm, but the fingers of that hand were carefully disposed in such a way as not to disarray his hair. He said, "Now, wait, Larri, would it be right to suggest that you tackled only easy cases? The really puzzling cases you might have made no attempts to explain?"

"You mean," said Larri, "that I shied away from anything that might spoil my perfect record or that might upset my belief in the rational order of the universe? – If so, you're quite wrong, Dr. Gonzalo. Most reports of apparent mystical powers are dull and unimportant, crude and patently false. I ignore those. The cases I do take on are precisely the puzzling ones that have attracted attention because of their unusual nature and their apparent divorce from the rational. So, you see, the ones I take on are precisely those you suspect I avoid."

Gonzalo subsided and Avalon said, "Larri, the mere fact that you can duplicate a trick by prestidigitation doesn't mean that it couldn't also have been performed by a mystic through supernatural means. The fact that human beings can build machines that fly doesn't mean that birds are man-made machines."

"Quite right," said Larri, "but mystics lay their claims to supernatural powers on the notion, either expressed or implicit, that there is no other way of producing the effect. If I show that the same effect *can* be produced by natural means, the burden of proof then shifts to them to show that the effect can be produced after the natural means are made impossible. I don't know of any mystic who has accepted the conditions set by professional magicians to guard against trickery and who then succeeded."

"And nothing has ever baffled you? Not even the tricks other magicians have developed?"

"Oh, yes, there are effects produced by some magicians that baffle me in the sense that I don't know quite how they do it. I might duplicate the effect by perhaps using a different method. In any case, that's not the point. As long as an effect is produced by natural means, it doesn't matter whether I can reproduce it or not. I am not the best magician in the world. I am just a better magician than any mystic is."

Halsted, his high forehead flushed, and

stuttering slightly in his eagerness to speak, said, "But then nothing would startle you? No disappearance like the one involving the salt shaker?"

"You mean that one?" asked Larri, pointing. There was a salt shaker in the middle of the table, but no one had seen it placed there.

Halsted, thrown off a moment, recovered and said, "Have you ever been *startled* by any disappearance? I heard once that magicians have made elephants disappear."

"Actually, making an elephant disappear is childishly simple. I assure you there's nothing puzzling about disappearances performed in a magic act." And then a peculiar look crossed Larri's face, a flash of sadness and frustration. "Not in a magic act. Just –"

"Yes?" said Halsted. "Just what?"

"Just in real life," said Larri, smiling and attempting to toss off the remark lightheartedly.

"Just a minute," said Trumbull, "we can't let that pass. If there has been a disappearance in real life you can't explain, we want to hear about it."

Larri shook his head. "No, no, Dr. Trumbull. It is not a mysterious disappearance or an inexplicable one. Nothing like that at all. I just – well, I lost something and can't find it and it – saddens me."

"The details," said Trumbull.

"It wouldn't be worth your attention," said Larri, embarrassed. "It's a – silly story and somewhat –" He fell into silence.

"Damn it," thundered Trumbull, "we all sit here and voluntarily refrain from asking anything that might result in your being tempted to violate your ethics. Would it violate the ethics of the magician's art for you to tell this story?"

"It's not that at all –"

"Well, then, sir, I repeat what Jeff has told you. Everything said here is in absolute confidence, and the agreement surrounding these monthly dinners is that all questions must be answered. – Manny?"

Rubin shrugged. "That's the way it is, Larri. If you don't want to answer the question we'll have to declare the meeting at an end."

Larri sat back in his chair and look depressed. "I can't very well allow that to happen, considering the fine hospitality I've been shown. I will tell you the story, but you'll find there's not much to it. I met a woman quite accidentally; I lost touch with her. I can't locate her. That's all there is."

"No," said Trumbull, "that's not all there is. Where and how did you meet her? Where and how did you lose touch with her? Why can't you find her again? We want to know the details."

Gonzalo said, "In fact, if you tell us the details, we may be able to help you."

Larri laughed sardonically. "I think not."

"You'd be surprised," said Gonzalo. "In the past –"

Avalon said, "Quiet, Mario. Don't make promises we might not be able to keep. – Would you give us the details, sir? I assure you we'll do our best to help."

Larri smiled wearily. "I appreciate your offer, but you will see that there is nothing you can do merely by sitting here."

He adjusted himself in his seat and said, "I was done with my performance in an upstate town – I'll give you the details when and if you insist, but for the moment they don't matter, except that this happened about a month ago. I had to get to another small town some hundred and fifty miles away for a morning show and that presented a little transportation problem.

"My magic, unfortunately, is not the kind that can transport me a hundred and fifty miles in a twinkling, or even conjure up a pair of seven-league boots. I did not have my car with me – just as well, for I don't like to travel strange roads when I am sleepy – and

87

the net result was that I would have to take a bus that would take nearly four hours. I planned to catch some sleep while on wheels and thus make the trip serve a double purpose.

"But when things go wrong, they go wrong in battalions, so you can guess that I missed my bus and that the next one would not come along for two more hours. There was an enclosed station in which I could wait, one that was as dreary as you could imagine – with no reading matter except some fly-blown posters on the wall – no place to buy a paper or a cup of coffee. I thought grimly that it was fortunate it wasn't raining, and settled down to drowse, when my luck changed.

"A woman walked in. I've never been married, gentlemen, and I've never even had what young people today call a 'meaningful relationship.' Some casual attachments, perhaps, but on the whole, though it seems trite to say so, I am married to my art and find it much more satisfying than women, generally.

"I had no reason to think that this woman was an improvement on the generality, but she had a pleasant appearance. She was something over thirty, and was just plump enough to have a warm, comfortable

88

look about her, and she wasn't too tall.

"She looked about and said, smiling, 'Well, I've missed my bus, I see.'

"I smiled with her. I liked the way she said it. She didn't fret or whine or act annoyed at the universe. It was a good-humored statement of fact, and just hearing it cheered me up tremendously because actually I myself was in the mood to fret and whine and act annoyed. Now I could be as good-natured as she and say, 'Two of us, madam, so you don't even have the satisfaction of being unique.'

"'So much the better,' she said. 'We can talk and pass the time that much faster.'

"I was astonished. She did not treat me as a potential attacker or as a possible thief. God knows I am not handsome or even particularly respectable in appearance, but it was as though she had casually penetrated to my inmost character and found it satisfactory. You have no idea how flattered I was. If I were ten times as sleepy, I would have stayed up to talk to her.

"And we did talk. Inside of fifteen minutes I knew I was having the pleasantest conversation in my life – in a crummy bus station at midnight. I can't tell you all we talked about, but I can tell you what we *didn't* talk about. We didn't talk about magic.

"I can interest anyone by doing tricks, but then it isn't me they're interested in; it's the flying fingers and the patter they like. And while I'm willing to buy attention that way, you don't know how pleasant it is to get the attention without purchasing it. She apparently just liked to listen to me, and I know I liked to listen to her.

"Fortunately, my trip was not an all-out effort, so I didn't have my large trunk with the show-business advertising all over it, just two rather large valises. I told her nothing personal about myself, and asked nothing about her. I gathered briefly that she was heading for her brother's place, that it was right on the road, that she would have to wake him up because she had carelessly let herself be late – but she only told me that in order to say that she was glad it had happened. She would buy my company at the price of inconveniencing her brother. I liked that.

"We didn't talk politics or world affairs or religion or the theater. We talked people – all the funny and odd and peculiar things we had observed about people. We laughed for two hours, during which not one other person came to join us. I had never had anything like that happen to me, had never felt so alive and happy, and when the bus finally came at 1:50 A.M., it was amazing how sorry I was. I didn't want the night to end.

"When we got onto the bus, of course, it was no longer quite the same thing, even though we found a double seat we could share. After all, we had been alone in the station and there we could talk loudly and laugh. On the bus people were sleeping.

"Of course it wasn't all bad. It was a nice feeling to have her so close to me. Despite the fact that I'm rather an old horse, I felt like a teenager – enough like a teenager, in fact, to be embarrassed at being watched.

"Immediately across the way was a woman and her young son. He was about eight years old, I should judge, and *he* was awake. He kept watching me with his sharp little eyes. I could see those eyes fixed on us every time a street light shone into the bus and it was very inhibiting. I wished he were asleep, but, of course, the excitement of being on a bus, perhaps, was keeping him awake.

"The motion of the bus, the occasional whisper, the feeling of being quite out of reality, the pressure of her body against mine – it was like confusing dream and fact, and the boundary between sleep and wakefulness just vanished. I didn't intend to sleep, and I started awake once or twice, but then finally, when I started awake one more time, it was clear there had been a considerable period of sleep, and the seat next to me was empty."

Halsted said, "I take it she had gotten off."

"I didn't think she had disappeared into thin air," said Larri. "Naturally, I looked about. I couldn't call her name, because I didn't know her name. She wasn't in the rest room, because the door was swinging open.

"The little boy across the aisle spoke in a rapid high treble – in French. I can understand French reasonably well, but I didn't have to make any effort, because his mother was now awakened and she translated. She spoke English quite well. she said, 'Pardon me, sir, but is it that you are looking for the woman that was with you?"

" 'Yes,' I said. 'Did you see where she got off?'

" 'Not I, sir. I was sleeping. But my son says that she descended at the place of the Cross of Lorraine.'

" 'At the what?'

"She repeated it, and so did the child, in French.

"She said, 'You must excuse my son, sir. He is a great hero worshipper of President Charles de Gaulle and though he is young he knows the tale of the Free French forces
92

in the war very well. He would not miss a sight like a Cross of Lorraine. If he said he saw it, he did.'

"I thanked them and then went forward to the bus driver and asked him, but at that time of night the bus stops wherever a passenger would like to get off, or get on. He had made numerous stops and let numerous people on and off, and he didn't know for sure where he had stopped and whom he had let off. He was rather churlish, in fact."

Avalon cleared his throat. "He may have thought you were up to no good and was deliberately withholding information to protect the passenger."

"Maybe," said Larri despondently, "but what it amounted to was that I had lost her. When I came back to my seat, I found a little note tucked into the pocket of the jacket I had placed in the rack above. I managed to read it by a streetlight at the next stop, where the French mother and son got off. It said, 'Thank you so much for a delightful time. Gwendolyn.'"

Gonzalo said, "You have her first name anyway."

Larri said, "I would appreciate having had her last name, her address, her telephone number. A first name is useless."

"You know," said Rubin, "she may

deliberately have withheld information because she wasn't interested in continuing the acquaintanceship. A romantic little interlude is one thing; a continuing danger is another. She may be a married woman."

"Have you done anything about trying to find her?" asked Gonzalo. "Certainly," said Larri sardonically. "If a magician is faced with a disappearing woman he must understand what has happened. I have gone over the bus route twice by car, looking for a Cross of Lorraine. If I had found it, I would have gone in and asked if anyone there knew a woman by the name of Gwendolyn. I'd have described her. I'd have gone to the local post office or the local police station."

"But you haven't found a Cross of Lorraine, I take it," said Trumbull.

"I have not."

Halsted said, "Mathematically speaking, it's a finite problem. You could try every post office along the whole route."

Larri sighed. "If I get desperate enough, I'll try. But, mathematically speaking, that would be so inelegant. Why can't I find the Cross of Lorraine?"

"The youngster might have made a mistake," said Trumbull.

"Not a chance," said Larri. "An adult, yes, but a child, never. Adults have accumulated enough irrationality to be very unreliable eyewitnesses. A bright eight-year-old is different. Don't try to pull any trick on a bright kid; he'll see through it.

"Just the same," he went on, "nowhere on the route is there a restaurant, a department store, or anything else with the name Cross of Lorraine. I've checked every set of yellow pages along the entire route."

"Now wait a while," said Avalon, "that's wrong. The child wouldn't have seen the words because they would have meant nothing to him. If he spoke and read only French, as I suppose he did, he would know the phrase as 'Croix de Lorraine.' The English would have never caught his eyes. He must have seen the symbol, the cross with the two horizontal bars, like this." He reached out and Henry obligingly handed him a menu.

Avalon turned it over and on the blank back drew the following:

"Actually," he said, "it's more properly called the Patriarchal Cross or the Arch-iepiscopal Cross since it symbolized the high office of patriarchs and archbishops by doubling the bars. You will not be surprised to hear that the Papal Cross has three bars. The Patriarchal Cross was used as a symbol of Godfrey of Bouillon, who was one of the leaders of the First Crusade, and since he was Duke of Lorraine, it came to be called the Cross of Lorraine. As we all know, it was adopted as the emblem of the Free French during the Hitlerian War." He coughed slightly and tried to look modest.

Larri said, a little impatiently, "I understand about the symbol, Dr. Avalon, and I didn't expect the youngster to note words. I think you'll agree, though, that any establishment calling itself the Cross of Lorraine would surely display the symbol along with the name. I looked for the name in the yellow pages and for the symbol on the road."

"And you didn't find it?" said Gonzalo.

"As I've already said, I didn't. I was desperate enough to consider things I didn't think the kid could possibly have seen at night. I thought, who knows how sharp young eyes are and how readily they see something that represents an overriding interest? So I looked at signs in windows, at street signs – even at graffiti."

"If it were a graffito," said Trumbull,

96

"which happens to be the singular form of graffiti, by the way, then, of course, it could have been erased between the time the child saw it and the time you came to look for it."

"I'm not sure of that," said Rubin. "It's my experience that graffiti are never erased. We've got some on the outside of our apartment house –"

"That's New York," said Trumbull. "In smaller towns there's less tolerance for these evidences of anarchy."

"Hold on," said Gonzalo, "what makes you think graffiti are necessarily signs of anarchy? As a matter of fact –"

"Gentlemen! Gentlemen!" And as always, when Avalon's voice was raised to its full baritone, a silence fell. "We are not here to argue the merits and demerits of graffiti. The question is: how can we find this woman who disappeared? Larri has found no restaurant or other establishment with the name of Cross of Lorraine; he has found no evidence of the symbol along the route taken. Can we help him?"

Drake held up his hand and squinted through the curling smoke of his cigarette. "Hold on, there's no problem. Have you ever seen a Russian Orthodox Church? Do you know what its cross is like?" He made quick marks on the back of the menu and shoved it toward the center of the table. "Here –"

He said, "The kid, being hipped on the Free French, would take a quick look at that and see it as the Cross of Lorraine. So what you have to do, Larri, is look for a Russian Orthodox Church en route. I doubt there would be more than one."

Larri thought about it, but did not seem overjoyed. "The cross with that second bar set at an angle would be on the top of the spire, wouldn't it?"

"I imagine so."

"And it wouldn't be floodlighted, would it? How would the child be able to see it at three or four o'clock in the morning?"

Drake stubbed out his cigarette. "Well, now, churches usually have a bulletin board near the entrance. There could have been a Russian Orthodox cross on the –"

"I would have seen it," said Larri firmly.

"Could it have been a Red Cross?" asked Gonzalo feebly. "You know, there might be a Red Cross headquarters along the route."

"The Red Cross," said Rubin, "is a Greek

Cross with all four arms equal. I don't see how that could possibly be mistaken for a Cross of Lorraine by a Free French enthusiast. Look at it –"

Halsted said, "The logical thing, I suppose, is that you simply missed it, Larri. If you insist that, as a magician, you're such a trained observer that you *couldn't* have missed it, then maybe it was a symbol on something movable – on a truck in a driveway, for instance, and it moved on after sunrise."

"The boy made it quite clear that it was at the *place* of the Cross of Lorraine," said Larri. "I suppose even an eight-year-old can tell the difference between a place and a movable object."

"He spoke French. Maybe you mis-translated."

"I'm not that bad at the language," said Larri, "and besides, his mother translated and French is her native tongue."

"But English isn't. *She* might have gotten it wrong. The kid might have said something else. He might not even have said the Cross of Lorraine at all."

99

Avalon raised his hand for silence and said, "One moment, gentlemen, I see Henry, our esteemed waiter, smiling. What is it, Henry?"

Henry, from his place at the sideboard, said, "I'm afraid that I am amused at your doubting the child's evidence. It is quite certain, in my opinion, that he did see the Cross of Lorraine."

There was a moment's silence and Larri said, "How can you tell that, Henry?"

"By not being too subtle, sir."

Avalon's voice boomed out. "I knew it! We're being too complicated. Henry, how is it possiable for us to achieve greater simplicity?"

"Why, Mr. Avalon, the incident took place at night. Instead of looking at all signs, all places, all varieties of cross, why not begin by asking ourselves what very few things *can* be easily seen on a highway at night?"

"A Cross of Lorraine?" asked Gonzalo incredulously.

"Certainly," said Henry, "among other things. Especially if we don't call it a Cross of Lorraine. What the youngster saw as a Cross of Lorraine, out of his special interest, we would see as something else so clearly that its relationship to the Cross of Lorraine would be invisible. What has been happening

100

just now has been precisely what happened earlier with Mr. Larri's trick with the coin and the salt shaker. We concentrated on the coin and didn't watch the salt shaker, and now we concentrate on the Cross of Lorraine and don't look for the alternative."

Trumbull said, "Henry, if you don't stop talking in riddles, you're fired. What the hell is the Cross of Lorraine, if it isn't the Cross of Lorraine?"

Henry said gravely, "What is this?" and carefully he drew on the back of the menu –

Trumbull said, "A Cross of Lorraine – tilted."

"No, sir, you would never have thought so, if we hadn't been talking about the Cross of Lorraine. Those are English letters and a very common symbol on highways if you add something to it –" He wrote quickly and the tilted Cross became:

"The one thing," said Henry, "that is designed to be seen without trouble, day or night, on any highway, is a gas-station sign. The child saw the Cross of Lorraine in this one, but Mr. Larri, retracing the route, sees only a double X, since he reads the entire sign as Exxon. All signs showing this name, whether on the highway, in advertisements, or on credit cards, show the name in this fashion."

Now Larri caught fire. "You mean, Henry, that if I go into the Exxon stations en route and ask for Gwendolyn –"

"The proprietor of one of them is likely to be her brother, and there would be no more than a half dozen or so at most to inquire at."

"Good God, Henry," said Larri, "you're a magician."

"Merely simple-minded," said Henry, "though not, I hope, in the pejorative sense."

URSULA CURTISS
Point of No Return

It was so astonishingly fast and simple that for a few moments Roger Corbin could scarcely believe it. He had brought about the most tremendous of all changes – the transition from life to death – and it had been almost like slapping shut a book in a fit of boredom. But then Vera's thin faded-blonde hair had obviously covered a thin skull.

The goldfish in their tank saw everything, and after a quick molten scurry they resumed their tranquil flickering through painted china arches and clusters of imitation white coral. They, and much later an unseen kitten at the edge of a dark field, were the only witnesses to the final disposal of Vera Corbin, and neither would ever speak.

In the morning, the face in the bathroom mirror certainly did not look like that of a wife-killer. the really sinister husbands – or so Roger Corbin had come to believe through novels and television – were the meek and rabbity kind, or the smooth and too-handsome, or the saintly pillars of the community.

He fitted into none of these categories. At a vigorous fifty-three, his big hard body and tanned square-jawed face under the close-cut gray hair were testimonials to his liking for the outdoors. Women, looking at the jaw, sometimes suspected a temper there, but they suspected it in the mysteriously intrigued and admiring way in which women often notice failings in any husband other than their own. Men were dryly amused at Roger's caution with his money – his luncheon companions usually left a surreptitious additional tip – but they liked his easy outspoken air and respected his shrewdness.

Less was known about Roger's wife, who spent a good deal of her time making complicated casseroles and polishing her ivy, but on the surface at least the Corbins had a reasonably normal twenty-five-year marriage. It was true that Vera, like many small excitable women, had been known to rush off in a huff for a week or so at a time, but this was regarded as a substitute for bowling or ping-pong.

As a result, no one at the office was surprised when Roger let it drop in a half annoyed, half humorous way that he wished his wife would get over her current fit of pique and come home again.

Howard Cooper and Dennis Thorne, married colleagues who prudently wanted no details of a domestic upset, merely raised their eyebrows and shook their heads noncommittally. It was left to doting Miss Wegby, Roger's secretary, to register her sympathy and indignation by a number of moist, warm glances and, the very next morning, by a yellow rosebud from her mother's garden.

Miss Wegby might have been designed by a committee of jealous wives. Although only in her late twenties, she had the overbosomed, broad-hipped figure of a matron twice her age. She was asthmatic and near-sighted, and in vain she administered layers of powder to her gleaming and earnest face, a practice which someone had unkindly likened to hiding her light under a bushel. But she was an expert shorthand typist, devoted and passionately loyal – she frequently took work home with her – and she was more comforting to Roger Corbin at this juncture of his life than any houri. Because hadn't someone said that no one knew a man as well as his secretary? And here was Miss Wegby bringing him bouton-nieres and Danish pastry for his midmorning coffee – "You can't be eating properly, Mr. Corbin," – and generally cherishing him to the top of her bent.

She needn't have worried about Roger's meals. He did think a little wistfully about Vera's casserole's – for a woman of almost no imagination she had been an extremely good cook – but the freezer was well stocked and his appetite had never faltered. He would return to the silent house at 5:30, set his dinner preparations in train, feed the knowledgeable goldfish with a steady hand, and settle down comfortably with a drink and the newspaper. Half hearted dinner invitations had been conveyed through their husbands by Mrs. Cooper and Mrs. Thorne, but Roger declined. "I'd better be at home, just in …"

Far from getting on his nerves, the empty house delighted him: it had somewhat the quality of a finally stilled faucet. Not that he took any liberties with the housekeeping: he was fully as property-minded as Vera had been, and used coasters and placemats and ashtrays with care. The cleaning woman had made her weekly visit, and a half hour every evening with dustcloth and mop kept the place almost as gleaming as when Vera had been in residence.

When eight days had gone by, he invited

young Derek Bingham, the only unmarried man in the office, for dinner. He had done this before in temporary bachelorhood and it was important to keep to the pattern. More than that, it was time to plant the first suggestion. Over an after-dinner beer, gazing pensively at the hearth where Vera had fallen after her head was sent crashing back against the stone edge of the mantel, he mused like a man thinking aloud.

"Maybe we ought to get away more week-ends. Vera and I," he explained to Bingham's somewhat baffled face – they had been talking about Vietnam a moment before. "Maybe that's what's been the trouble."

Bingham looked uncomfortable and studied his beer as attentively as though it had just spoken to him.

" Oh, no real trouble – good lord, you don't throw twenty-five years out the window," said Roger with too much cheerfulness and too much confidence. He brooded. "I guess the damn columnists are right and a woman gets feeling taken for granted. I thought she was all wrapped up in the house" – his gaze swept over the textured lemon carpeting, the gleams of mahogany, the paintings selected to match the slipovers – "but – well." He slapped the arms of his chair decisively and made a wry face. "Those are deep waters, and you haven't even got your feet wet yet. Don't let it put you off that very pretty girl I saw you with at lunch today. How about another beer?"

Predictably, Bingham fled.

The first move had been made.

If Roger should presently announce tidings of a divorce, who would gainsay him? Not family – Vera's widowed mother, had died ten years before and Vera had quarreled bitterly with some cousins who had sheltered the old lady and been remembered in the modest will. They had received the money and Vera had inherited two paltry lots in a slum section of Newark, New Jersey, and since then there had never been so much as an exchange of Christmas cards.

Close friends were not a hazard, because Vera had none. After their eleven months here Roger was far better known than she, and if he did not raise a hue and cry, who would? It wasn't as though he intended to remarry – Vera had cured him of that. Neither were there any financial considerations. They had a joint checking account, but at some future and judicious time he would simply change banks.

Although he and Vera had made out mutual wills at the time of their marriage, unrevoked through the years of corrosive dislike, he wasn't losing anything there. To any questions he would merely say – and it must often happen this way – that his wife had severed all communication with him and he had no idea where she was to be found.

... Found.

Unlikely, in the newly plowed field ready for planting two miles away. Roger didn't even know the owner, which seemed in itself a safeguard. As for Vera's old green Volkswagen – driven deep into the trees along a ditch-bank and containing the suitcase she had packed so furiously with her own hands – the car was far more likely to be striped in that area than reported to the police.

And if it were reported? One more case of a woman foolish enough to have picked up a hitchhiker, or to have driven at night with the passenger door unlocked. Volkswagen and body were well over a mile apart, but surely the police would waste considerable time in dragging the obvious place, the ditch. They could investigate the house and Roger to their heart's content. There had been surprisingly little blood on the hearth where Vera had stood and said the one unforgivable thing, and he was confident that his own small-hours' scrubbing, the cleaning woman's ministrations, and several open fires had taken care of that. As to his own life, the deepest probing could not produce any indication of monetary gain or any interest in another woman, because neither existed.

And there were certainly no witnesses to the growingly acid domestic scenes, the peculiar deadlock about divorce although there had been no religious barrier. In Vera's world, divorced women were subtly disgraced – and in a community-property state Roger was grimly determined not to part with half the reward of his thirty years' work. They were bound forever by their wall-to-wall carpeting and copper-colored kitchen appliances and Vera's philosophy of life, of which perhaps the high point was an insistence on cloth napkins instead of paper.

Why, the police would have to ask themselves, would a husband of twenty-five years suddenly not be able to stand it a single moment longer?

Roger had once read somewhere that by tracing a finger gently and unceasingly over the same place on the skin it was possible to produce bleeding. Vera had done that, only at the end she had not used a gentle finger but the sharpest kind of knife...

Roger Corbin was an only child, his father dead before he was born. Marguerite Corbin was an attractive and ambitious woman who found her adoring son an asset until he was twenty-five and a distinct liability thereafter. Was this great and prematurely graying creature to contradict her punishing diets, her facials, her cunning hair tints? She found Vera Beasly, and said to Roger in her fluttery voice, "Darling, it isn't *right* of me to monopolize your life – it's the kind of thing that gives mothers a bad name. I would like to see you settled down, you know, perhaps in the kind of home where" – she smiled at him bravely – "I might someday be welcome now and then."

A little bewildered, frightened at his mother's mysterious air of courage, Roger had married Vera, small and energetic and blonde. Mrs. Corbin, unencumbered, presently went off with a dubiously titled Italian and sank, along with all hands, on his yacht off the coast of Sicily.

Vera was all twitters and comfort, and alluded only three or four times to the fact that, far from leaving an estate, Mrs. Corbin had bequeathed them a few debts. She took a course in shorthand and typing, got a job in a wholesale drug house, and at the end of five years was office manager. The rise to this position was reflected at home in a new and critical crispness, a sharper eye on time-wasting habits like a late Saturday-morning sleep. Roger, beginning to make a respectable income, was also beginning to feel like an erring typist. He insisted that Vera give up her job.

A mistake? Possibly, because her new aggressiveness was now unleashed at home. On the other hand, she had been well on the way to becoming a female dictator, with "absenteeism" and "waste motion" routine parts of her conversation. Deprived of a public outlet for her energy, she sat back triumphantly to see just how well Roger was going to provide for them – and the fact that he did so with increasing success seemed to gall her.

At the end of ten years there were no children, a fact at which Roger was by now obscurely relieved. Vera was less reticent, but for a different reason. "There's so much in heredity, and, well, we know about my people but we don't know a thing about your father, do we? I mean, perhaps it's just as well..."

This carried a deep sting which Roger was careful not to let his wife see. As a child he had asked the usual questions about his

112

father, only to be confronted by a pretty little handkerchief applied to his mother's eyes. "My treasure mustn't ask me about that. Such a wonderful man, such a tragedy – oh, I simply can't talk about it!" Once she indicated that his father had pined away of tuberculosis. On another and forgetful occasion Mrs. Corbin mentioned a fire in a theater where he had given his life to save women and children. Long before her death, Roger had accepted the strong possibility that he was illegitimate.

Far from undermining his devotion to his mother's memory, the delicate insinuations about any irregularity in her marital status only deepened his Roger's dislike of Vera, already well begun. If it had become hatred at that point, or even if Vera, perversely, had not been such an excellent manager, the marriage might have come to a quiet and bloodless end. But his aversion was still like a familiar but scratchy sweater – nothing to make a man rip the garment off – and in Vera's careful hands their net worth was becoming very comfortable.

So the point of no return was reached, unnoticed, and passed. The negative aspects of their marriage were in a curious way as binding as their possessions. Vera could not complain that Roger drank to excess or

113

abused her physically or gambled or ran around with other women; indeed, he didn't even run around with her, and this formed the basis for her furious little departures. To her querulous demands as to why they couldn't go away occasionally for a vacation – even a weekend at some nice resort – Roger merely answered implacably that he was going fishing or hunting instead; surely it had penetrated even her head that some kind of physical exercise was considered imperative for men of his age?

It was incredible to him that she should seriously expect him to spend time and effort and money to closet himself in a strange place with a woman who was only and barely tolerable in seeing to his comforts at home. And because it was so very obvious he never bothered to say it.

For his part, Roger could not point to any neglect of the house, or any frittering away of money. Nor had Vera let herself go. At forty-nine she was nothing more than plump and well girdled, and she dressed with fussy care – so much so that no collar or pocket or waistline ever suited her, but had to be smoothed and plucked and tugged at with office-manager firmness. Apart from two small deep vertical lines between her eyebrows, her skin was still almost girlish;

her blonde hair, although faded, was carefully curled. It was a tribute to the Corbins' peculiar expertise and perhaps to their surroundings that, on the rare occasions when they entertained, Vera's wifely little sharpnesses and Roger's sardonic retorts made them seem all the more solidly and comfortably married.

On that evening eight days before, up until the very last seconds, they would not have had the appearance of killer and victim.

It had not been a good day at Slade Enterprises where Roger worked. At 4:30 he even had occasion to snap at the usually faultless Miss Wegby. Arriving at the foot of his driveway at 5:30, in the moodiness that springs from remorse, he discovered that Vera had failed to bring in the newspaper and that it had been run over by some vehicle with disastrous results. He had backed and swerved with grim speed and driven to the nearest store, returning at 6:00 with an edition from which the owners of the store had torn the pages containing their own and their competitors' ads, and was informed by Vera that dinner would be ready in a matter of minutes.

Roger's blood pressure had slid up a notch. For the last several weeks, in her disapproval at the fact that his pre-dinner Scotches were gradually creeping from two to three, Vera had been stealthily advancing the dinner hour. "Well, *I* won't be ready in-a-matter-of-minutes," he had said shortly, mimicking her briskness. "After having to go nearly back to town to get the blasted paper, I'm going to have a drink in peace."

Vera's brows went up at his use of the singular, but she only said, "I'll do what I can with the chicken hash" – in a tone implying that she would put down some kind of insurrection – and departed for the kitchen.

She was back almost at once, her arms folded militantly. When Roger didn't glance up from his mutilated newspaper she said in a high bright voice. "I'm sorry about the paper – it must have been the dishwasher repairman. It broke down this morning and I called them at once, and of *course* he didn't come until midafternoon and of *course* he didn't have the proper part on the truck and of *course* it was too late by then for him to go back to the shop and get it. All this charming mañana!" finished Vera with biting scorn. "Why, I wonder, is it considered so charming to be lazy and late about everything but the bill?"

All, so far, had gone largely according to

pattern except that they were both a little more tense than usual. The finger-snapping, efficiency-watching Vera simply didn't fit into this leisurely suburb, reflected Roger, forgetting his own temper at delay. "If this is a prelude to suggesting that we move back East, forget it," he said, walking to the kitchen to make his second drink. "We've got a lot of money invested in this place. My God, look what you've got here!" His gaze swept appreciatively over hanging ivy and coppper and stainless steel.

"I *have* looked. A broken dishwasher," said Vedra, prim and icy.

The quarrel, although it was hardly more than routine procedure, continued through dinner and after. Both said what they had said a hundred times before, and Vera's face acquired a mottled flush. She was not a woman, if such a woman existed, whom anger became. They had reached the familiar point of, "If you're so bent on going away, why don't you? Nobody's stopping you," and "All right, that's exactly what I will do!" when Vera added something new. Flinging a sponge dramatically into the spotless sink, wheeling to pass him, she said with quiet deadliness, "Do you know something, Roger? I'm sure nobody at the office would dare tell you, but you are getting *very odd.*"

On that she had departed for the bedroom. Thump, click, rustle: she was packing like a wet hen, until the ultimate respectability of a husband should appeal to her again. Roger interjected a fresh note of his own, shouting through the closed door, "Do me a favor and take a lot of clothes with you. Along with your bank book."

In one sense, this savings account was a thorn in his flesh as it was solely in Vera's name and not subject to the community-property law, representing income from the New Jersey lots left to her by her mother. On the other hand, it financed these little expeditions of hers.

Ostentatiously, while the sounds of preparation went on in the bedroom, he finished his coffee, consulted the paper, and switched on the television set. He was the picture of unconcerned comfort when there was a suitcase-sounding thump in the entrance hall and Vera, gray-suited, wearing a small black-and-white hat and black pumps, stalked past him across the lemon carpeting to the mantelpiece.

"I'm leaving Mrs. Tafoya's key here. If you want her to clean on Thursday, put it under the middle pot of ivy outside the front door."

"What? Oh, the middle pot. Right," said

Roger, gazing sedulously at the television screen. Vera, one white glove on, was now smoothing on the other with the tiny interminable pushings that accompanied this act. Her anger was almost visible in the room as a shimmer of heat. "Shall I tell you something else, Roger?"

"Do. I have always lacked the Beasley culture and stand ready to be instructed. I have never," said Roger – Vera's father had owned a small feed-and-grain store – "quite understood the difference between chick feed and mash."

He was on his feet – polite, receptive. Vera's face hardened and she lifted her head. "I've finally figured out why your mother never told you about your father. She obviously didn't know who he was – Don't you *dare* touch me, Roger Corbin, don't you dare lay a fing –"

That was when the goldfish began their molten scurry...

Barring any immediate family or close friends to make an outcry, people were, Roger discovered, rather easily lost. Now that he paid attention to the subject, the newspapers seemed full of tiny casual items about bones stumbled across by hunters or picnickers or exploring children.

119

Vera's mail, for instance, presented no problem. Advertisements from local stores, a card advising Vera that her dentist had moved his office to a new address, a darkly worded statement that two library books were overdue. Roger found and returned the books and paid the fine to a high-school girl he had never seen before.

The way now seemed clear – particularly as young Bingham could testify to his presentiments – for a rueful announcement that he had heard from Vera in Reno and she meant it after all: she was divorcing him

"Twenty-five years," he would repeat, shaking his head unbelievingly, but he knew from experience that his acquaintances would shy away from details and his secretary think him the most wronged of men.

It was the sheerest accident that he did not carry out this plan. Returning uncustomarily to the house at noon one day because he had forgotten his reading glasses, and automatically scooping the mail from the box, he took a cursory look before he left. Mortgage payment, electric-light bill, a political circular – and a letter, airmailed, for Mrs. Vera B. Corbin from Paget & Maybank, the Newark attorneys who handled the rental property.

A thorough scrutiny with the letter held against the light told Roger nothing except that there was no check enclosed. But in this climate envelopes came unstuck with ease, and with only a little coaxing this one did. In his speculation over the lack of people who might make pressing inquiries about Vera he had forgotten all about this area of her life, and the omission frightened him; his fingers were trembling as he unfolded the single stiff white sheet.

And learned that the two insignificant lots had stood in the way of a new bank building and parking lot under an urban renewal plan. Thanks to Vera's already-sent power of attorney, the sale had ben consummated for $50,000.

Roger didn't dare take the afternoon off – it was something he had never done before – but he looked at production records and signed the morning's dictation in a daze of rage and bewilderment. $50,000! How could such a thing possibly –? But of course it was Vera who visited the mailbox on weekdays and she had simply sequestered everything that had to do with the sale of the lots. Business-minded, she knew very well, that this windfall didn't come under the community-property law, and she had kept the earlier bargaining stages secret.

What else – *who* else – might there be that he didn't know about or hadn't thought of?

Back in the house at 5:30 – the house that might be teeming with destructive forces – Roger didn't even pause to make a drink but commenced a search at once. He spent very little time at the desk where Vera had paid the household bills and written letters and Christmas cards; she would have kept nothing clandestine there. The bedroom? That was the obvious place – or no, it wasn't. The kitchen.

The letters from Paget & Maybank, four of them in a period of more than a year, were curled neatly in the innermost of a nest of cannisters in the cupboard under the sinks. Besides being lodged behind an almost impenetrable barrier of frying pans and chafing dishes, the cannisters were vessels Roger would never use no matter how long he cooked for himself.

On the heels of panic came a kind of appalled fury at Vera. It was safe now to pause for a drink, but clearly she could not be trusted one inch. By midnight, however, with three more drinks and a gulped-down hamburger along the way, he had searched the house so thoroughly that he was confident there were no more secrets.

Today's letter no longer frightened him in itself; it asked no questions and didn't even require an acknowledgment. And four communications in over a year did not suggest that Paget & Maybank were feverishly preoccupied with the affairs of Vera B. Corbin. As they had her power of attorney, it might and probably would be months before they instituted any inquiry as to the whereabouts of their client. Months before Vera was found dead and her will became effective and $50,000 passed into Roger's bereaved hands.

He snatched his mind from that thought as he would have snatched his hand from a high-tension wire.

But it came back, and with it, like the frill on a lamb chop, came the idea of triumph over Vera. But first – and Roger shuddered when he recalled how close he had come to announcing that he had heard from her in Reno – first he must consider the risks.

Provided that Vera were disinterred quite soon, the date of her death could be established to have been substantially earlier than the glad tidings from Paget & Maybank, so there was no real problem of motive on his part. As to the actual disposal of her body – unflinchingly, he sent his mind back.

A small woman, she had fitted quite easily

into the back seat of her Volkswagen. It hadn't been late – not much after 9:00 – but he had been met by very few oncoming cars and, in that quiet area of alfalfa fields and tiny adobe houses, had been passed only once. The headlights had died around a curve; he had sat tensely in the Volkswagen to make very sure of that before pulling in at the edge of the plowed field.

The mewing kitten? A dog would have worried him, with the vision of someone at the end of a leash, but people here did not walk cats. On the contrary, they abandoned unwanted ones.

It had taken a surprisingly long time to dig deep enough, even in the loose earth, and more time to fill in, moving backward on hands and knees and raking roughly with his fingers so that the earth should not look tamped down. In the dark he could only guess at his success. Then off to the ditch a mile away, the green Volkswagen driven deep into green, and this time there were no headlights at all and almost no house lights showing. It had been a long walk home, again without encounter.

The car. That was the safe and indirect way. Arrange to have the car reported, so that the police would come to him with the initial disadvantage of having to deliver gravely disturbing news. An abandoned car, a suitcase packed as only a woman could pack it, the ditch . . .

In the morning Roger cruised by the ditch, gazing with an informed eye through the mask of tamarisks and cottonwoods. The Volkswagen didn't seem to be there, oddly, although even by night he could not have been mistaken –

Dangling binoculars casually, he left his car, pushed his way through undergrowth, gazed disbelievingly at heavy tire tracks in the sandy soil. At the time he had thought complacently that the Volkswagen would be stripped of its tires and battery and possibly even its engine, and that there would be a juvenile conspiracy not to report the car to the authorities.

But they had taken, or towed, the car itself – the whole car. And with it Vera's suitcase, the tangible argument that she had left her home of her own volition. Car theft thrived in this locality; the Volkswagen, its engine number filed off, was probably spray-painted behind somebody's house.

But the suitcase: what had they done with that? Combed it for valuables, emptied it into the ditch? *That* was a sweat-producing thought; although there were no edible fish to be caught, little boys might well be out with rods, perhaps hooking a blouse or a slip, running proudly home: "Look, Mom!"

With the vanishing of the car, Roger was a man reduced to a course he distrusted and feared, and on too-short notice – but the $50,000 beckoned, and there was now the threat of premature discovery as well. He would have to do what countless men before him had done: humble himself before the police, tell them that his wife had left him after a quarrel, and that he feared for her safety.

He would do it from his office. Calling about such a matter from there would have an open, aboveboard, nothing-to-hide air.

He was spared the trouble. His detour, plus a wild sand-ridden wind that made driving slow and parking lights necessary, brought him to Slade Enterprises late. When he entered his office, Miss Wegby, spectacularly sallow in maroon, was apparently bidding goodbye to a man in a deputy sheriff's uniform.

"Oh, Mr. Corbin, you're just in time," she cried asthmatically. "I know this gentleman is only doing his duty, but it's so ridiculous! I've just told him that Mrs. Corbin was in yesterday after closing hours to pick up the money for her trip."

The room took a small lurch before Roger Corbin's eyes. He made himself look directly at the deputy. "I'm afraid I don't understand. Has there been some question...?"

"You know how it is," said the deputy ruefully; he studied his shoes with embarrassment. "New administration, new broom. We get a call from some catty female to see is your wife all present and accounted for, and we have to check it out. I tell you, we get all kinds. Well –" He touched his wide-brimmed hat. "I wish they were all as easy as this. Morning, ma'am... Mr. Corbin."

Roger could not move at once; an abyss so deep and black that he couldn't even begin to see the bottom of it had just opened up in front of him.

Loyal Miss Wegby. Snapped at on the day that mattered, rushing over to his house in her car with the missing report, seeing him depart with Vera's body. Passing him on that dark quiet road, stopping at a careful distance, coming back.

Watching.

She was eyeing him steadily now. Vast-bosomed, broad-hipped, sallow, asthmatic, she was giving him a look which contained far more than secretarial devotion – a look of yearning love. Because of the high winds and her asthma, her breath made little mewing sounds, like an unseen kitten at the edge of a dark field.

DANA LYON

The Good Companions

Greg and Anne Hayward were the only friends I had at the time they moved away from the city and that left me with none. My sister Rose had been the one who made all the friends, working in an office the way she did, with me staying home and keeping house for her. But when she died last year none of her fine friends bothered to come around and see me or invite me to their homes after they'd paid their condolence calls. So there I sat, alone, living on Rose's pittance from her insurance and the remains of our father's legacy, until Anne and Greg moved in next door. Why they paid so much attention to someone like me, I'll never know – maybe just because they were kind and felt sorry for me.

Well, of course I was kind to them, too, like the time I took Greg some of my homemade soup when he had the flu and Anne was working – he was a writer, so he didn't have to go to work – and I guess some other times, too, though I can't place them.

They were young, in their late twenties, and they didn't have too much of a social life. They seemed to be satisfied just to be with each other, except they'd drop in to see me quite often – to borrow an egg or use my phone if theirs was out of order or chat a bit.

I missed them badly when they left, but they said they couldn't stand the city noises any longer, they just had to get away, and they'd write.

"Dear Susie," Anne wrote shortly after they'd left, "we've found the most wonderful bit of land, a little clearing in some trees with a tank house on it (the regular house burned down some time ago) and real privacy. We're camping out now, but we're going to fix up the tank house until it's *darling* and then you must come to visit us. Best –

"Anne and Greg."

Well, I didn't hear from them after that for ages, and then along came a letter from them Special Delivery.

"Susie dear –

"We're about to ask a great favor of you, though we think you might enjoy it, too. Greg has got to take a trip up north to see his family – his father is quite ill – and we don't want to leave the place alone now that we've

130

fixed it up. Especially our two darling dogs – of course we wouldn't leave them alone under any circumstances, but they hate the kennels where we take them occasionally when we go into the city, and they droop around for days afterward.

"How would you like to have a little vacation here amidst the pines and sycamores or whatever, in the company of two wonderful dogs? They're no trouble at all, are wonderful protectors and good companions. Do say yes and let us know as soon as possible. We would have called, but we can't get a phone this far out. Will be waiting to hear. Love,

"Anne and Greg."

Well, of course I said yes, even though they hadn't invited me to visit until I could be of some service to them. I hadn't been away from the apartment overnight since I could remember and I felt I needed a change but couldn't afford to go away. Besides, I was curious to see what kind of place they had. No doubt they had exaggerated, young people being what they are, always talking about their wonderful experiences and opportunities that usually boil down to nothing much. So I took a bus and three hours later I was there.

Everything was as they'd described it – the small two-storey tank house was now painted a pale blue with white trim with pink geraniums planted all the way around it, the small clearing, the pine trees rising in the distance. And the dogs, who were introduced to me as Rex and Regina, one a huge German shepherd, the other a small, prancing, beautiful collie. They came up to me while Anne and Greg looked on smiling, and I reached out a hand to touch the big dog on his head. He had been standing there looking amiable but now suddenly he changed, without seeming to move a muscle. There was something different and withdrawn about him, like a polite child you're going to kiss who doesn't want to be kissed.

I turned to little Regina, who had been dancing alongside him, also seeming amiable, but she too had changed although I hadn't made a move to touch her. It was as if she were blindly following the other dog's lead.

Now I can't say I don't like dogs, it's just that I've never had any experience with them, having lived in an apartment for the last thirty years. And I can't say my experience with other people's dogs has been too good. They always jumped up on me or growled or made messes in the wrong place

132

or something, and I got so I couldn't help feeling that people who devoted their lives to their animals had something a little bit wrong with them, like not liking people but needing something to love.

Anne showed me around. "All you have to do," she said, "is feed the dogs morning and evening and they'll be happy. Oh, and keep their water dish full outside. Here's the dog door –" a big square hole in the back door with a flap over it "– let them come in and out as they please." She laughed. "We let them sleep wherever they want, usually in the living room, but they're very neat, perfectly housebroken, they don't claw the furniture or get it dirty, so they have their way with us." She paused. "I hope you won't get too lonely here. The freezer is stocked with all kinds of food and everything is in good working order –"

She led the way up the narrow spiral stairs and showed me to one of the two bedrooms – the smaller one, naturally – which was clean as a whistle and fresh with sunshine.

"You'll have to go through our bedroom to get to the bath. This place is so tiny, that's the only way we could manage a bath at all," she added apologetically. "I do hope you'll have a good rest while you're here. If you want to walk in the woods, take the dogs with you; there's nothing to be protected from, really, but they're good company. Have fun."

Later the two of them waved goodbye and were gone in their little compact car, disappearing almost instantly through the tall dark trees.

There were plenty of things for me to do, as Anne had pointed out: walks in the woods, a color TV set although it could receive only two channels – but color! I'd always wanted one but couldn't afford it. And there were shelves full of books in the tiny living room, also a small fireplace to sit in front of during the chilly evenings.

I roamed outside and poked around a bit. I could see trees spreading off in all directions with only a narrow dirt road leading to the highway, and I couldn't help wondering why some people have all the luck. I would have loved a home like this – well, just for summers, perhaps – with a little car of my own and fresh air and country living. I couldn't help the touch of bitterness in me at the thought that people like Anne and Greg, so young and beautiful and free, with their lovely homemade house and beautiful surroundings, seemed to have everything. While I had nothing.

I looked through the books in the living room and selected a mystery that was years old. I sat down with it but couldn't put my mind on it. Restless, I got up and went to the kitchen, fixed myself a can of soup and some buttered toast, then went back to the living room, where I turned on the TV – and a whole new world opened up before me. I'd never enjoyed Westerns in black and white, but now with the color, the landscapes, the mountains in the distance, all the blues and greens and yellows seemed to fill the room. I was lost in another dimension, far from the city and my dingy apartment and my colorless life as housekeeper for my busy sister, now gone. So dull since she died, so almost poverty-stricken. Again the thought came, why couldn't *I* have something like this all my own?

Then suddenly there was a dark shadow in front of the set, blotting out the picture, and I was frightened until I realized it was Rex, the German shepherd, just standing there looking at me. Regina moved up beside him and they baoth stared at me. What on earth, I thought, then glanced at my watch. Eight-thirty, the windows dark now, no light in the room except from the flickering screen.

"Get out of the way," I said to the dogs,

but they sat there, unmoving. Oh, good heavens, I suddenly remembered, I forgot to feed them! Anne had said, "First thing in the morning you give each of them some canned dog food and at five o'clock a dish of kibble." And now it was more than three hours past their suppertime.

I got some kibble out of the large paper sack under the sink, plunked down their dishes, then rushed back to the TV set.

Next morning when I came downstairs, there was a horrid smell. On the living-room rug was a mess that one of the dogs had left, and I can tell you I was furious. Anne had assured me they were housebroken. They sat and looked at me and I could feel the contempt in their whole beings – an extension of what caused the mess in the first place – which enraged and frightened me at the same time. I picked up the nearest thing I could find, the hearth broom, and chased them out of the house.

"You nasty creatures!" I yelled. "Get out of here if you can't behave yourselves!"

They scurried out through the dog door and I decided to punish them by not giving them their breakfast; they'd just have to wait until suppertime. That would teach them.

I cleaned up the mess and settled down to

the TV again, though there wasn't much on except children's shows and women interviewing other women. All young, of course, nothing to interest a woman in her fifties. Well, I'd just have to wait until night to see a good show.

After the first day or two there wasn't much to do. I went for walks in the woods and the two dogs trailed behind me, but when they chased a skunk right across my path and I tried to get them to go after it, they just sat there and did nothing. Nothing but stare at me.

Weeks of waiting here, I was beginning to think, before Anne and Greg would be back. No human company. No traffic sounds. No one to talk to. Nothing to do but look at TV and read old books. Well, I decided after a few hours of idleness, maybe I'll make myself a pie with some of the berries in the freezer – Anne had told me that she and Greg had picked them themselves.

I spent the whole morning on two pies and put them on the table to cool, then went back to TV again – even the silly woman shows were better than nothing. Vaguely, through my absorptioin, I heard a slight noise in the kitchen but when I went out there later I didn't notice anything at first. then – my pies! They had been carefully eaten down to the tin plates.

"Get out of here!" I screamed at the two skulking dogs, beating them with the broom. "Get out and stay out!"

But I couldn't make them stay out because there was no way to lock the dog door. They came in again and sat looking at me. I tried to stare them down but they just sat there and looked at me. Then Regina touched her nose to Rex's – communicating, I suppose – and went outside and I could hear her lapping water. She came in and sat down, staring at me again, and Rex went out and had some water.

"All right," I said at last, "if that's the way you want it, you can just go to bed tonight without your kibble. That ought to teach you."

After supper I sat down in front of the TV again and the dogs were quiet.

Suddenly I remembered having seen a bottle of sherry in the kitchen, and I thought maybe a little would quiet my nerves, so I stood up to get it. The result was disastrous, for Regina had been sleeping at my feet, almost as if keeping watch on me; but I hadn't known she was there and as I stood up I stumbled over her and she yelped and I lost my balance and started to fall. As I did so I grabbed the floor lamp beside me but it wasn't enough to stop my fall, and it came down with me.

I sprawled out on the floor with the dogs carrying on, the lampshade broken, and me with a bruise on one leg. I was frightened and terribly nervous and, most of all, enraged.

"Get *out* of here!" I yelled at the dogs. And hardly knowing what I was doing, I kicked out at Regina, hit her in the ribs, and she yelped again and the two dogs ran out of the room and through the dog door to the outside.

I got up, too shaken to know what I was doing, and limped my way to the kitchen, where I had half a glass of sherry to quiet my nerves. Then I went upstairs to bed.

It was quiet during the night.

Next morning, when I came down, the two dogs were waiting for me at the foot of the stairs. Just sitting there silently, as if they had been waiting for me a long time. I was in no mood for amiability.

"Get out of the way," I said, but they didn't move and I started to go past them. Rex stirred slightly and the way was blocked, so I stepped past Regina, but Rex was there, too. "You crazy! Don't you want me to feed you?"

Again I tried to move past them, but they didn't budge. "Get out of my way!" I said again, raising my voice. "Move! Out of the way!" They didn't stir.

I started to push past them, and now there was a long deep growl, the first I had heard from Rex, and when I looked at him his eyes seemed almost red. He pulled back his lips a bit and I could see the long fangs. I tried to push past Regina. She didn't growl, she simply snapped her sharp little teeth together, and it made a dreadful sound. Now they inched closer to me; now they were the aggressors, not I; now they were not blocking my way to the lower floor, they were pushing me upstairs.

"No," I said. "No. Good dogs, good dogs. I want to feed you, let me come down," and I moved down the stairs again – but there was that little collie snapping at my ankles and the big dog with the low growl in his throat. I moved back. It wasn't enough. Again the snapping and the growl until, step by step, I backed up into the hall above and was pushed against my bedroom door.

The dogs were on both sides of me now. Growl, snap, snap, growl – and finally I was in my room, the door closed quickly behind me, and those two terrible beasts on the other side. Now I breathed more easily, though I was still shaken and trembling.

Why hadn't Anne and Greg told me they were dangerous? How dare they leave me alone and unprotected with these dreadful creatures? What did they have against me that they must lure me here and leave me at the mercy of two dangerous beasts? I tried opening the door a wedge several times, but there were my antagonists, just sitting and looking at me.

After a while I grew hungry. And thirsty. I opened the door carefully, wider this time, but again came the low growl and I could see them both sitting there, watching, waiting. I closed the door again. Now that I knew I couldn't reach water, my thirst became acute. I must get to the bathroom off the other bedroom.

I put my ear to the door and heard nothing. But I felt the two uncanny creatures on the other side. There was silence, but they were there. Why? Why were they keeping me imprisoned like this? What did they want?

I thought, I must get out of here? Perhaps if I made a break for it? Opened the door suddenly and ran down the stairs? No, that wouldn't do, they could tear me apart. I'd just have to try my luck getting into Anne's and Greg's room where the bathroom was so that I could get some water for my parched throat.

I opened the door a crack, slowly, carefully. A growl, a snap. They were still there. But *they* would have to eat! They needed food even more than I did, for by now my appetite was gone, though I still craved liquid. I'd wait until they went for food – perhaps they'd finally realize that I was the one who fed them and would let me out for that purpose. They'd have to.

Or would they? They surely couldn't get at the canned dog food, but now I had a sudden picture of the large paper sack of kibble in the cupboard under the sink. And the cupboard door didn't quite close. They could eat the kibble and they had water in the pan outside. How long would the kibble and water last?

My watch had stopped – I had forgotten to wind it. I didn't know what time it was, although I could see the shadows changing when I glanced out the window. My thirst grew, and now I was also beginning to feel the first pangs of hunger. I looked out the window again and there was Regina, capering about as if she had just eaten and now felt active and playful.

142

I opened my door. Rex sat there. Later I opened it again and Regina sat there. Alone. While Rex was eating, I suppose. "Nice doggie," I said, reaching out a hand to pat her on the head. The snap was sudden and dangerously close to my hand. She seemed to be smiling – although I know, of course, that dogs can't smile; but her eyes, those golden eyes into which one could gaze forever without reaching the bottom of the pit, were not smiling; they were deadly.

And so the two dogs imprisoned me, in shifts. Always one of them was outside my door. Rex could have torn me apart; Regina couldn't have, but she could have ripped my legs to shreds. Singly or together, they were my keepers.

I couldn't last long without water. Often I went to the door and listened, afraid to open it, but I always knew one of them was there. I could hear the soft shhh-ing sound when they stirred. I could almost hear their breathing. I didn't know how much time had passed. I knew there was daylight and then dark, twice, and my throat was parched and my body weak.

Then one day the sky clouded over and grew dark, and off in the distance I heard the rumble of thunder and saw an occasional flash of faroff lightning. I stood dully at the window, thankful for anything to break the monotony, too far gone in despair to realize what this storm could mean to me. But suddenly, when the huge drops spattered down, I came back to myself and reached my hands out frantically, cupping them for the cherished water. There was so little of it I could catch! I looked frantically about the room for any kind of receptacle, and my eyes fell on a small, pretty glass bowl meant for flowers but now empty. I reached it out through the window and the rain lasted until the bowl was half full, and then I sipped, rationing the water until I could plan some way out of my prison.

Occasionally, when there was complete quiet beyond the door, I would open it a crack; but instantly both dogs, or one of them when the other was busy eating or drinking or exercising, would leap up and stand there, no longer growling or baring fangs but looking like polite, well trained pets. Smiling at me. It seemed. Once I tried opening the door enough to let myself through and I could feel rather than see the tenseness in their bodies, the preparation for attack, the guardedness that came over them when they sensed I might escape.

Another time, when there had been quiet for several hours outside my door, an idea came to my mind. I went to the window and looked down at the ground. Fifteen feet? Too far to jump with safety, but – I ran to the bed, ripped the sheets off, tore them into strips, knotted them together, then tied one end to the foot of the bed and threw the other out the window. It dangled to within a few feet of the ground. I pulled hard on my self-made rope and it held.

Then I went to the window and leaned over the sill and looked down. And there was Rex, sitting below, looking up at me, looking pleasant, looking amiable, smiling, smiling.

I don't know how long it has been now.

The weakness of hunger pervades me, now that the greater pain of thirst has been relieved, and I move about listlessly, or else sit on the bed and do nothing. There is no TV here, no radio, no reading material. Nothing but quiet and stillness and loneliness, and death by inches.

Once I came out of my lifeless lethargy at a sound outside my window. A horrible sound. Ravening. I went and looked out and Rex was below, tearing a small animal apart, blood on both of them. So the kibble must have given out. But that still wasn't important enough to those two creatures to cause them to let me out so that I could feed them.

Strangely, hungry as Rex must have been, he didn't devour all the rabbit, but left part of it and trotted off around a corner of the house. In a moment Regina came capering around, full speed ahead, and fell on the meat that Rex had left for her. She glanced up once, as if to say, *See what you're missing?* – and went on with her meal.

They survive well.

I do not. I am unkempt, with no way to clean myself, and with hope deteriorating fast. I am hungry, I am growing thirsty again as the water slowly disappears from my bowl, and there is nothing to occupy my mind.

Except one thing: why are the dogs doing this to me? Revenge? Fear? Savagery? Mindless behavior of the jungle? No, not this last. Their behavior is not mindless . . .

My thoughts wander, then center on the one thing that is beginning to take over all that is left of my mind. *Why?* Rex could have killed me at any time, with one leap at my throat. He could have crunched my ankle when they were herding me upstairs. Regina could have torn my legs to shreds if she had wished. But instead they are keeping me here as a prisoner, not knowing, or perhaps not

146

caring, that I can die here, die on the wrong side of a door that can lead to freedom.

The thought keeps coming back, over and over again – for what else do I have to think about? They could have killed me at any time, so why didn't they? Because they need me to feed them in order to keep themselves alive? No. They are managing without me, they can survive without my ministrations, they are totally self-sufficient. Then why don't they kill me, any time I open the door, kill me and be done with it?

Finally I knew. The reason they didn't kill me outright was that then there would have to be an accounting. When their masters returned and found me dead in my room, they would not blame the dogs; they would only be sorry the dogs had been neglected while poor Susie lay dead of natural causes in their absence. But if I were found torn apart by their darlings' fangs, then there would be retribution, perhaps even execution. Like humans, I thought, the idea coming slowly and painfully into being – like humans. Like humans. *Do your deed, evade the consequences.*

Monsters, I thought ... and now the final grip on my sanity is going. Monsters. To let me die slowly, in torture, so that they will not be held accountable!

147

I ran to the door and beat on it, screaming, "Monsters! You beastly human monsters!"

On the other side of the door there was silence, except for a soft pattering, a soft movement, a soft sound, gentle but unyielding . . .

L. E. BEHNEY

The Sound of Women Weeping

The houses faced each other across the dingy
street; one was weathered, white-painted,
two-storied, the other squat, drab-brown,
with a wide veranda and a screened-in side
porch. They seemed to regard each other
with suspicious eyes – the two-story one
from narrow windows pinched beneath a
high, white-walled forehead, and the squat
one from beneath the beetling veranda roof
that projected like a thick, dark brow. the
pale and wintry light of the late afternoon
sun made barred shadows across the dead
lawns. The street was quiet. Only an
occasional car scuttled by, crisping through
the fallen leaves.

Ed Crossman stood behind his front
windows and gazed with somber gray eyes
across the street at the brown house. He was
a tall, broad-shouldered man with a gentle
and deep-lined face. The black suit he was
wearing was too small for him and smelled
faintly of moth spray. He drew his hand over

149

his face with a gesture of inarticulate grief and turned from the window to the stairs.

At the bottom of the steps he leaned against the banister and listened to the silence of the old house. In the kitchen the refrigerator hummed monotonously; beneath the floor some timbers creaked faintly; against the outside wall the thin cold wind drove a branch with a stealthy tapping – all the sounds seemed to intensify the hollow emptiness of the rooms. The house seemed to be waiting, listening – for the gay laughter and skipping feet that would never come again.

Since that night of horror, Ed Crossman had never been alone to think of the future, to plan the things that must be done. Doctor Miller had come first and then the police and the ambulance crew. Later the neighbors had appeared, and the relatives with their tears and their shocked faces, and inevitably the reporters with their notebooks and cameras, and finally the curious with their prying eyes and pointing fingers. Carloads of them had come, staring and whispering under the bare-limbed elms that lined the street.

It was over now – the unbelievable, the unbearable thing that had happened; and he and Ellie must face the long darkness that lay ahead. Ed Crossman straightened his

150

shoulders and climbed the stairs. He tapped at the door of the front bedroom, and when there was no answer he pushed open the paneled door.

His wife lay motionless on the big fourposter bed. She hadn't changed her dress after the funeral and the limp, black silk made her small body look shrunken and shapeless. Her eyes were closed and her hands folded inertly on her breasts. She lay so quietly that the man hurried to her side with a sudden cold fear. He touched her cheek and felt the burning dryness of her skin. She opened her eyes and stared dully up at him.

"Everybody's gone," he said. "We're alone, Ellie."

He sat on the bed and took her fevered hands in his – small hands, work-hardened hands, good hands, busy hands; through all the years of their marriage they had never been idle until now.

"Get her up, get her busy," Doctor Miller had said. "Don't let her lie there and brood about it. Make her angry, make her cry, make her feel something. She needs to cry. If she doesn't, she may drift away from us into a world of unreality."

But Ellie Crossman hadn't cried – not since that night.

151

"Ellie," said Ed Crossman. "Do you hear me, Ellie?"

Her eyes stared at him blankly.

He shook her gently. "Ellie, I want to talk to you. We've got a lot to do, a lot to decide."

She looked at him. "Why?" she asked. "What does anything matter?"

"You can't give up." he said. "We've got to go on living and the sooner we get at it the better for both of us?"

Ellie closed her shadowed eyes. "I don't care any more, Ed. She was all we had. There's nothing left."

"I know how you feel . . . she was my daughter too. My life. Everything." The words were hollow dust in his mouth. He said, "I want to do something that is very hard for me – right now, this afternoon. And I need you. I need you with me where you've always been."

"Not today, Ed. Let me be."

"Today, Ellie, while I have the strength. Tomorrow bitterness may be too much a habit. I want to go see Steve and Alice."

Her body jerked and tensed, her fingers dug into his hands, her eyes blazed at him. "Why?" she cried. "How can you forget? How can you even speak their names?"

Ed Crossman shook his head. "It wasn't their fault, Ellie. You can't blame them any more than you can blame yourself. None of us knew what was going to happen. If we'd stayed home, if we hadn't left her alone... None of us knew there was any danger – in this house, in this quiet street, in this peaceful town. It was one of those stupid, senseless things, without reason or meaning. We can't live the rest of our lives blaming ourselves – or blaming anyone."

He stood up and crossed the room to the front window. He looked down on the dry front lawn and suddenly it was spring and long ago. The grass was green, the flower beds blazed with color, and children played with shrill laughter in the golden sunlight. He remembered the day so long ago and so long forgotten – Steve's son, Carl, standing by the hedge, his still eyes watching, his dark face frowning.

Had Ed felt a cold premonition even then? The vision was so real that he felt again the swelling half awed pride he had known that day as he had watched his chubby blonde-headed little daughter. So beautiful and perfect she had always been to him...

His eyes lifted now to the squat brown house across the street, and the happy voices were silent, the withered lawn empty and cold.

A car came slowly down the street and

clattered up the opposite driveway. A small man got out of the car and stood a moment leaning against it. His thin body was stooped and aged and the wind sent his wisps of dark hair flying.

Ed Crossman turned from the window and spoke to his wife. "Steve just came home and I'm going over there. Come along, Ellie. They're still our friends. They've got awful trouble."

The woman moaned and covered her face with her hands. "What's their trouble compared to ours? Our child is dead! I hate them, Ed. I'll hate them as long as I live and I don't want to ever see them again. How can you be so – so – unfeeling?"

The man rubbed the side of his face. His big hands shook. He said slowly, "Ellie, I know I'm asking a lot. Too much, maybe. But look at it this way. If the kids were sick or got hurt in an accident, wouldn't you and Alice comfort each other? If our Joanie died and Carl was terribly injured, wouldn't you do all you could to help Alice?"

The woman turned on the bed and stared at him with burning eyes. "It's not the same, Ed."

"No," the big man agreed heavily. "It's worse. Our pain and sorrow are clean things and all our memories of our daughter are

154

tender and good. But think of Steve and Alice. What will they have to remember all the rest of their lives? Come with me. Please, Ellie."

The woman shook her head and buried her face in the bedclothes. Ed Crossman covered his wife with a blanket and went out of the room and down the stairs.

The wind was cold and damp on his face when he reached the street. There was a feel of fog in the air, and a trace of rising mist paled the thin light of the sun. Ed Crossman walked slowly through the rustling leaves. How Joanie had loved to tumble in the big leaf piles! How she had shrieked with delight as she raced the falling leaves, her eyes blue as the sky, her yellow curls flying. It was as if the recent years had never been, as if he remembered her most vividly as a child. Sometimes she seemed to skip beside him, her small warm hand clasping his. In these moments his crushing sense of loss was so great it seemed unbearable.

He stood before the brown house. The windows were dark, the shades drawn, the porch leaf-littered. With leaden feet he climbed the porch steps. He was sweating coldly. Beyond the closed front door some malevolent presence seemed to lurk. He knew it was only his tortured mind that made it seem so, but it was with the greatest difficulty that he forced himself to raise his hand to the knocker.

He tapped gently. No answer. He struck the knocker more firmly. This house where he had always come and gone almost as though it were his own had become an unfriendly thing.

The house remained coldly silent. Almost with relief he turned away. And turning, he heard the savage chuck-chuck of a hoe in the back yard. He went down the steps and around to the back.

Steve Parkson was wielding the tool with violent slashing strokes as he dug into the earth of his vegetable garden.

Ed Crossman watched him a moment, then called his name.

The small man swung around. He had been crying and the pale light glinted on his thin, tear-streaked cheeks. He stared at Ed with incredulous eyes and his face twisted in an anguished grimace. Then their hands met.

Steve Parkson said huskily, "You didn't need to come, Ed. I know how you must feel and, God, I can't blame you. I can't believe it's happened. It's a damn dream, a nightmare. I keep thinking I'll wake up and – and I'll see Carl and Joanie."

"I know, Steve, I know."

"Maybe it wouldn't be so bad if we'd had other kids. But I guess it wouldn't matter. It'd be the same. I got to talk to someone. You, Ed? You want to talk? You got time?"

"I've got time, Steve."

The men sat on a stone bench in the fading sunlight. Behind the back-yard fence and out of the wind the sun had a faint warmth. They were silent for a time, each buried in his own thoughts.

"I went to see the boy today," Steve Parkson said with a shuddering effort. "They got him in a cage like an animal. He walks up and down, up and down. He said he's sorry and if I saw you I was to tell you he didn't mean it. He didn't mean to hurt Joanie. He said something just sort of snapped. He loved her. I guess he always did, even when they were kids, only it was play then."

"If he loved her," Ed Crossman cried, "how could he kill her?"

"I don't know, Ed. I don't know." Steve Parkson pounded his fist on the stone bench. "I tried to raise him right, teach him right from wrong. I guess I'm not much of a teacher. Inside I knew there was something wrong. He was such a quiet boy, but he had a temper – he always did even when he was a little kid. You know how it is, you can't

157

believe there's anything wrong with your own kid. Other people's kids, yes – but not your own. sometimes he was such a good boy. Helped his ma, helped me. And always when I'd see him growing so big and handsome and strong, it was like a flame warming me, my pride in him. I loved everybody because he was my son."

"I know, Steve, I know." The big man put his arms around the small man's shoulders.

"I knew something was wrong with him. But I just wouldn't believe it." The small man choked, tears sliding dowh his cheeks. "I saw a lot of things. I kept making excuses for him. I'ts my fault. If I'd beat it out of him, maybe? I don't know. I did lick him good once,the time I saw him burn Mrs. Carter's cat in the incinerator. He swore up and down he didn't, but I saw him. The cat scratched him. I liked him more because he lied to me, I guess, and then I was scared because he'd do a thing like that. If I'd taken him to the doctor then, maybe this wouldn't have happened."

"You didn't know, Steve. You can't take all the blame on yourself for what happened. Maybe if we hadn't left her there alone ..."

The night of the lodge party. He and Ellie had wanted to go. It had seemed safe enough. Joanie had laughed at his fears, called him

158

her Darling Worry Bug. "I'm sixteen," she had laughed. "I don't need a baby sitter. For goodness' sakes, Father, I'm practically grown up!" He could see her face, the smooth curve of her cheek, the roundness of her slender neck. Looking at his daughter from the open door, Ed had felt an urge to go back and kiss her goodbye, to tell her how much he loved her. All the rest of his life he would have that deep regret...

"Why did he kill her? What did he tell you" Ed asked with slow pain.

Steve Parkson looked far up into the opaque and empty sky as though he too searched for an answer. "He talked to me today," he said. "He never told the police anything except that he killed her. He told me that he loved her. Nobody could ever understand how much. She wouldn't be true to him, he said. She wanted to date other fellows."

, "She was just a youngster, just past sixteen!" Ed Crossman cried.

"He says he saw you and Ellie leave and he went over to talk to Joanie. That was all he meant to do, just talk. They had quite an argument about it. Finally Joanie told Carl to leave. He says that's when he – well, when something snapped. She looked so pretty when she was mad, with her eyes full of sparks and her cheeks all pink. He tried to kiss her. He told her if he couldn't have her nobody else would either. She pushed him away and ran into the kitchen. She tried to get out the back door. Next thing the boy knew, he was standing over her with a kitchen knife in his hand and Joanie was on the floor – and blood over everything.

Ed Crossman closed his eyes. They had come home early, driven by his unrest. It had been a night of brilliant full moon, clear pale light, and velvet shadows. He had been putting the car into the garage when Ellie had begun to scream. Rushing up the walk, he had found her kneeling over Joanie's body. Bright red blood on the black and white tiles of the kitchen floor.

The unbelievable nightmare had begun then and it would never end. It would never end for Steve and Alice either. All their lives were caught up in this one senseless, maniacal act.

It was hard, hard not to hate. Ed drew in a deep breath and put his hand on his friend's thin shoulder. "I'm sorry for all of us," he said. "Most of all for Joanie. Her life would have been such a happy time. To her everything was wonderful. I know she wouldn't even – even hate Carl for what he did to her. And because it wasn't in her to

160

hate, I can't either – not and be fair to her. I'll do what I can for your boy, Steve. Taking his life isn't going to bring back Joanie. Maybe I can help. I'll do what I can."

Along the back fence a row of bronze chrysanthemums bloomed in bright defiance of the coming winter. The dying sun touched the top flowers and they glowed bright gold. Like Joanie's hair, Ed Crossman thought with a quick stab that tightened his throat.

Parkson touched his arm almost timidly. "Thanks, Ed," he said. "There aren't many guys in the world would say what you just did."

"We've been friends and neighbors – thirteen years, isn't it, since you moved in here?"

"The fall of forty-eight." Parkson hesitated. "How's Ellie?"

Ed Crossman rubbed his cheek. "She's still feeling the effects of the shock, Steve. She and Joanie were very close. She's upstairs in bed now."

The big man stood up. The air was rapidly growing colder and pale mists were gathering in the still air. The bare trees along the street raised skeleton arms. "I've got to go home, Steve."

"I'd ask you in, but Alice – she don't feel so good either. She hasn't slept since we

161

heard about the boy. At night I feel her lying so stiff and full of pain beside me. I know she's thinking like I am – of all the things we did we shouldn't and what we didn't do we should have. She never cried, not even when I told her – she just stared at me. She keeps it all bottled up inside her. She won't go to see the boy. She doesn't even ask about him. It's like he never was. You know what she does, Ed? She cleans house like it's killing her. We've got the cleanest house this side of hell."

The small man looked at Ed Crossman. "I'd like to ask you in but Alice, she says she don't want to see anybody."

"Sure, Steve. I understand."

Their hands met and Ed Crossman turned away. He looked across the street and saw Ellie coming toward them through the chilly dusk. She had changed her black silk for a clean starched housedress and her soft, graying hair was brushed back neatly. She walked with a firm step and her grief-lined face was calm. She saw the men and came toward them. "Hello, Steve," she said. "Where's Alice?"

Steve Parkson nodded toward the house. Ellie looked at her husband. "You were right, Ed," she said. She leaned forward and her dry lips brushed his cheeks. "I saw you and Steve sitting together, talking together, and I knew this can't be the end of things for us. I belong with you."

Ed Crossman looked at his wife and knew that he had never loved her more. She climbed the back stairs and let herself in the back door. she called, "Alice! Oh, Alice! It's me, Ellie!"

The men heard the sound of women weeping.

LUNA WOLF

The Kind and Considerate Murderer

"How would you like it if we went on a cruise?"

She smiled at him gently. "If you feel like it, dear."

Of course she'd go, even though she knew he would try to kill her.

It sadened her immeasurably to realize that he was so eager to get rid of her. Her own love for him had steadily grown over the eighteen years of their marriage. Yes, it was much greater now than it had been at the beginning, she thought as she gazed at him with such devotion he lowered his eyes.

It was just a fluke that none of his previous attempts had worked. Not, she sharply told an imaginary interlocutor, for want of cooperation on her part.

She had soon guessed what was happening and was resigned to it. Not merely resigned but accepting it as his wish. More than anything she wanted him to be happy. She smiled when he expressed worry about her

164

new accident-proneness, when he seriously urged her to be extra-careful, when he even suggested psychoanalysis. To establish, no doubt, that there was something wrong with her mind. That, too, she accepted and dutifully went to see the analyst he chose for her.

She wanted so badly to let him know that she knew, so that their last days together would not be spoiled by lies. And she desperately wanted to ask him why.

Yes, why? Hadn't she always been an admiring, devoted, compliant wife? Had she ever by word or deed indicated dissatisfaction? If on occasion she had vaguely regretted the need to give up her career for his sake, these moments of regret had been brief. She'd felt deeply that it had been well worth the sacrifice. And she had made quite a satisfactory life for herself, reading a lot, occasionally writing some poetry – not very good, she knew, but rather satisfying – painting a little, working in her garden. Yes, she knew how to keep busy.

So why did he want to kill her? Could her depression and poor health of the past year have annoyed him to that degree? She tried so hard not to be a burden, to behave as normally as possible. Or had he fallen in love with someone else? She couldn't believe it, but, if so, wouldn't the usual thing have been for him to ask for a divorce? But of course he knew that she could never live without him.

She tried to explain some of her feelings to the analyst, a tall dry man whom she found intimidating.

"He's such a wonderful person. Intelligent, sensitive, considerate, passionate, and tender – everything a woman can want."

"Then you consider your marriage a happy one?"

"Oh, yes, marvelously happy. True, we've never had any children but that doesn't matter. My husband fills my life completely."

"And yet you have been suffering from depression for a year. We must find the cause of that."

"My poor health is the cause."

"What's been wrong?"

"Nothing very much, just bad headaches, indigestion, and terrible, terrible fatigue, so that sometimes I can hardly drag myself around."

"But your physician found nothing organically wrong?"

"No, he said it was – well, he said it was nerves."

"So seemingly it is not your physical state

that causes the depression but rather the other way around."

"I have no reason to be depressed. I told you how happy I am! Why, the longer I know my husband the more I love and appreciate him. I don't even need other people, don't like parties or anything like that."

"Do you have any close friends?"

"Well, of course I know some people but they're not exactly intimate friends. I told you that all I really want is to be with my husband. And he doesn't at all mind not having a social life – he sees so many people at the college."

"He teaches at Blakeham, doesn't he?"

"That's right. He's chairman of the English department and loves his work."

"Are there any tensions or resentments on his part that you know of?"

"Towards me? Definitely not. Very early in our marriage he was a little self-conscious because he is smaller than I am, but that's long since gone."

She had never intended to tell the doctor about her husband's attempts on her life but one day he forced it out of her.

"You seriously believe your husband is trying to kill you? Why?"

"I don't know. That's the only thing that bothers me. Why."

"The only thing? Surely you're bothered by his desire to kill you, or at least your belief in it?"

"I've always lived to make him happy; I don't mind dying if that will make him happy."

"I see. Now, what makes you so sure he has tried to kill you?"

"I can't help being sure. The evidence is overwhelming."

And she went on to tell him about the time he tried to push her down the cellar stairs, pretending to steady her when she stumbled.

"But maybe he did try to steady you."

"I felt him push. It was just chance that I managed to grab a wall hook."

Then there was the incident of the mushrooms. He was a fine amateur mycologist and they'd been eating the mushrooms he had picked for years. That last time, maybe three or four weeks ago, she hadn't been feeling well and he'd especially gone out to get her some, to cheer her up.

"I usually love them in a nice cream sauce on toast, but this time I simply couldn't swallow. To please him I ate a little, all I could force down. That night I was horribly sick. If I'd eaten more I'd be dead."

"Did your husband eat any of the mushrooms?"

"A mouthful that I saw. He claims he finished what I left."

"Did he get ill."

"No, of course not. He knew what to avoid."

"All mushrooms look alike cooked in a cream sauce."

"Well, he managed it somehow since I got sick and he didn't."

The third happening was in a way the most frightening.

"You see, I suffer from claustrophobia and he knows it. He's such a very kind person that I can't understand his doing this. I was standing just inside the linen closet in a sort of a mezzanine alcove we have when I heard him call out that he was leaving for work. I leaned around the closet door. He was halfway up the eight steps and we said goodbye. I heard the front door slam shut – he's always slamming doors, the only ungentle thing he does – and then a few seconds later the closet door slammed shut on me. It was terrifying. I would have suffocated if it hadn't been the cleaning woman's day to come in."

169

And she shuddered violently.

If she could not convince the doctor that these were genuine attempts to kill her, neither could he persuade her that she was wrong. Not that she cared what the man thought. she hadn't wanted to tell him about the incidents; actually she didn't want to see him at all and only did it to please her husband.

So when she told the analyst about the proposed cruise and he smugly pointed out how concerned her husband was about her welfare, she just shrugged. What did it matter? It gave her great satisfactioin to think that the fool doctor would soon know he'd been mistaken, that she would have the last laugh.

As the days passed, she began looking forward more and more to the cruise. To get away from the snow and the cold! To die in the sun, that was really all she asked for. She loved the sun – she had never really been comfortable in the severe New England winters.

"My Mediterranean blood," she often joked, referring to her Southern French ancestry.

She went about humming, happily taking their summer things out of storage, airing, washing, ironing them under her husband's pleased gaze.

"That's what you've been needing all this time, sweetheart," he once said, hugging her, "a bit of nice warm sunshine."

"Ah, sunshine, sunshine," she'd crooned, leaning against him.

How nice it was of him, she reflected, to think of killing her in warmth. Once in a while she wondered how he'd do it but the answer was obvious and she shied away from it. She'd always been afraid of water and couldn't swim. He knew that, of course, and she was convinced that he was too kind simply to let her drown. No doubt he'd see to it that she was unconscious at the time.

And finally it was the day of their departure. She stood looking for the last time at her lovely home, at the expanse of lawn surrounding it, and nostalgically thought she'd never see the garden bloom again. This time she almost turned to her husband to ask him why. But what difference did it really make?

The ship looked festive, all white and flagged in the sun, and she felt irrepressibly gay as they stepped on board. It was good that their last days together would pass joyfully. She hoped he'd let her have a few days of basking on the deck and, knowing him so well, she was confident he would. Perhaps he'd even wait until the return voyage.

Life on board was just as she'd envisioned it. Though she didn't mingle much with her fellow passengers, their holiday spirit wafted over her like a delicious scent. The weather was superb and she sat in a deck chair all day long, just lying there in a semi-doze.

Her husband would occasionally come to sit by her side, taking her hand and stroking it, not even urging her to join him in the various shipboard games. Happy as they'd been before, they now achieved truly perfect happiness – not the excited bliss of their early days together but a profoundly tranquil and honeysweet felicity. This was surely the pinnacle of their marriage.

But for all this, she never doubted for a moment that he would go through with his plan. She was more grateful to him than ever for delaying its execution. But as they started on their way back she grew just a little restive. He was cutting it awfully fine, and something might happen at any moment to spoil the perfection of the cruise.

Three days before the end of the voyage she finally knew the time had come. He'd been particularly tender and attentive all day and

172

she knew he would kill her that night. In a sudden great surge of affection she decided that she'd help him all she could. It would be terrible for him to endure another failure. In any case, she could wait no longer.

That evening after supper they strolled arm in arm on deck. But it was too early; there were still too many people around. It would happen later , after he had his evening game of chess. As they had every night since they'd embarked, they would meet in the lounge at 10:30 for a nightcap, then take a final walk before going to bed. Except that tonight she wouldn't be going to bed.

As she sat in her usual deck chair in the silvery night, barely aware of the dance band in the lounge, she reflected that he'd probably drop some sleeping pills into her drink. But that wouldn't give them enough time to work, she suddenly realized with a surge of terror. Digging into her purse she took out her own supply of capsules and quickly swallowed six. That was much better. She'd hate to be plunged into that black water fully conscious.

Soon she was totally relaxed and slightly drowsy. She mustn't on any account fall asleep before it was time to go down. The sudden loud rhythm of the band jarred her out of her reverie. It might be better to walk around a little, to clear her head just a little.

Unsteadily rising from the chair, she made her way to the railing and looked down into turbulent phosphorescence. Not very inviting, she shuddered. Where would he do it? She was quite heavy to push over the side and he, poor darling, wasn't very big. He must have picked a spot where the railing was lower, probably on the upper deck, where the lifeboats were. She turned toward the stairs and pulled herself up, then zigzagged to the place she had in mind.

She was getting terribly sleepy. What a shame he wasn't here now. She didn't think she'd be able to keep awake much longer. Then, with sudden striking clarity, she realized there was no need to wait. Helping him was not enough! She'd do the job for him! Gratefully closing her eyes she leaned over farther and farther.

Footsteps sounded in her straggling mind, just behind her. So he'd come. She tried to twist back, but her unsteady feet slipped and she lost what balance she had.

As she went over she felt more than saw his arm reach out toward her.

STANLEY ELLIN

The Betrayers

Between them was a wall. And sinced it was
only a flimsy, jerry-built partition, a
sounding board between apartments, Robert
came to know the girl that way.

At first she was the sound of footsteps, the
small firm rap of high heels moving in a
pattern of activity around her room. She
must be very young, he thought idly, because
at the time he was deep in *Green Mansions*,
pursuing the lustrous Rima through a
labyrinth of Amazonian jungle. Later he
came to know her voice, light and breathless
when she spoke, warm and gay when she
raised it in chorus to some popular song
dinning from her radio. She must be very
lovely, he thought then, and after that found
himself listening deliberately, and falling
more and more in love with her as he
listened.

Her name was Amy, and there was a
husband, too, a man called Vince who had
a flat, unpleasant voice, and a sullen way
about him. Occasionally there were quarrels

which the man invariably ended by slamming the door of their room and thundering down the stairs as loud as he could. Then she would cry, a smothered whimpering, and Robert, standing closer to the wall between them, would feel as if a hand had been thrust inside his chest and was twisting his heart. He would think wildly of the few steps that would take him to her door, the few words that would let her know he was her friend, was willing to do something – anything – to help her. Perhaps, meeting face to face, she would recognize his love. Perhaps –

So the thoughts whirled around and around, but Robert only stood there, taut with helplessness.

And there was no one to confide in, which made it that much harder. The only acquaintances he numbered in the world were the other men in his office, and they would never have understood. He worked prosaically enough, in the credit department of one of the city's largest department stores, and too many years there had ground the men around him to a fine edge of cynicism. The business of digging into people's records, of searching for the tax difficulties, the clandestine affairs with expensive women, the touch of larceny in every human being – all that was bound to have an effect, they told Robert, and if he stayed on the job much longer he'd find it out for himself.

What would they tell him now? *A pretty girl next door? Husband's away most of the time? Go on, make yourself at home!*

How could he make them understand that that wasn't what he was looking for? That what he wanted was someone to meet his love halfway, someone to put an end to the cold loneliness that settled in him like a stone during the dark hours each night.

So he said nothing about it to anyone, but stayed close to the wall, drawing from it what he could. And knowing the girl as he had come to, he was not surprised when he finally saw her. The mail for all the apartments was left on a table in the downstairs hall, and as he walked down the stairs to go to work that morning, he saw her take a letter from the table and start up the stairway toward him.

There was never any question in his mind that this was the girl. She was small and fragile and dark-haired, and all the loveliness he had imagined in her from the other side of the wall was there in her face. She was wearing a loose robe, and as she passed him on the stairway she pulled the robe closer to her breast and slipped by almost as if she were afraid of him. He realized with a start

177

that he had been staring unashamedly, and with his face red he turned down the stairs to the street. But he walked the rest of his way in a haze of wonderment.

He saw her a few times after that, always under the same conditions, but it took weeks before he mustered enough courage to stop at the foot of the stairs and turn to watch her retreating form above; the lovely fine line of ankle, the roundness of calf, the curve of body pressing against the robe. And then as she reached the head of the stairs, as if aware he was watching her, she looked down at him and their eyes met. For a heart-stopping moment Robert tried to understand what he read in her face, and then her husband's voice came flat and belligerent from the room. "Amy," it said, "what's holdin' you up!" – and she was gone, and the moment with her.

When he saw the husband he marveled that she had chosen someone like that. A small, dapper gamecock of a man, he was good-looking in a hard way, but with the skin drawn so tight over his face that the cheekbones jutted sharply and the lips were drawn into a thin menacing line. He glanced at Robert up and down out of the corners of blank eyes as they passed, and in that instant Robert understood part of what he had seen in the girl's face. This man was as dangerous as some half tamed animal that would snap at any hand laid on him, no matter what its intent. Just being near him you could smell danger, as surely the girl did her every waking hour.

The violence in the man exploded one night with force enough to waken Robert from a deep sleep. It was not the pitch of the voice, Robert realized, sitting up half dazed in bed, because the words were almost inaudible through the wall; it was the vicious intensity that was so frightening.

He slipped out of bed and laid his ear against the wall. Standing like that, his eyes closed he strained to follow the choppy phrases, he could picture the couple facing each other as vividly as if the wall had dissolved before him.

"*So you know,*" the man said. "*So what?*"

"*. . . getting out!*" the girl said.

"*And then tell everybody? Tell the whole world?*"

"*I won't!*" The girl was crying now. "*I swear I won't!*"

"*Think I'd take a chance?*" the man said, and then his voice turned soft and derisive. "*Ten thousand dollars,*" he said. "*Where else could I get it? Digging ditches?*"

"Better that way! This way . . . I'm getting out!"

His answer was not delivered in words. It came in the form of a blow so hard that when she reeled back and struck the wall, the impact stung Robert's face. *"Vince!"* she screamed, the sound high and quavering with terror. *"Don't, Vince!"*

Every nerve in Robert was alive now with her pain as the next blow was struck. His fingernails dug into the wall at the hard-breathing noises of scuffling behind it as she was pulled away.

"Ahh, no!" she cried out, and then there was the sound of a breath being drawn hoarsely and agonizingly into lungs no longer responsive to it, the thud of a flaccid weight striking the floor, and suddenly silence. A terrible silence.

As if the wall itself were her cold, dead flesh Robert recoiled from it, then stood staring at it in horror. His thoughts twisted and turned on themselves insanely, but out of them loomed one larger and larger so that he had to face it and recognize it.

She had been murdered, and as surely as though he had been standing there beside her he was a witness to it! He had been so close that if the wall were not there he could have reached out his hand and touched her. Done

180

something to help her. Instead, he had waited like a fool until it was too late.

But there was still something to be done, he told himself wildly. As long as this madman in the next room had no idea there was a witness, he could still be taken red-handed. A call to the police, and in five minutes...

But before he could take the first nerveless step Robert heard the room next door stealthily come to life again. There was a sound of surreptitious motion, of things being shifted from their place; then, clearly defined, a lifeless weight being pulled along the floor and the cautious creaking of a door opened wide. It was that last sound which struck Robert with a sick comprehension of what was happening.

The murderer was a monster, but he was no fool. If he could safely dispose of the body now during these silent hours of the night he was, to all intents and purposes, a man who had committed no crime at all!

At his door Robert stopped short. From the hallway came the deliberate thump of feet finding their way down the stairs with the weight dragging behind them. The man had killed once. He was reckless enough in this crisis to risk being seen with his victim.

What would such a man do to anyone who confronted him at such a time?

Robert leaned back against his door, his eyes closed tight, a choking constriction in his throat as if the man's hands were already around it. He was a coward, there was no way around it. Faced with the need to show some courage he had discovered he was a rank coward, and he saw the girl's face before him now, not with fear in it, but contempt.

But – and the thought gave him a quick sense of triumph – he could still go to the police. He saw himself doing it, and the sense of triumph faded away. He had heard some noises, and from that had constructed a murder. The body? There would be none. The murderer? None. Only a man whose wife had left him because he had quarreled with her. The accuser? A young man who had wild dreams. A perfect fool. In short, Robert himself.

It was only when he heard the click of the door downstairs that he stepped out into the hallway and started down, step by careful step. Halfway down he saw it, a handkerchief, small and crumpled and blotched with an ugly stain. He picked it up gingerly, and holding it up toward the dim light overhead let it fall open. The stain was bright sticky red, almost obscuring in one corner the word *Amy* carefully embroidered there. Blood. *Her* blood. Wouldn't that be evidence enough for anyone?

Sure, he could hear the policeman answer him jeeringly, *evidence of a nosebleed, all right,* and he could feel the despair churn in him.

It was the noise of the car that roused him, and then he fled down the rest of the stairs – but too late. As he pressed his face to the curtain of the front door the car roared away from the curb, its taillights gleaming like malevolent eyes, its license plate impossible to read in the dark. If he had only been an instant quicker, he raged at himself, only had sense enough to understand that the killer must use a car for his purpose, he could easily have identified it. Now, even that chance was gone. Every chance was gone.

He was in his room pacing the floor feverishly when within a half hour he heard the furtive sounds of the murderer's return. *And why not,* Robert thought; *he's gotten rid of her, he's safe now, he can go on as if nothing at all had happened.*

If I were only someone who could go into that room and beat the truth out of him, the thought boiled on, *or someone with such wealth or position that I would be listened to . . .*

But all that was as unreal and vaporous as

his passion for the girl had been. What weapon of vengeance could he possibly haved at his command, a nobody working in a...

Robert felt the sudden realization wash over him in a cold wave. His eyes narrowed on the wall as if, word by word, the idea were being written on it in a minute hand.

Everyone has a touch of larceny in him – wasn't that what the old hands in his department were always saying? Everyone was suspect. Certainly the man next door, with his bent for violence, his talk of ten thousand dollars come by in some unlikely way, must have black marks on his record that the authorities, blind as they might be, could recognize and act on. If someone skilled in investigation were to strip the man's past down, layer by layer, justice would have to be done. That was the weapon: the dark past itself, stored away in the man, waiting only to be ignited!

Slowly and thoughtfully Robert slipped the girl's crumpled handkerchief into an envelope and sealed it. Then, straining to remember the exact words, he wrote down on paper the last violent duologue between murderer and victim. Paper and envelope both went into a drawer of his dresser, and the first step had been taken.

But then, Robert asked himself, what did he know about the man? His name was Vince, and that was all. Hardly information which could serve as the starting point of a search through the dark corridors of someone's past. There must be something more than that, something to serve as a lead.

It took Robert the rest of a sleepless night to hit on the idea of the landlady. A stout and sleepy-eyed woman whose only interest in life seemed to lie in the prompt collection of her rent, she still must have some information about the man. She occupied the rear apartment on the ground floor, and as early in the morning as he dared Robert knocked on her door.

She looked more sleepy-eyed than ever as she pondered his question. "Them?" she said at last. "That's the Sniders. Nice people, all right." She blinked at Robert. "Not having any trouble with them, are you?"

"No. Not at all. But is that all you can tell me about them? I mean, don't you know where they're from, or anything like that?"

The landlady shrugged. "I'm sure it's none of my business," she said loftily. "All I know is they pay on the first of the month right on the dot, and they're nice respectable people."

He turned away from her heavily, and as
185

he did so saw the street door close behind the postman. It was as if a miracle had been passed for him. The landlady was gone, he was all alone with that little heap of mail on the table, and there staring up at him was an envelope neatly addressed to Mrs. Vincent Snider.

All the way to his office he kept that envelope hidden away in an inside pocket, and it was only when he was locked in the seclusion of his cubicle that he carefully slit it open and studied its contents. A single page with only a few lines on it, a noncommittal message about the family's well being, and the signature: *Your sister, Celia.* Not much to go on.

But wait, there was a return address on the stationery, an address in a small upstate town.

Robert hesitated only a moment, then thrust letter and envelope into his pocket, straightened his jacket, and walked into the office of his superior. Mr. Sprague, in charge of the department and consequently the most ulcerated and cynical member of it, regarded him dourly.

"Yes?" he said.

"I'm sorry, sir," said Robert, "but I'll need a few days off. You see, there's been a sudden death."

Mr. Sprague sighed at this pebble cast into the smooth pool of his department's routine, but his face fell into the proper sympathetic lines.

"Somebody close?"

"Very close," said Robert.

The walk from the railroad station to the house was a short one. The house itself had a severe and forbidding air about it, as did the young woman who opened the door in answer to Robert's knock.

"Yes," she said, "my sister's name is Amy Snider. Her married name, that is. I'm Celia Thompson."

"What I'm looking for," Robert said, "is some information about her. About your sister."

The woman looked stricken. "Something's hapened to her?"

"In a way," Robert said. He cleared his throat hard. "You see, she's disappeared from her apartment, and I'm looking into it. Now, if you . . ."

"You're from the police?"

"I'm acting for them," Robert said, and prayed that this ambiguity would serve in place of identification. The prayer was answered, the woman gestured him into the house, and sat down facing him in the bare and uninviting living room.

"I knew," the woman said, "I knew something would happen," and she rocked piteously from side to side in her chair.

Robert reached forward and touched her hand gently. "How did you know?"

"How? What else could you expect when you drive a child out of her home and slam the door in her face! When you throw her out into the world not even knowing how to take care of herself!"

Robert withdrew his hand abruptly. "You did *that?*"

"My father did it. *Her* father."

"But why?"

"If you knew him," the woman said. "A man who thinks anything pretty is sinful. A man who's so scared of hellfire and brimstone that he's kept us in it all our lives!"

"When she started to get so pretty, and the boys pestering her all the time, he turned against her just like that. And when she had her trouble with that man he threw her out of the house, bag and baggage. And if he knew I was writing letters to her," the woman said fearfully, "he'd throw me out, too. I can't even say her name in front of him, the way he is."

"Look," Robert said eagerly, "that man she had trouble with. Was that the one she married? That Vincent Snider?"

"I don't know," the woman said vaguely. "I just don't know. Nobody knows except Amy and my father, the way it was kept such a secret. I didn't even know she was married until all of a sudden she wrote me a letter about it from the city."

"But if your father knows, I can talk to him about it."

"No! You can't! If he even knew I told you as much as I did..."

"But I can't let it go at that," he pleaded. "I have to find out about this man, and then maybe we can straighten everything out."

"All right," the woman said wearily, "there is somebody. But not my father, you've got to keep away from him for my sake. There's this teacher over at the high school, this Miss Benson. She's the one to see. And she liked Amy; she's the one Amy mails my letters to, so my father won't know. Maybe she'll tell you, even if she won't tell anybody else. I'll write you a note to her, and you go see her."

At the door he thanked her, and she regarded him with a hard, straight look. "You have to be pretty to get yourself in trouble," she said, "so it's something that'll never bother me. But you find Amy, and you make sure she's all right."

"Yes," Robert said. "I'll try."

At the school he was told that Miss Benson was the typewriting teacher, that she had classes until three, and that if he wished to speak to her alone he would have to wait until then. So for hours he fretfully walked the few main streets of the town, oblivious of the curious glances of passers-by, and thinking of Amy. These were the streets she had known. These shop windows had mirrored her image. And, he thought with a sharp jealousy, not always alone. There had been boys. Attracted to her, as boys would be, but careless of her, never realizing the prize they had. But if he had known her then, if he could have been one of them . . .

At three o'clock he waited outside the school building until it had emptied, and then went in eagerly. Miss Benson was a small woman, gray-haired and fluttering, almost lost among the grim ranks of hooded typewriters in the room. After Robert had explained himself and she had read Celia Thompson's note, she seemed ready to burst into tears.

"It's wrong of her!" she said. "It's dreadfully wrong of her to send you to me. She must have known that."

"But why is it wrong?"

"Why? Because she knows I don't want to talk about it to anyone. She knows what it would cost me if I did, that's why!"

"Look," Robert said patiently, "I'm not trying to find out what happened. I'm only trying to find out about this man Amy had trouble with, what his name is, where he comes from, where I can get more information about him."

"No," Miss Benson quavered, "I'm sorry."

"Sorry!" Robert said angrily. "A girl disappears, this man may be at the bottom of it, and all you can do is say you're sorry."

Miss Benson's jaw went slack. "You mean that he – that he *did* something to her?"

"Yes," Robert said, "he did," and had to quickly catch her arm as she swayed unsteadily, apparently on the verge of fainting.

"I should have known," she said lifelessly. "I should have known when it happened that it might come to this. But at the time . . ."

At the time the girl had been one of her students. A good student – not brilliant, mind you – but a nice girl always trying to do her best. And well brought-up, too, not like so many of the young snips you get nowadays.

That very afternoon when it all happened, the girl herself had told Miss Benson she was going to the principal's office after school hours to get her program straightened out. Certainly if she meant to do anything wicked she wouldn't have mentioned that, would she? Wasn't that all the evidence anyone needed?

"Evidence?" Robert said in bewilderment.

"Yes, evidence. There had been that screaming in the principal's office, and Miss Benson had been the only one left in the whole school. She had run to the office, flung open the door, and that was how she found them. The girl sobbing hysterically, her dress torn halfway down; Mr. Price standing behind her, glaring at the open door, at the incredulous Miss Benson.

"Mr. Price?" Robert said. He had the sense of swimming numbly through some gelatinous depths, unable to see anything clearly.

Mr. Price, the principal, of course. He stood glaring at her, his face ashen. Then the girl had fled through the door and Mr. Price had taken one step after her, but had stopped short. He had pulled Miss Benson into the office, and closed the door – and then he had talked to her.

The long and the short of what he told her

was that the girl was a wanton. She had waltzed into his office, threatened him with blackmail, and when he had put her into her place she had artfully acted out her little scene. But he would be merciful, very merciful. Rather than call in the authorities and blacken the name of the school and of her decent, respectable father, he would simply expel her and advise her father to get her out of town promptly.

And, Mr. Price had remarked meaningfully, it was a lucky thing indeed that Miss Benson had walked in just in time to be his witness. Although if Miss Benson failed him as a witness it could be highly unlucky for her.

"And he meant it," Miss Benson said bitterly. "It's his family runs the town and everything in it. If I said anything of what I really thought, if I dared open my mouth, I'd never get another job anywhere. But I should have talked up, I know I should have, especially after what happened next!"

She had managed to get back to her room at the far end of the corridor, although she had no idea of where she got the strength. And as soon as she had entered the room she saw the girl there, lying on the floor beneath the bulletin board from which usually hung the sharp, cutting scissors. But the scissors

193

were in the girl's clenched fist as she lay there, and blood over everything. All that blood over everything.

"She was like that," Miss Benson said dully. "If you reprimanded her for even the littlest thing she looked like she wanted to sink through the floor, to die on the spot. And after what she went through it must have been the first thing in her head: just to get rid of herself. It was a mercy of God that she didn't succeed then and there."

It was Miss Benson who got the doctor, a discreet man who asked no questions, and it was she who tended the girl after her father had barred his door to her.

"And when she could get around," Miss Benson said, "I placed her with this office over at the county seat. She wasn't graduated of course, or really expert, but I gave her a letter explaining she had been in some trouble and needed a helping hand, and they gave her a job." Miss Benson dug her fingers into her forehead. "If I had only talked up when I should have. I should have known he'd never feel safe, that he'd hound her and hound her until he . . ."

"But he isn't the one!" Robert said hoarsely. "He isn't the right man at all!"

She looked at him wonderingly. "But you said . . ."

"No," Robert said helplessly, "I'm looking for someone else. A different man altogether."

She shrank back. "You've been trying to fool me!"

"I swear I haven't."

"But it doesn't matter," she whispered. "If you say a word about this nobody'll believe you. I'll tell them you were lying, you made the whole thing up!"

"You won't have to," Robert said. "All you have to do is tell me where you sent her for that job. If you do that you can forget everything else."

She hesitated, studying his face with bright, frightened eyes. "All right," she said at last. "All right."

He was about to go when she placed her hand anxiously on his arm. "Please," she said. "You don't think unkindly of me because of all this, do you?"

"No," Robert said, "I don't have the right to."

The bus trip which filled the remainder of the day was a wearing one, the hotel bed that night was no great improvement over the bus seat, and Mr. Pardee of Grace, Grace, & Pardee seemed to Robert the hardest of all to take. He was a cheery man, too loud and florid to be properly contained by his small office.

He studied Robert's business card with interest. "Credit research, eh?" he said admiringly. "Wonderful how you fellas track 'em down wherever they are. Sort of a Northwest Mounted Police just working to keep business healthy, that's what it comes to, doesn't it? And anything I can do to help . . ."

Yes, he remembered the girl very well. "Just about the prettiest little thing we ever had around here," he said pensively. "Didn't know much about her job, of course, but you got your money's worth just watching her walk around the office."

Robert managed to keep his teeth clenched. "Was there any man she seemed interested in? Someone around the office, maybe, who wouldn't be working here any more? Or even someone outside you could tell me about?"

Mr. Pardee studied the ceiling with narrowed eyes. "No," he said, "nobody I can think of. Must have been plenty of men after her, but you'd never get anything out of her about it. Not with the way she was so secretive and all. Matter of fact, her being that way was one of the things that made all the trouble."

"Trouble?"

"Oh, nothing serious. Somebody was picking the petty-cash box every so often, and what with all the rest of the office being so friendly except her it looked like she might be the one. And then that letter she brought saying she had already been in some trouble – well, we just had to let her go.

"Later on," continued Mr. Pardee pleasantly, "when we found out it wasn't her after all, it was too late. We didn't know where to get in touch with her." He snapped his fingers loudly. "Gone, just like that."

Robert drew a deep breath to steady himself. "But there must be somebody in the office who knew her," he pleaded. "Maybe some girl she talked to."

"Oh, that," said Mr. Pardee. "Well, as I said, she wasn't friendly, but now and then she did have her head together with Jenny Rizzo over at the switchboard. If you want to talk to Jenny go right ahead. Anything I can do to help..."

But it was Jenny Rizzo who helped him. A plain girl dressed in defiant bad taste, she studied him with impersonal interest and told him coolly that she had nothing to say about Amy. The kid had taken enough kicking around. It was about time they let her alone.

197

"I'm not interested in her," Robert said. "I'm trying to find out about the man she married. Someone named Vincent Snider. Did you know about him?" From the stricken look on her face Robert realized exultantly that she did.

"Him!" she said. "So she went and married him, anyhow!"

"What about it?"

"What about it? I told her a hundred times he was no good. I told her just stay away from him."

"Why?"

"Because I knew his kind. Sharp stuff hanging around with money in his pocket, you never knew where it came from. The kind of guy's always pulling fast deals, but he's too smart to get caught, that's why!"

"How well did you know him?"

"How well? I knew him from the time he was a kid around my neighborhood here. Look," Jenny dug into a desk drawer deep-laden with personal possessions. She came out with a handful of snapshots she thrust at Robert. "We used to double-date together, Vince and Amy, and me and my boy friend. Plenty of times I told her right in front of Vince that he was no good, but he gave her such a line she wouldn't listen. She was like a baby that way; anybody was nice to her, she'd go overboard."

They weren't good photographs, but there were Vince and Amy clearly recognizable. "Could I have one of these?" Robert asked, his voice elaborately casual.

Jenny shrugged. "Help yourself," she said, and Robert did.

"Then what happened?" he said. "I mean, to Vince and Amy?"

"You got me there. After she got fired, they both took off. She said something about Vince getting a job downstate a-ways, in Sutton, and that was the last of them. I could just see him working at anything honest, but the way she said it she must have believed him. Anyhow, I never heard from her after that."

"Could you remember exactly when you saw her last? That time she told you they were going to Sutton?"

Jenny could and did. She might have remembered more, but Robert was out of the door by then, leaving her gaping after him, her mouth wide open in surprise...

The trip to Sutton was barely an hour by bus, but it took another hour before Robert was seated at a large table with the Sutton newspaper files laid out before him. The town's newspaper was a large and respectable

199

one, its files orderly and well kept. And two days after the date Jenny Rizzo had given him, there was the news Robert had hoped to find. Headline news emblazoned all across the top of the first page.

Ten thousand dollars stolen, the news report said. A daring, lone bandit had walked into the Sutton Bank and Trust, had bearded the manager without a soul around knowing it, and had calmly walked out with a small valise containing ten thousand dollars in currency. The police were on the trail. An arrest was expected momentarily.

Robert traced through later dates with his hands shaking. The police had given up in their efforts. No arrest was ever made.

Robert had carefully scissored the photograph so that Vince now stood alone in the picture. The bank manager irritably looked at the picture, and then swallowed hard.

"It's him!" he told Robert incredulously. "That's the man! I'd know him anywhere. If I can get my hands on him ..."

"There's something you'll have to do first," said Robert.

"I'm not making any deals," the manager protested. "I want him, and I want every penny of the money he's got left."

"I'm not talking about deals," Robert said. "All you have to do is put down on paper that you positively identify this man as the one who robbed the bank. If you do that the police'll have him for you tomorrow."

"That's all?" the man said suspiciously.

"That's all," Robert said.

He sat again in the familiar room, the papers, the evidence, arranged before him. His one remaining fear had been that in his absence the murderer had somehow taken alarm and fled. He had not breathed easy until the first small, surreptitious noises from next door made clear that things were as he had left them.

Now he carefully studied all the notes he had painstakingly prepared, all the reports of conversations held. It was all here, enough to see justice done, but it was more than that, he told himself bitterly. It was the portrait of a girl, who, step by step, had been driven through a pattern of betrayal.

Every man she had dealt with had been an agent of betrayal. Father, school principal, employer, and finally her husband, each was guilty in his turn. Jenny Rizzo's words rang loud in Robert's ears. *Anybody was nice to her she'd go overboard.*

If he had spoken, if he had moved, he

could have been the one. When she turned at the top of the stairs to look at him she might have been waiting for him to speak or move. Now it was too late, and there was no way of letting her know what these papers meant, what he had done for her.

The police were everything Robert had expected until they read the bank manager's statement. Then they read and reread the statement, they looked at the photograph, and they courteously passed Robert from hand to hand until finally there was a door marked LIEUTENANT KYSERLING, and behind it a slender, soft-spoken man.

It was a long story – Robert had not realized until then how long it was or how many details there were to explain – but it was told from start to finish without interruption. At its conclusion Kyserling took the papers, the handkerchief, and the photograph, and pored over them. Then he looked at Robert curiously.

"It's all here," he said. "The only thing you left out is why you did it, why you went to all this trouble? What's your stake in this?"

It was not easy to have your most private dream exposed to a complete stranger.

Robert choked on the words. "It's because of her. The way I felt about her."

"Oh." Kyserling nodded understandingly. "Making time with her?"

"No," Robert said angrily. "We never even spoke to each other!"

Kyserling tapped his fingers gently on the papers before him.

"Well," he said, "it's none of my business anyhow. But you've done a pretty job for us. Very pretty. Matter of fact, yesterday we turned up the body in a car parked a few blocks away from your place. The car was stolen a month ago, there wasn't a stitch of identification on the clothing or anything; all we got is a body with a big wound in it. This business could have stayed up in the air for a hundred years if it wasn't for you walking in with a perfect case made out from A to Z."

"I'm glad," Robert said. "That's the way I wanted it."

"Yeah," Kyserling said. "Any time you want a job on the force you just come and see me."

Then he was gone from the office for a long while, and when he returned it was in the company of a big, stolid plainclothesman who smiled grimly.

"We're going to wrap it up now,"

203

Kyserling told Robert, and gestured at the man.

They went softly up the stairs of the house and stood to the side of the door while Kyserling laid his ear against it for some assurance of sound. Then he briskly nodded to the plainclothesman and rapped hard.

" Open up!" he called. "It's the police."

There was an ear-ringing silence, and Robert's mouth went dry as he saw Kyserling and the plainclothesman slip the chill blue steel of revolvers from their shoulder holsters.

"I got no use for these cute little games," growled Kyserling, and suddenly raised his foot and smashed the heel of his shoe hard against the lock of the door. The door burst open, Robert cowered back against the balustrade of the staircase –

And then he saw her.

She stood in the middle of the room facing him wildly, the same look on her face, he knew in that fantastic moment, that she must have worn each time she came face to face with a betrayer exposed. Then she took one backward step, and suddenly whirled toward the window.

"Ahh, no!" she cried, as Robert had heard her cry it out once before, and then was gone through the window in a sheet of broken

glass. Her voice rose in a single despairing shriek, and then was suddenly and mercifully silent.

Robert stood there, the salt of sweat suddenly in his eyes, the salt of blood on his lips. It was an infinity of distance to the window, but he finally got there, and had to thrust Kyserling aside to look down.

She lay crumpled on the sidewalk, and the thick black hair in loose disorder around her face shrouded her from the eyes of the curious.

The plainclothesman was gone, but Kyserling was still there watching Robert with sympathetic eyes.

"I thought he had killed her," Robert whispered. "I could swear he had killed her!"

"It was his body we found," said Kyserling. "She was the one who did it."

"But why didn't you tell me then!" Robert begged. "Why didn't you let me know!"

Kyserling looked at him wisely. "Yeah?" he said. "And then what? You tip her off so that she gets away; then we really got troubles."

There could be no answer to that. None at all.

"She just cracked up," Kyserling said reasonably. "Holed up here like she was, not knowing which way to turn, nobody she could trust... It was in the cards. You had nothing to do with it."

He went downstairs then, and Robert was alone in her room. He looked around it slowly, at all the things that were left of her, and then very deliberately picked up a chair, held it high over his head and with all his strength smashed it against the wall.

ROBERT L. FISH

Adventure of the Disappearance of Whistler's Mother

It was seldom, indeed, that the successful conclusion of a case left my friend, Mr. Schlock Homes, dissatisfied and unhappy; but one such affair did occur in the latter part of '66, and I relate the case to demonstrate how the best intentions of the finest of men can at times lead to unwanted results.

The months preceding this particular affair had been busy ones, and reference to my case-book for that period reveals numerous examples in which his analytical genius was given full opportunity for expression. There was, for example, his brilliant solution to the strange affair of the American baseball manager who went berserk, which I find noted as *The Adventure of the Twisted Lip;* and shortly thereafter his attention was drawn to the mysterious curse placed upon the south forty of a local grange owned by a prominent manufacturer of stomach drugs. I am sure my readers will recognize the case, which I later delineated as *The Adventure of the Bane in the Lower Tract.*

One might reasonably have imagined, this being so, that when at long last a dropping off of activity afforded my friend a well needed chance for rest he would have been pleased; but such was not the case. Boredom was always distasteful to Homes, and I was not surprised, therefore, to return to our quarters at 221B Bagel Street one late blustery afternoon in October to find my friend, hands thrust deep into the pockets of his dressing-gown, sprawled out in a chair before the fireplace, glowering fiercely into the flames.

Nor did he greet me in his customary manner, but came to his feet at my entrance and moved to the window restlessly, scowling down at the pavement.

I set aside my bag, removed my greatcoat and bowler, and was just turning to the sideboard when a sharp ejaculation caused me to swing about and contemplate Homes. He was leaning forward, staring down at the street in sudden excitement, his entire attitude expressing inordinate interest.

"Homes!" I exclaimed. "What is it?"

"Come here, Watney," said he, and drew the curtains further apart as I obediently hurried to his side. His thin finger pointed downward, quivering with excitement. "What do you make of that poor fellow there? Harrowed, is he not?"

My glance followed the direction of his finger. The figure to which Homes was referring was dashing madly from one side of the street to the other, studying the numerals of the houses in obvious agitation. Despite the dank chill of the day, he wore neither cape nor beaver; his hair was tousled, his waistcoat awry, and his manner extremely disturbed.

"Harrowed?" I repeated wonderingly, watching the eccentric path woven by the man below. " In my opinion, medically speaking, he appears not so much harrowed as ploughed."

"No matter," Homes replied with barely concealed triumph. "The important fact is that he is coming to visit us, for you will note he has paused before our doorstep, and even now is entering. And here, if I am not mistaken, is our visitor now."

Homes was, as usual, correct, for there was the sound of footsteps pounding loudly on the stairs, and a moment later the door burst open. The disheveled man stood panting upon the threshold, casting his eyes about wildly until they lit on Homes.

"Schlock 'Omes!" he cried in a thick French accent. "Thank *le bon Dieu* I 'ave found you in!"

At closer sight of our visitor, Homes's eyes widened in sudden recognitioin. He hurried forward, taking our perturbed guest by the arm and leading him to an easy chair beside the fireplace.

"Duping!" he cried. "My Lord man, what is the trouble? What brings you to London? And in this sorry state?" He turned to me, his eyes glowing.

"Watney, this is none other than my old friend from Paris, Monsieur C. Septembre Duping! You may recall that back in '41 I was able to be of some slight assistance to him in that sinister business of the simian with the inclination for strangling women and stuffing them up chimneys."

"Of course," I replied warmly, my eyes fixed upon our famous visitor with admiration. "As I recall, I even recorded the case in my notes as *The Adventure of the Monk's Habit.*"

"Precisely," Homes agreed, and swung back to our guest, dropping into a chair across from him and leaning forward sympathetically. "Septembre, pray tell us what is bothering you."

The man seated facing him took a deep

breath and then nodded. The warmth of the room after the raw weather outdoors had obviously done much to relax him, as well as the fact that I had hastened to furnish him with a whisky, taking one myself to keep him company.

"Yais," he said heavily, and raised troubled eyes to my friend's face. "'Omes, a terrible thing 'as 'appened. I know you are too *occupé* to come to Paris, but I still wished for ze benefit of your analytical brain."

"Of course," Homes replied warmly. "What is the problem?"

Our guest laid aside his empty glass and hesitated a moment, as if to emphasize the extreme gravity of the matter. When at last he spoke, the very quietness of his tone impressed us with his seriousness.

"'Omes," he said slowly, *"Whistler's Mother 'as been stolen!"*

If he had expected any great reaction from Homes, he was surely disappointed, for other than a slight narrowing of his eyes, caused by a puff of smoke from the fireplace, my friend's face remained impassive. "Ah? Most interesting. Pray continue."

"Yais." Duping sighed deeply, and then plunged ahead. "Well, ze facts are zese. *Hier*, at ze Louvre, zey 'ave a *réception* for a new painter 'oo is visiting Paris, and to make ze

211

affair properly impressive, zey arrange it in ze form of a musical *soirée*, calling ze programme "'Ello, Dali.' I mention zis fact only to explain why zere was so unusual-large a crowd zere. How you say, *normalment* at zis hour ze Louvre is quite empty. Well, to make a long story *court*, at nine o'clock, when ze *musicale* is start, Whistler's Mother is zere, where she 'as been for years. At ten o'clock, when everybody leave –" He spread his hands. "Gone! Wizout a clew!"

Homes nodded, his eyes fixed on the other's unhappy expression. "I see."

"Yais. Well, I imagine you will want ze description." Our visitor thought a moment, assembling the data in his mind, and then continued. "A black background, and gray. 'Er size, in your English measurements, *approximativement* five-foot-four by four-foot-nine. As you can well understand, a 'eavy frame, of course. What else? Ah, yais – ze age. About ninety-five years, I believe." He shook his head sadly. "Let us 'ope she is in good condition when returned, and not damaged or smashed."

Homes nodded and sprang to his feet, beginning to pace the room, his thin hands clasped tightly behind his back. After several turns, he came to stand before our guest, staring down with a frown on his face. "And has a reward been offered?"

Duping shrugged. "Money is no object, 'Omes. We will pay anyzing for ze return." He also rose, moving in the direction of the doorway. "We 'ave ze suspicion zat Whistler's Mother may already 'ave been smuggled out of France, possibly 'ere to England."

"A natural conclusion," Homes agreed. "And where are you staying in England?"

"I do not stay. I return at once to Paris. I came only to ask your 'elp."

"And you shall have it! You may expect to hear from me quite soon, giving you my solution to this puzzle. I shall get right to it this very evening, my dear Septembre."

"But, 'Omes – I mean, Homes," I interrupted in disappointment. "You have forgotten. We have tickets for Albert Hall tonight. The Rome Flood-Control Chorus is doing 'Hold That Tiber'."

He waved aside my objection almost impatiently. "Duty before pleasure, Watney," he replied a bit coldly. "Besides, I am not particularly interested in a programme consisting solely of popular tunes."

"But there is also classical music," I insisted, a bit stung by his tone. "Cyd Caesar

213

is completing the programme by playing the 'Etude Brutus'."

Homes thought a moment and then shook his head. "In that case, it is a pity, but I have already given my word." He returned his attention to our guest. "One last question, Septembre," he said softly, staring at the other intently. "And once the return is effected –?"

"We shall 'ang 'er, of course," Duping replied simply, and closed the door behind him.

No sooner had our guest left than Homes flung himself back into his chair, tenting his fingers, and staring across them towards me with a dark frown on his hawklike features.

"A tragedy, is it not, Watney?"

"Indeed it is," I readily agreed. "An old woman kidnaped!"

"No, no!" He shook his head at me impatiently. "You missed the entire point! The tragedy is that a poor wine-stewardess in a nightclub should face such a penalty for the mere pilfering of several bottles of wine. Particularly since the poor soul was under the influence at the time and scarcely liable for her actions."

"I beg your pardon?" I asked, bewildered. "I heard nothing today of nightclubs or wine-stewardesses. In fact, with the small amount of information Monsieur Duping furnished, I do not see how you can possibly hope to come up with the any answer to the puzzle."

"Small amount of information? Really, Watney, at times I despair of you! Duping gave us more information than we really needed. For example, there was his description of the woman. Obviously, if she is five-foot-four by four-foot-nine there was no need to inform us that she has a heavy frame. Similarly, if they plan to hang her when and if they get her back, it was scarcely necessary to tell us that her background was black. And being ninety-five years of age, one could automatically assume she would be gray. No, no. Watney! Duping gave us all we require. The real problem is how to handle it."

He swung himself about and stared fiercely into the flames of the fireplace, speaking almost as if to himself.

"There is a possibility, of course, that we cannot only satisfy Duping but still save the poor old lady's life. If only –" He nodded to himself several times, and then turned around to face the room, glancing at his timepiece. "A bit early to make our move, though."

"Really, Homes," I said, deeply annoyed. "I honestly believe you are pulling my leg. That business before of wine-stewardesses and nightclubs! And now this mysterious muttering you are indulging in! What move, pray, is it too early to make?"

"Why," Homes replied, surprised, "to break into Professor Marty's digs, of course." He noted the expression on my face and suddenly smiled in a kindly fashion. "No, Watney, I am not teasing you. We have at least an hour to spare, so let me explain this sad case to you." He leaned in my direction, ticking his points off methodically on his fingers.

"Let us start with Duping's description of the place where the old lady was last seen, and from which she disappeared, this place called the Louvre – or, in English, The Louver. That the place is a nightclub is instantly discernible: the fact that normally it was deserted between the hours of nine and ten, long before the most frivolous of French patrons would think of beginning their evening's entertainment; the presence of music in the form of this 'Hello, Dali' revue; and most important, the name, so typical, and so similar to The Venetian Blind or The Window or The Cellar or others which we know to be so popular in Soho today. I

216

should not hesitate to predict that their decor consists of louvers painted in green against a puce background. But no matter – let us continue."

A second finger was bent over to join the first while I listened in open-mouthed wonder to his brilliant deductions.

"Now, precisely what was this elderly lady doing in this nightclub? Obviously, she was not merely an habitué. Duping's exact words were, 'Where she 'as been for years.' Had she been a client, even the most constant, he almost certainly would have worded it differently. He would have said, 'Where she 'as been in ze 'abit of dropping in for years,' or something of that nature. Therefore, not being a client, we are forced to the conclusion that she is – or was, rather – an employee of the establishment, and one of long standing, at that.

"But in what position?" He shrugged before continuing. "Well, considering her age and her measurements, I believe we can safely eliminate the positions of waitress and hat-check girl, both of which demand a certain degree of beauty. Matron in the Mesdames? Again, I believe we can disregard this possibility; her exact presence or absence at any particular hour would scarcely have been noted with the exactitude that

217

Duping indicated. And the same holds true, of course, for any of the kitchen staff. Cashier? With her black background it is doubtful if the owners would permit her near the till. There is, therefore, only one position left: Mrs. Whistler could only have been the wine-stewardess!"

A third finger was depressed as I listened, amazed, to this startling demonstration of incontrovertible logic. Homes's eyes remained half closed as he cointinued to clothe the thin facts given by his friend with the warm flesh of his impeccable analysis.

"Now, Watney, consider: How could an old lady like this manage to subject herself to a penalty as severe as hanging in the short period allowed her between the hours of nine and ten? Certainly her crime was not murder, for which the French still maintain the guillotine. It must therefore have been something equally severe in the eyes of her accusers, but short of murder. It must also, of necessity, be something within her power to perform. Recalling that her position was that of a wine-stewardess, and that she had no access to any of the funds of the club, we can only reach one conclusion: that her crime consisted of taking some of the wine stocks. Undoubtedly rare and precious, and therefore probably cognac."

"But, Homes!" I objected. "Hanging? Just for stealing a few bottles of wine?"

He smiled at me pityingly. "It is apparent you know little of human nature, Watney. In the American colonies, as I am sure you are aware, the penalty for stealing a horse is hanging. And not so long ago punishment even more severe was reserved for anyone taking the King's deer. Why should France, where their national pride in their liqueurs is paramount, feel any less strongly? No, no! It is the only conclusion consistent with all the facts, and therefore must be the correct one. You know my dictum: when all theories but one have been eliminated, that remaining theory, however improbable – indeed, however impossible – must be the truth – or words to that effect."

I nodded dumbly. "Now," Homes went on, "when Duping told us that she had been stolen, you assumed his poor English prevented him from using the word 'kidnaped.' Actually, his poor English prevented him from stating what he truly meant – not that she had been stolen, but that she, herself, had stolen something."

I could not help but accept the faultless conclusion. "But, Homes," I said hopefully, "you suggest there were mitigating circumstances?"

"Yes. As I have already said, the poor woman was obviously under the influence of alcohol. You may recall Duping stating that he hoped she would not be 'smashed' when apprehended. It is an American slang term apparently becoming popular even in France. In any event, his very fear of this indicates that she stole the bottles in order to drink them – proof positive that her excessive thirst caused her crime in the first place. That she chose a moment when everyone was concentrating on the revue is easily understood. Under normal conditions she would have been too busy serving customers to have succumbed to the temptation to imbibe."

"But you say you hope to be able not only to satisfy Duping but also save the old lady?"

"There is that possibility."

"And this somehow involves Professor Marty?"

"Exactly." He considered me somberly. "It will mean a bit of a risk tonight, but there is nothing else for it. If you do not care to join me in this venture, I shall not hold it against you. The Professor is undoubtedly the most dangerous man in all England."

"Nothing on earth could stop me from accompanying you, Homes!" I declared stoutly, and then frowned. "But where does

Professor Marty come into this at all?"

He shook his head impatiently at my lack of perception. "Please, Watney! You may recall that when Duping suggested the old lady might even now be in England, I readily agreed. Why? Because the name Whistler is certainly not French, but rather English, and in times of trouble to whom would she return, if not to her son in England? We can scarcely believe that with her black background her son is free of a taint of malfeasance, and no criminal in England is beyond the scope or knowledge of Professor Marty. No, no! If Whistler's mother is in England at the moment, you may be sure the Professor is well aware of it. By entering his rooms after he has left on his nightly foray againt society, I hope to find proof of the fact. And possibly turn it to the advantage of that poor soul!"

"Bravo, Homes!" I cried, and could not help applauding both his motives and his infallible logic. Unfortunately, at the moment I was holding both a glass and a bottle, and while I shamefacedly hastened to clear up the debris, Homes disappeared into his room to change into more suitable raiment.

It was past the hour of ten when our hansom dropped us around the corner of Professor Marty's darkened rooms in Limehouse. The night had turned cold, which afforded us a good excuse to keep our collars high and our faces hidden from the denizens of the district, who slunk past us to fade into the growing miasma rising from the river beyond.

With a glance in both directions, Homes chose a moment when a swirl of fog momentarily hid us from any passers-by to swiftly mount the steps and apply his skill to the lock. A moment later he was beckoning me to follow; scant seconds more and he had closed the door, and his bull's-eye lantern was casting its restricted beam about the empty room.

"Quickly, Watney!" he whispered urgently. "We have little time! You take the den and the bedroom while I examine the kitchen and bath." He took one look at my opening lips and added coldly, "We are looking for anything that might indicate the presence of the old lady here."

I nodded and began to close my mouth when I remembered something else. "But I have no lantern, Homes."

"Use vestas, then, if need be, but hurry!"

He disappeared even as I was fumbling

beneath my cape, and an eerie chill swept over me until I had the first one lit and spied a taper on the mantelpiece. A moment later I was shielding the flickering flame and studying the room in which I stood. To me it appeared as any other room, and my heart sank as I realized how ill-equipped I was for a search of this nature, and that I might very well fail my friend. To bolster my spirits, I went to the liquor cabinet, and at that moment the beam of Homes's lantern joined by weaker candle as he returned to the den.

"There is nothing," he said in a dispirited voice, and then his tone sharpened. "Watney! What are you doing?"

"Nothing –" I began guiltily, but before I could offer my excuses he had dropped down beside me and was reaching past my arm for the contents of the cabinet. A moment later and he was pounding my back in congratulation.

"Watney, you have done it! Good man!"

I stared in bewilderment as he began withdrawing bottles and examining them, muttering half to himself as he did so. "Cordon Bleu, Remy Martin, Napoleon, Courvoisier – excellent! With any luck, this should do it!"

"But, Homes!" I interjected. "I don't understand. Do what?"

He swung to me with a fierce light of triumph in his eyes. "My dear Watney! When Duping expressed fear that the old lady would be apprehended in an inebriated state, he was not worrying about *her*, since he gave no indication of reducing the penalty for her crime. No, he was fearful that the cognacs would be consumed, for they are his main interest. By returning these to him, it is well possible that he will allow the matter to drop, and stop his pursuit of the poor woman."

His eyes swung about the room. "Quickly! Find me something in which to package these bottles while I pen a brief note to Duping to enclose. The packet to Le Havre leaves on the midnight tide, and by hurrying we can just make it."

While he bent over the escritoire, I hastily searched the room for wrapping materials, but despite my efforts the best I could find was an old roll of canvas that had been shoved behind a bookcase. I brought it forward hesitatingly and showed it to Homes.

"Ah, well," he said, shrugging, "it is certainly not the cleanest, for somebody has smeared it with tar or something. However, we have no time for further delays – it will have to do. Help me roll these bottles in it

224

and we will be on our way to the dock. With any luck these will be in Duping's hands tomorrow, and our problem will have been solved."

Our exertions of the previous evening kept us both late abed, and it was close to the hour of noon before I came into our breakfast room to find Homes already at the table. He nodded to me pleasantly and was about to speak when our page entered and handed Homes a telegraph form.

I seated myself, unfolded the afternoon journal, and was just reaching for the curried kidney when a sharp exclamation of dismay caused me to glance up. Homes, his face ashen, was staring in horror at the slip of paper in his hand. "Homes!" I cried. "What is it?"

"I am an idiot!" he muttered bitterly. "An abysmal idiot! I should have anticipated this?"

"Anticipated what, Homes?" I enquired, and for an answer received the telegraph form flung across the table. I read it hastily; its message was succinct. HOMES, YOU HAVE DONE IT AGAIN. WHISTLER'S MOTHER IS ONCE AGAIN IN OUR HANDS AND HUNG. THANKS TO YOU. "But, Homes!" I exclaimed. "I don't understand!"

"No?" he replied scathingly. "It is easily enough understood. I failed to take into account that the old lady might follow her booty back across the channel and thus fall into their hands! I am a fool! Rather than save her, I actually led her to her death."

"You must not blame yourself, Homes," I said with warm sympathy. "You did your best, and no man can do more."

"I did far too well," he replied balefully. "Without my help Duping might have searched for the old woman and her cognac for years." He tried to shake off his black mood, shrugging, "Ah, well! It is too late now to cry over spilt milk. Tell me, Watney, is there anything of a criminal nature in today's journal to help take my mind from this terible fiasco?" I hastily abandoned my kidney, perusing the newspaper instead, running my eyes rapidly down one column after another, but without too much success. There was, however, one weak possibility, and in lieu of a more interesting case I offered it.

"There is this, Homes," I said, studying the article further. "It seems that a very valuable painting was stolen from the French National Gallery; but the dateline is several days old. It may very well be that by this time the trail is much too cold."

The renewed sparkle in Homes's eyes told me that he was already well on the road to recovery.

"The time element makes no difference, Watney! A crime is a crime, and the more difficult the case, the better I like it! Besides, we have one bit of information the Sûreté lacks: we know that Professor Marty could not have been involved, for we would have come upon some evidence of it during our search. And eliminating this adversary takes us quite a step forward! A telegram to the authorities offering my services, Watney, if you will!"

MABEL SEELEY

The House That Nella Lived in

Steve Karakas was in a small town, mowing
'em down. The town's name was Maple
Valley. It had exactly one beer joint, and
that's where he was now, back to the bar,
heel caught on the rail. Steve Karakas – short
and quick and genial, and as ruthless as a
bullet. Close around him the local boys
leaned on each other, hair unstuck and
ragged over their foreheads, eyes bugged.
Punks, thought Steve, who didn't know a
thing.

"So then we get down along Mexico, see.
May-hee-ko, they call it. Well, the boat stops
at this dump for three hours, unloading, and
I says to myself, in three hours I unload too.
I hikes out along a main drag till I get to this
house, see, that has a balcony on it. With a
dame. Young, black hair, big black lamps –"

At the important part a hoarse crow went
up around him, of envy and second-hand
pleasure. But naturally there was a heckler.

"I noticed it happened a long ways off,"

this heckler said. He was a burnt-nose kid, standing a little way off by himself up the bar. Taller than Steve, but he didn't have a muscle.

"Oh, yeah?" Steve asked, easy but letting his shoulders roll. "Wanna make something of it?"

"Heck, no," the kid said, throwing it smart. "I ain't no plug-ugly."

"You play it all your own way," Steve threw it back smarter. "I ain't so crazy about getting my fist into a red ripe tomato. I mean like that one out front of your face."

The nose went up quick and a good laugh broke out all around. Oh, Steve knew how to handle 'em.

"Beer?" he asked. "Guess I'm good for another round. Talking about women always makes me thirsty." A laugh went up on that one, too.

When they'd got their beer they were friendly, relaxed. Now, thought Steve, was the right time.

"Ah, the heck with that stuff, anyways," he tossed in. "Me, I'm done with it. Gettin' old. Twenty-seven. What I'm doin' from here on is to settle down. Find some gal with the moola and get hitched. Say a widda. How's this town fixed for widdas with dough?" This was as artless as the rest, his voice said; only his eyes spoke a difference.

The crow went up again.

"Ah, there's no dough in this burg," he said.

"Say, who you kiddin'? We got old Mrs. Crunenback, ain't we? You'd go for old lady Crunenback, mister. Twenty thousand insurance. Eight-six years old."

"How about Mrs. Winty? Two farms. Kind of fat, maybe, but –"

"Yeah, and you wouldn't have to go out for her, neither. She'd go out for you!"

"Aw, have a heart, fellas," Steve cut in, still pretending that it was no more than a joke. "Ain't there a little dough somewheres that ain't tied to witches?"

They all talked at once. Naw, they said; if there was, he didn't think it would be laying around for strangers, did he? But then in the middle of it the heckler with the red nose stuck in his oar again. Quiet and funny, as if he meant something different from what he was saying.

"We got Nella Melstrom," he said.

The other boys shut up quick, looking at their beer.

"She ain't a widow, exactly," the tall boy drawled out. "But she's as close to rich as

230

you'll find in this town. She ain't old, and she ain't bad-looking, either."

The boys wore slammed doors in their faces.

"What's the matter?" Steve made it careful. "Her mama's a jungle snake?"

"Nope. Nella's an orphan."

"Your cast-off, huh?"

"Not mine. Sure, I went out with Nella a bit, once. I quit, though."

" You did, huh. Why'd you quit?"

"I just decided she wasn't quite safe for me, that's why."

"You decided – Say, what are you, anyhow? A yellow-bellied – She wouldn't get *me* that way. What is she, a weight-slinger? If you'd like to make a bet –"

"Why not? It could be fun, seeing this hot stuff you throw around."

Steve looked at the faces, now grown jeering, expectant, all turned to the other side.

"Nobody has to dare me twice't," he said. "Just you show me where this Nella hangs out."

The red-nosed boy loosened himself from the bar. "That's where you'll find Nella." At the front window of the bar, his pointing finger singled out a white house showing distantly against green-black pines, halfway

231

up a bluffside, south beyond the village rim. "Yep, that's where you'll find Nella," the boy said it over. "Lives there alone, too. All alone, except for an old woman does up her housework."

"Nella, just you wait for me, I'm comin'," Steve said.

"That's right, you go up. Nella won't mind," the boy said. "We'll be seeing you. Or then again, maybe we won't."

The crowd shuffled around, hanging back, but another boy said, "Sure, you go to it, hot stuff. We'll keep our eyes open."

"You'll get 'em full, all right," Steve promised, and that was that.

He'd got what he wanted from them. Slamming into his beat-up convertible, parked handy in front of the beer joint, he shot fifty feet up the street to a café that said *Nelson's*.

"Say, you know any folks in this village named Melstrom?" he asked the old geezer who dumped the pork chops down. The old gink was red, too, but only his hair had the color. His face was much paler with freckles."Kin of yours?" the man asked, kind of short.

"My cousins, or something. My mom

used to mention 'em. Maple Valley. I'm sure that's the town. Maple Valley."

"Just one girl left. That's Nella. Folks got killed in a car smash."

"Did, huh? Say, that's too bad. Only Nella left. Poor kid, hope she gets along."

"Oh, she gets along, Nella. Sold out her dad's bank. Good price, too, I guess."

Steve tried hard to get it. Good price. Her dad's bank. But the way she'd been put to him, there was a catch – there must be.

He inched it to Nelson, but Nelson clammed up. Well, nothing like seeing for yourself.

It wasn't seven yet; he drove straight for the steep road that wound up the bluffside. Halfway up, there was a grade where the pull of gravity at his front wheels was almost as much back as down; he had a half sick thrill in the pit of his stomach. After that, the climb eased, turned, and brought him to a house with a porch.

The girl had cushions around her in a long chair, and she was reading. But when the car swung alongside she sat up, looking eager.

Baby! Steve said to himself, swearing it. He couldn't be seeing straight. This girl was as small as a ten-year-old kid. She had a kid's face, too – funny, smiley, and blue-eyed. Blonde hair, pale and silky, pulled up at the

233

sides and curled under in back. But plenty grown up, too. You saw that from her neck down.

"Baby, you're knocking me cold," he told her, and this time he wasn't swearing it. "I came up here to see a girl named Nella. Nella Melstrom. I didn't expect to run into anybody who would knock the sunspots off Jane Russell."

"Why, I'm Nella," the girl said, simple and surprised and even more eager, getting up to hold the porch screen open. "Who're you?" The way she put it she couldn't be anything but all-over small town – a girl who'd never catch onto a thing. He stuck out his hand.

"Why, Nella, hello! I guess I'm your cousin, a couple of times back. Steve Karakas, my name is; my mother used to say we had kin in these parts. Melstrom, she said; I remember that. Melstrom. So when I was driving through here –"

The kid smiled so all-over she wriggled. "Isn't that funny? I can't remember dad ever – or mother – but there's nobody else here named Melstrom."

"I sure hope I'm not mistaken."

"You do?" She was so pleased with him he had a great big lift; he didn't have to get any further along than this to know he'd have no trouble with her. No trouble at all!

"Do sit down," she was telling him. "No, not there. Here, by me. Have you lived near here?"

"I've lived everywhere, I guess." What more could he ask? He sat by her and began to spin it out. He took her to Rio and Agua Caliente; he took her to 'Frisco and Hollywood, to a jail in Las Vegas and down into Panama City. He'd realy been there and he could do 'em good. He left out the women and put in things he'd heard about. She sat right where she was until the August evening was dark, listening so close he almost had her ears in his teeth.

When it got to ten or so, he pulled out of it, stretching and smiling at her.

"Shagging around, that's my stuff. I'm not much for sticking in one place."

"Why, it's late!" she said then, waking up. "And I've not even – I haven't even offered you a drink!"

He let her go, willing; when she came back she handed him a glass. Lemonade. Her idea of a drink. Lemonade. An old woman pattering after her offered him cookies.

"Martha, this is Steve Karakas. I've learned he's my cousin," Nella was chattering, while he got a good look at the woman. Short and fat, mouth pursed into a buttonhole. Sixty-five if a day.

"Hello, Martha," he greeted her, getting up, friendly, but the old dame beat it like a frightened rabbit. It gave him another big lift – she wouldn't bother him, either.

"You mustn't mind Martha," Nella was telling him. "Her teeth hurt; she never does wear them except when she's eating. She's bashful."

"Say," he asked, pushing it. "Aren't you two afraid up here all alone by yourselves? So far out?"

"Goodness, no." She stared at him, surprised, and laughed. "I can't be afraid here. My house looks afer me."

"Your house – say, that's good!"

He waited, expecting her to laugh again; instead, she said the thing over, in the simple way she said everything.

"My house is different from all other houses. I love it, and it loves me." She'd sat down with her lemonade, but the white-painted brick wall was where she could reach it; she stretched out to give the wall a little pat. "My house was built for me, didn't you hear of that? Dad and mother weren't married until I was born, but of course you know that much. Everyone around here would tell you. I hadn't been born long,

236

though, when grandfather died and daddy got the bank and married mother and me. He built the house then. It's taken care of me ever since."

The catch. That was it – she was off her nut. For a minute his head stopped short; the wheels wouldn't spin around. Then when they did start up they moved in short jerks; his plans jolted around in his head. The muscles moved a little on his bones, too. Crazy people were something he'd always steered clear of; you never knew what they would do.

When he stared at her, though, he just couldn't believe it. There she sat, tiny and quiet, eyes shining in the moonlight, and after a while his muscles smoothed down a bit. Her size now – that made it safer. Just the same, he wanted to get away a minute. Where he could think.

"Wish there was some house would look after me," he joked. "Right now I could use a bed –"

"Mr. Nelson's got two rooms," she said, still all eager. "Oh, I hope –"

"At Nelson's? You mean – the café?" He was leaving it open.

"You've just *got* to stay a while," she urged, anxious, like any girl who wanted a boy friend. "You could eat with me – we'd picnic – we'd swim in the river –"

"Say, you make it sound good."

He still wasn't promising, and going down the bluff he drove slowly; that steep strip could give him the willies. Nelson wouldn't hurt him, though, and Nelson was glad enough to rent him a stuffy little room with a bed and a rocker and a dresser. Lying on the patchwork quilt with his shoes off, he got to thinking. He knew now what scared the boys.

If Nella had heft to her – but she didn't. If she went on a tear he could takle her down with one hand. That stuff about the bank – good price, Nelson had said. Living alone the way she did, she should have hung onto all the dough. Stocks, bonds – something he could turn into cash in a hurry. He'd been bumming around now for seven months, since the last one, and not finding a thing. That ear he'd got in Juarez wasn't helping him any, and his belly wasn't as flat as it once was – a man twenty-seven was getting along. Nella had looks, too. Cute and little. She'd fit his hands –

In the morning, roaring south past the beer joint, he kept his chest out and a grin on his face; no worry that the boys wouldn't have heard where he was last night, and how late he'd stayed; no worry they'd see where he went now. He'd show 'em who had guts. Besides, it wasn't as if the kid was so far off the beam.

When he swung onto the plateau, she was ready and waiting, dressed up in starchy pink, hopping out to his car like a bunny. "Oh, Steve! I'm so glad you stayed! I'm so glad you're here! I waited my breakfast, a special big breakfast. I'm terribly hungry – I hope you're right next door to starving –"

The door went wide, drawing him in. He stepped warily, not that he believed anything, but it didn't pay to be careless. Just the same, a jolt came to him. Not a jolt coming from anything Nella said, but the other kind. He'd been in plenty of swell places – nightclubs and like that – but this house was different. The hall was painted yellow, pale yellow; the dining room green and cream. Not colors that screamed money, but that had a kind of clean freshness. Flowers, some in fabric and some real. Chairs, little tables, bright silver.

"You have to think my house is lovely," Nella said, and there she went again, cheek to the creamy enamel of a doorframe, hugging it.

"It sure is, babe," he said carefully.

"Swell." For a minute there, with her hugging the foorframe, he was seeing things – a sunshine that centered on her, alive and tender, flowing back and forth over her like breath.

"Now you've got me going," he protested, and shook himself. A good thing he did, too. He saw then that the room was just any room, that's all – in very nice shape, of course, but only a small dining room with a lot of bright sunshine coming in through the curtains to lie quietly on the table and the dishes and the silver. No more flowing back and forth.

That's the way it went after breakfast, too. Everything was all right, almost. They drove in his car to the river that curved along the east side of the valley; they lay beside it, lazy in the shade. When some boys and girls came along he borrowed trunks and dove in with them, racing and tagging – kid stuff, but a chance for him to keep his eyes open. Nella, he could see, was treated different; not as if the kids were afraid of her, though – more as if they were respectful. They tagged her, but while they pushed each other under water they didn't push Nella. Nella did a dive and they all yelled it was awful. When they went home Nella looked after them, lonesome, but then she looked back at him and became cheerful and asked him back up to the house for lunch.

That time there wasn't anything about the house at all. As for the way Nella spattered words – well, that was girl stuff, no dizzier than any dame. He decided she wasn't any more than simple-minded. Someone – her mother, maybe – had sold her a bill of goods about the house.

Then he forgot that, too. Once they'd finished eating, she dared him to race her to the bluff-top. Out in the sand and thin grass, and among the boulders between the trees, she could swing herself up like a monkey in rigging. At first, he kept abreast, but after a while he began to lag, blowing hard. At the very top was a huge rock with steep sides. She seemed to slide up, but he had to crawl, itching and hot, his shirt ripped and his hands skinned, while she laughed at his troubles from above.

"You devil," he told her, when he'd made it at last. "You'll pay for this!"

She laughed when he caught her, laughed in his arms, laughed against his hair, against his mouth. He pulled her down the rock and she lay laughing in the grass at its feet, provoking him with her constant laughter.

They went down the bluff holding hands.

Crazy? This kid crazy? Crazy like a fox,

that's all. She knew what she wanted. Wild, was what she was. Too wild for the mud hunks in this town. But okay with him. He liked 'em wild.

"It's nice you love me. I'm glad you love me. Last night I thought maybe you *would* love me if you stayed." She kept stopping to rub her cheek on his sleeve.

"You're not hard to take, baby," he let her know, making his voice deep. "You're about the swellest kid I ever met." He could tell 'em when he wanted to. All the rest of that day he spent seeing to it she knew a good Joe when she had one. Lying beside her in the porch chair, eating dinner on the porch, too. Spinning more yarns about the world.

"You don't want I should go back to Nelson's, do you, honey?" he coaxed, when she turned sleepy and nuzzling. He might just as well cinch it now. "Why don't I just stay with you up here?"

"Oh, no!" she said it so quick she stopped a yawn in the middle, sitting up tight, and he knew then what was coming. "You can't sleep here, Steve. My house wouldn't like it."

Right after he'd decided she was okay, too! No jolt this time – it just made him sore. He stood up, flexing his muscles. "Feel that

bicep, kid. Think your house could do anything to that?"

"Carl had muscles, too. Carl was *very*
strong. The house didn't like it when *he*
stayed."

That stopped him cold, almost.

He asked, "Who's Carl?"

"Carl's a boy who used to love me."

"Why, you –" He stopped, speechless.
Innocent! Innocent little punk! And here she
was standing up close to him, on this porch
of hers, handing him baby stares, talking
about it as if it was nothing at all.

"It seems like forever since Carl went
away."

So that was it. A past. "She ain't a widow,
exactly." Something like that was the way
she'd been put to him. All over town it must
be, the way this Carl had been going with
her, and then beat it, probably afraid he'd
have to marry her. No wonder the kid was
– well, not nuts exactly, but right next door
to it.

Anyway, it was no skin off his nose.

"Aw, babe." He hugged her. "That's
tough. That guy was a rat. You don't have
to worry that I'll beat it. I'll see a judge
anytime you say."

"He wasn't a rat. He was nice. I liked him.
I was sorry when he went. I got lonesome."

243

"Sure you did, you poor kid. You don't have to be lonesome no more, though. We'll get married tomorrow if you want." Usually he let them bring up the wedding deal, let them be the anxious ones. This Carl business, though, was an opening.

She strained against his arms. "No, we mustn't get married. Not ever."

For the second time in one evening he didn't think he was hearing straight. "What do you mean, not get married?"

"I like you this way."

Bats, at that. More than one way, too.

He tried joking her out of it. "You mean you stay alone up here, and me at Nelson's, in that dump?"

"You can be here all day."

"Nights, I'm talking of."

"My house is much stronger, nights. You mustn't even go in my house, nights. That's why we're out here on the porch."

"Babe, listen. Don't you love me?" He put all the trembles in that one.

"You're fun. I love fun. But not nights."

"You're a silly kid. Here, kiss papa." He pulled her up close again.

He slept, though, at Nelson's.

He slept every night at Nelson's. Exasperating. He couldn't get it. He pushed her

244

away and walked in through her house once, at nine in the evening, full dark, and not a thing happened to him. She tagged along at his heels, actually crying, pulling him back to the porch again, not believing even when he'd showed her how safe it was. He just couldn't get it, because in every other way no kitten was ever easier. She was affectionate and full of life, never getting enough swimming or hiking or climbing or any of that small-town stuff. Of course, it wasn't too bad a life for a change – all he could eat, and his belly was flattening, and Nella was entirely gone on him.

But she wouldn't change.

One night, when he got back to Nelson's, late, Nelson was still hanging around at the lunch counter.

"Havin' a cup of coffee," Nelson said. "You want one?"

"Sure. Thanks." Wires tightened on his spine, though; he'd been expecting this. This was where a small town tried sticking its nose in his business.

"I hear you been seein' a lot of your cousin." Nelson poured out the coffee.

"Every day," Steve answered him promptly. "Anything to you?"

"Oh, no, no." Nelson swallowed down

half his own cupful. "Funny thing about Nella. Bad luck with her boy friends."

"That so?"

"Yeah." Nelson wasn't looking at him. "Young fella named Viney. Carl Viney. Father still farms here – three, four miles out. Carl went with Nella pretty steady for a while. Got kind of thick, I guess. Then one night he went away. Never been seen or heard of since."

"Well, the dirty skunk," Steve said.

"Don't get me wrong." Nelson was in a hurry now. "I ain't saying a word against Nella. Nice kid –" he let it drift into silence.

"You don't have to worry that I'll stand her up," Steve made it strong enough to be definite. "I'm arranging to marry her, right now."

"That's fine," Nelson said, lukewarm.

When Steve went upstairs, Nelson's eyes didn't lift to his back, but there was warning in Nelson, all right. After that, he always stopped when he came in, daring Nelson to start something, but Nelson never peeped again. Just the same, it made him want to hurry things.

"Say, Nelson was talking to me about you last night," he told Nella, again from a porch chair. "He says you're an heiress."

"You mean, about my money? Isn't it nice I have money, Steve? If I didn't, I could never live up here –"

"I'll say you're lucky. You handle it all by yourself?"

"Oh, no. Mr. Chandler – that's Mr. Chandler who bought the bank – takes care of it. Invests it for me. There's about seventy thousand now, Mr. Chandler says. He's very good about money; he puts it in farm mortgages, mostly. I never spend much of it – only my income." She was as open about this as about anything else he had asked.

He whistled. "Baby! You got any idea how *much* dough that is? Baby, how you could live in the big time!" He was galvanized, almost awestricken. Seventy gees! Better, much better, than he'd expected. Better, much better, than anything he'd ever come in for before. "Why're you sticking in this dead dump?"

"You know why, silly. I can't leave my house, can I?"

"You'll be leaving it soon, kid, just as soon as we're hitched. And we're not stalling, either. We –"

"But you *know* we're not getting married. Ever."

"I tell you what." He didn't dare look at her, because if he did, with this guff she

247

forever threw back at him – and right now when he'd found out how big the stake was, too – he'd have to start slapping her down. Patience! If people wanted to find out about patience, they ought to take lessons from him.

"I tell you what – I'll give you my car for a present. Right now. It ain't what it once was – you can trade it in on a new one. Then we'll be all set for when we do get hitched, and in between we can take us some real trips around here."

She grabbed at it, anxious to be done with quarreling. "That's generous of you, Steve – I've never had a car. I don't know – after daddy and mother – but there's no reason –"

A trip to the bank for the money meant he could cinch a few things.

"This is Steve Karakas. Steve's giving me his old car. I want to trade it in on a new one if I can have the money." As always, Nella put out all she had all at once.

Mr. Chandler shook hands with Steve. A soft, moon-faced man, easy-going.

"I don't know why not, Nella," Mr. Chandler said. "You got money around you're the boss of."

Chandler, a guy he could handle with one hand, too. And the money was there.

They drove to Red Falls with the certified check and came back with the brand new car. He taught Nella to drive it. She drove, when she caught on, like a hummingbird flying. They went two hundred, three hundred miles in a day. But they were back, nearly always, at night. Right up to the day in October.

Steve was at the wheel, on that day, when they began a seventy-mile drive to a movie. Beside him, Nella kept squeezing his arm. The minute he'd met her that day he'd known she was lifted up. Her cheeks shone red-hot and her eyes were dark.

"What do you think, Steve?" She was always ready to babble. "I've been talking to Martha. Martha thinks I may be getting a baby."

"You're kidding." The words jolted out of him.

"Why, Steve, what's the matter? It'll be wonderful for me when you're gone and I'm there in the house again. I won't be alone, really – not if I have a baby. I never had a baby before. This will be the first time."

He stopped her.

"That cuts it. That cuts all this talk about your being alone in the house, too. You're marrying me, see? And from then on you do what I say.

The half sick thrill, the one from halfway up the bluffside, was back in him, slapping this way and that like a gone-wild wave. One thing he hadn't tried, ever, was getting rid of a dame who was having a kid. People noticed things like that. It'd soon show on Nella, little and thin the way she was. They might trace him. He'd have to work quick now. Nor could he give it all up and go off by himself. Not this time – he needed that dough. Everything he had was sunk into this. Paying Nelson, giving her the car. He was flat.

"But Steve –"

"Look here, girl. You've got to get hitched now. Don't you see that?" Imagine having to argue with a girl, the shape she was in.

"But I don't want to. We mustn't. You don't know what my house would –"

"You don't think your crazy talk makes any difference to me, do you?" He leaned toward her, letting her see what his face was with the friendliness off. He picked up her right hand. "Leave me know when you've had enough," he said, and began twisting.

She looked at him, not believing – the way women did when you had to get tough the first time. Her eyes turned bluer and wider and wet, but she took it plenty. He thought for a while he'd have to break her arm. That wouldn't have been so good, either.

"Steve," she whispered at last.

He stopped the twist right away, glad to. "So you got the idea."

"I guess I can just as well marry you." She didn't look bewildered any more. Or even frightened. Just white and quiet. He started the car quickly, before she could change her mind, heading for the county seat. She sat hunched up, not looking at him, not saying anything. But when they got to Red Falls she told him where the courthouse was, and went along like a lamb, giving all the right answers to the license clerk and the Justice of the Peace.

Then she sat quiet in the car, going back.

"Maybe it'll be better," was the only thing she said, once. "Maybe it'll be better for the baby. I can tell the people in town. Or it might be in the papers."

"Sure, it'll be in the papers," he told her. "Cheer up, kid. They'll all know you're married, now."

But she wouldn't cheer up. As soon as they got to her house, he told Martha. Martha looked at him, her mouth, toothless as usual, working a little. Then she turned around without saying anything and went off to the kitchen. It was dark when they got home;

entirely dark. He walked in the house the same way he had that one other time, bold as brass, and again nothing happened. What was there to happen? From a plain house, with lights on?

And Nella came after him, quiet. Not crying, not pulling him back. He'd showed her.

"Your house, see" – he held both arms out – "it likes me."

She wouldn't answer, not even while they ate. the gloom got on his nerves. He'd showed her, all right, and she'd have to take it. But he still had to work on her. You'd think she knew what was coming to her, the way she was acting. But she couldn't. How could she? They never did.

"This ain't no funeral. Come on, sit by papa." When she stood up after dinner, he put his arm around her, walking her toward the living room. "The trouble with you is you're fed up, same as me. It's this town. What you want is to get your dough out of that silly bank and go places where it'll mean something. Get away from this town, from this house. I don't blame you, it gives you the willies."

The lights dimmed, then came back on steady.

"See," he told her. "A burg like this, even

the lights are no good. Baby, you should see a big town. Lights to put your eyes out. You could go places in a big town, too, baby. You're young, you got looks. Say, babe, your life's not even started. What do you say we beat it out of here, huh?"

"Maybe," she said.

That's the stuff!" This was the most she had ever given in. He'd get around her, all right. He pulled her with him to an armchair. She sat limp, unresisting, her head heavy on his shoulder.

"See, babe, this is what we'll do . . ."

For the rest of the evening he spun it out. Lights. Drinks. Real drinks. Shows. Nightclubs. Big-town life. She took it in, quiet.

When he couldn't stand any more, he stood up, stretching. "Well, baby, let's turn in. Your wedding night – it only comes but once."

She sprang up then, clutching his arm, her eyes big and terrified, right back to what she'd been.

"Steve, don't stay tonight! Even if we are married, go back down to Nelson's like always! Don't stay here!"

"Say, what is this?" he asked, incredulous. "Now, listen, baby. You wouldn't want I should have to get tough with you, not on your wedding –"

She dropped his arm, the terror and everything else going out of her face. "All right," she said.

They went up the carpeted stairs. She slept alone up there, she said – Martha had a room off the kitchen. For the first time he went into her room – white and big, with blue on the bed and the floor, and a lot of thin curtains around it, like veils. When he stepped over the doorsill the lights dimmed once more, as they had downstairs, and for a minute a chill fog surrounded him, but then the lights came back up and it was all right – just a silly girl's room.

In bed, Nella lay stiff in his arms.

"Aw, cut it, kid," he said. "Relax."

"I'm sorry, Steve."

"Sorry? What've you got to be sorry about?"

"I'll be lonesome when you're gone."

Oh, well, no reason he shouldn't kid her along. "Can't you get it in your silly little head? I'm going away, sure. So are you."

"That's what Carl said, too."

"*Carl* said. Say, is that nice? Talking about another guy on our wedding night."

"I was lying here looking at him in the
254

moonlight, just like this, and he went. He didn't even take his clothes along."

A tiny prick of caution stirred in him.

"What?"

"He didn't even take his clothes."

"Say, what is this?" Muscles were tightening now. "What're you getting at? What happened to his clothes?"

"We hid them, and then when he never came back Martha burned them in the furnace."

He hadn't been afraid when he walked in from the porch; he hadn't been afraid at their late dinner, or in the living room, or coming upstairs. But now a great surge of something washed over him – all the uneasiness he had ever felt with her collected to stormy power. She lay in his arms, small, pale, and still, looking helplessly at him from wide eyes. There was no fear in her face, only expectation – an expectation that reached out to him.

His muscles gathered, his arm squirmed from under her, his hands got her throat. "What happened to that guy? If you think you're pulling anything on me, it don't go, see? I'm a big-town guy –"

A grayness was gathering around him – that fog, again. His mind and his hands leaped to new strength, he clamped with

255

grimmer purpose on her throat. But her voice went on, even and sorrowful.

"I'll forget about today, Steve. I'll forget my arm. I'll tell the baby you were nice, Steve. I'm sorry about the house – it's just that it loves me and it's jealous and it won't let anything bad happen to me. It was the house that took Carl away – I know it, I felt it. I was here, just like this, and he – Steve! Steve!"

She cried out, a thin cry breaking against the night, because he was no longer there. The hands on her throat were gone; the shoulder she had clutched was gone. In the pillow were the wrinkles where his head had been, but his head wasn't there. She put out her hand. The warmth of his body was still in the bed – but he was gone. She rose on one elbow to look over the side of the bed to where he had thrown his clothes on the floor.

They were there.

She lay back, then, eyes wide, face not rebellious, only wistful and curious – as if she wondered not why but with what invisible hands her house had, for a second time, taken a lover from her.

There was nothing in the room to answer. Moonlight lay along the ceiling as reassuring as a smile, and a white window curtain, blowing over the bed, touched her shoulder like a caress.

VERONICA PARKER JOHNS
Homecoming

Bebe watched the drake breast its way through the browning grass. He was white with shocking-pink trimmings – a Muscovy, she remembered, one of those her father had most treasured, not the mongrel breed which had taken over since his death. It wore the bracelet of yellow plastic with which Pop had banded his flock. I, too, have a bracelet, she thought, glancing down at the circlet of emeralds and diamonds for which half the police in the Middle West were searching. I have a bracelet and I have Max, and all the police in the world must be looking for *him*.

The drake paused in his foraging to stare over his shoulder at the girl, his beady eye unblinking.

"What's that you say, duck?" she asked huskily. "You don't want I should mention Max, not while you're eating? You got a point there. I'm sort of beginning to feel that way about him myself."

The drake turned and edged nearer, curiosity obviously overcoming its natural

258

wariness. How long had it been, until this week, since a human voice had sounded on the farm? Pop died more than three years ago, and Granny hadn't talked to herself more than three or four months after that before the lawyer mailed the deed to Bebe, telling her she was now the only one left to pay the taxes.

Mom – if you could call anyone you knew so slightly by such a chummy name – had hightailed it out of there with a horn-player when Bebe was six years old and known as little Amantha Evans. Amantha! That would sure have looked silly on the marquee of a movie theater, providing she'd ever been able to get it that far off the ground. It had even looked foolish in the fine print used for chorines at the Dipsydoodle Club, where Max had found her, had taken her away from all that, and had taken all that away from her.

Or was it she who had found him? During the sixth and final routine that Saturday night, with the cold, gray Chicago dawn waiting for her outside the alley door, had she found the hot dark eyes, the strong arms (growing flabby now) which fraudulenty promised warmth. It didn't matter any more who had done the finding. It had all happened so long ago – eight years by the calendar, at least forty times that by any accurate form of reckoning.

Quit beefing, she scolded herself. There's a certain amount of prestige in being Maxie Swanson's girl. Better than dying in a four-bit rooming house with some hophead horn-player, as you mother did, and as Granny had kept promising you would too. A helluva promise to make, day in and day out, to a little kid, and Granny made it with such straight-from-the-feedbag certainty that Amantha had rushed away at fourteen to become Bebe.

Now she was back in residence. Should she run up the flag as they do for home games? Hardly. Maxie wouldn't like that. Maxie would like it if you didn't have to breathe so often, so you wouldn't stir up so much air and people would be less likely to notice. Since that last job, the one that had included the diamond-and-emerald bracelet, he was a mighty shy guy. He just wanted to rusticate – okay, hide out, to use the vulgar expression – on Bebe's farm, the rest of his life if need be, although it probably wouldn't amount to that.

Well, she could stand it, the better than he could maybe. But only if she was able to make the place look more presentable, more like it had been when her father was alive.

It was so ratty now, so needy that it made her want to cry – the rose bed choked by weeds, the shrubs strangled by honeysuckle, and the stinking poison ivy pulling its tricks all over the joint.

She'd need tools to work with; the ones her father had used were little more than rust. Maybe Maxie would let her make a trip into the neighboring town to get some. There was little chance that she would be recognized. Not much of a fourteen-year-old face is left when you reach twenty-two, not when the meantime has been so real lowdown mean.

Even before she got the tools, she could tackle the eight-foot ragweed that hedged the house with her bare hands – bare, that was, but for a three-and-a-half-carat diamond and a horse-choking star sapphire. She tugged at the first stalk fiercely, hating it, crowding in all the hate she felt for other things, other persons, for Maxie, for, dear God, herself most of all.

At her fury, the drake took flight – down toward the pond, which was probably still there although you couldn't see it through the overgrowth. Near the pond, she remembered, was her father's pride and joy, inherited from his father before him, the dewberry patch. Not just an ordinary dewberry, which isn't exactly ordinary to begin with, but a dewberry cross that Grandfather Evans had bred, with which he used to win a medal every year at the county fair.

People always asked for cuttings and Grampa wasn't stingy with it, but "Funny thing, Amantha" – she could hear his cracked old voice and the high-pitched laughter that set the dewberry jelly glasses to quivering –"it won't thrive noplace except on our own land. Puny little pea-size berries is all the others get, without a fairy's thimblefull of juice in a dozen of them."

There probably wasn't a berry bush left to keep his memory green. Poor Grampa. Poor Pop. Poor Amantha, dear Lord knows how many years; buried, calendarwise, eight.

Maxie Swanson lay sprawled on the horse-hair sofa in a crumpled white linen suit, like a stain in the Evanses' parlor, like spilled milk worth the crying over. His shoes, size thirteen, were neatly set upon the floor beside him. That's one thing to my credit, Bebe thought as she paused in the doorway; Granny wouldn't let Pop and Grampa put their feet up on that sofa, and I raised enough of a hassle so that Maxie don't dare do it with his shoes on.

"The bugs in this house is terrible," he

complained querulously, as if he'd been lying there thinking about them a long time, and blaming Bebe.

"They're clean, country bugs," she came to their defense. "Not like the bedbugs and worse you grew up with."

Maxie was always quick with his hands. He drew a bead on a horsefly, scooped it out of the air and into a peachblow rose bowl, held his palm flat against the top. The fly buzzed frenziedly, batting against the opaque glass.

"You fixing to pick off its wings, Maxie?" she asked caustically.

"No. Just thought if you were so fond of country bugs I'd catch you one for a pet. Better than you feeding that blasted cat that keeps mooching around."

"The cat's starved," she protested. "His people don't take care of him properly. You can't expect me not to –"

"Can't I?" he asked, half kiddingly, swinging his feet to the floor. Using the hand pressed against the rose bowl for leverage.

"Watch out!" she shouted. "You want to break that vase? It's an antique, you clumsy ape!"

He held it inverted in his hand for a moment, then pitched it through the open window. She heard it smash against a stone,

263

and ran to look out at the blue-green fragments. She whimpered, in impotent rage.

"Don't cry, little girl," Max purred. "I'll buy you another fly. I'll buy you anything in the lousy world you want. You know that, don't you, baby."

He could reach her now without getting off the sofa, and he put out an arm and drew her to him.

"You know that, don't you, baby?" he repeated, rubbing his forehead against her bare shoulder. "All you gotta do is ask Maxie pretty. Only I want you should stop feeding that cat. You wouldn't want him to put the finger on me, would you?"

"That's kind of farfetched, Max," she said, not weakening yet, not allowing herself to feel the way he had always been able to make her feel.

"No, it ain't," he contradicted in the little voice, the kid voice, the one that got her. "The people he belongs to would be sure to notice him putting on weight, and they might see him heading for this place day after day. It would seem kind of funny that a cat could get a handout in a house that's been empty three years. You wouldn't want them to check up and find me, would you, honey?"

He stroked her ribs gently. "What's

264

more," he said, "maybe the cat's folks like him skinny, like I like you. Don't you never let me catch you with your face in some other guy's saucer of cream. You're my girl, Bebe. Ain't you glad?"

He held her closer, his head an inch or two below her chin. After a while she lifted a hand and thrust it into his dark, thick, tantalizing hair.

"Sure, Maxie," she whispered. "I'm glad, I guess."

She had dropped off into a shallow slumber from which the car awakened her. Max had not been asleep and, as she opened her eyes, had rushed across the room to get the Luger. He cocked it toward the door, crouching, nostrils taut with his drawn-in breath. Fool! she thought. How scary can you be? Couldn't he recognize the motor of his own bodyguard's car?

Bat – Jean Baptiste Larue – never even glanced at the gun when he walked in and dropped the first load of packages. Max put it back on the curly-maple table, beside the basket of wax fruit under a dome of glass.

"What in hell took you so long, Bat?" he asked suspiciously. "You been shooting the breeze with the local yokels again?"

For a muscle man, for just about the

hardest hood on two feet, Bat had a surprisingly soft voice. "Sure, boss," he said. "It's like I told you – I've got to do it. It's the custom around here to pass the time of day. Was I to buy my stuff and get the hell out, people would get nosey."

"But what do you find to yak about?" Max asked with the bewilderment of a man who had never needed small talk.

Bat laughed. "About myself. Not Bat Larue, if you follow me, but the fellow I want them to think I am." He perched on the arm of the Boston rocker, continuing. "That's one sweet guy, that one. Always buying stuff for the other people in the camp." Bat lived in a trailer parked at the Maple Rest a couple of miles down the road. "Like more food than a lone bachelor could possibly eat. Like that oven for the oil stove Bebe wanted. I said it was for a dear old lady who's shoving off for California tomorrow."

"Did you get it, Bat?" Bebe broke in. "Honest?"

"I sure did."

"Gee," she breathed. "And the ham, a big one?"

He nodded.

"Which one's the ham?" she asked. "Boy, is it going to taste good! It'd be better,

266

of course, if I could use the big old coal stove –"

Max spoke harshly. "Will you for the love of Pete quit harping on the coal stove? I told you you couldn't light it, and that's that. Do you want to send up smoke signals to the neighborhood like some silly Indian?"

"Awright, already," she snapped. "We use the oil stove. I guess it'll do, since it has to. How big's the oven, Bat? I wonder if I could squeeze in some popovers in Granny's iron pan."

"Popovers!" Max snorted. "You think you're a baker or something?"

"I'm a very good baker," she informed him. "Granny taught me how. I can bake a pie any day as good as hers, and she was top prize-winner at the fair."

"Cripes, what hick stuff," Max said contemptuously. Bat looked at her as though she had flipped her wig, and no wonder. Back in Chicago she'd never set foot inside the kitchen, and here she was getting all excited about an oven.

"I'll get your toy, Bebe," Bat said, and went back to the car.

It was a good dinner. It was the best meal any one of them had had since Max, with Bat's assistance, stuck up the jewelry store on Michigan Avenue last week. That job was the biggest they'd ever pulled and the loot should net them enough to live high on the hog the rest of their lives; but until now the pickings had been poor.

Maxie's plans always worked smoothly because he kept them simple and figured out all the angles in advance. He would have been a success even in a legitimate business if his fancy had happened to turn in that direction.

He never did the obvious. No getaway car for him, in which to be trapped in city traffic. He scheduled the Marlowe job for a quarter hour before closing time, herded the clerks into the vault, having to shoot only one of them to prove his point. The other three who died weren't on Max's conscience because they wouldn't have suffocated if help had been a little quicker in reaching them. Nevertheless, he acted as if he felt real sorry when he read of their deaths in the next afternoon's papers.

One of them had been married less than a month to a girl who must have been quite a looker, if you allowed for the fact that her eyes were pretty puffy from crying and newspaper pictures aren't exactly flattering. It was she who had phoned the police around four-thirty in the morning to say her

268

husband hadn't come home. It hadn't seemed odd, even to a bride, before then. You had to hand it to Maxie. He'd picked a night when there was a jewelers' convention in town, when visiting firemen would be blamed for keeping papa out late. What with Bat's having disconnected the alarm system and the telephone, the three guys in the vault didn't have much of a prayer.

After Max had made a smart selection from the cases, he and Bat went out onto the Avenue, at the moment when thousands of others were doing that very thing. They'd taken the shuttle bus to the parking lot out by Soldier's Field, where a car had waited since morning. Then, like hundreds of commuters, they'd headed south across the line into Indiana, then east to the meeting with Bebe.

She had been waiting in Bat's car – to which was attached the shabby old trailer – at the spot marked X on her map, the side road through the dunes leading to a lake in which the other car could be submerged. Max stepped into the trailer with better than a half million worth of glitter and ate the bowl of soup she'd heated over a can of Sterno.

That's the way it had been ever since – soup until it came out of your ears, and delicatessen stuff. Then, after Bat bought the oil stove yesterday, chops, pan fried. But now that she had the oven there were no limits.

She poured the coffee, set the pot upon the table, and put on a kettle of water for dishes. It was good clear spring water, and thank the Lord Pop had at least run pipes into the kitchen, even if that was as much plumbing as the house had to offer. It was funny how finicky you could get about a bowl, a pitcher, and a privy in eight years. Maybe if she handled him right, Max would blow the house to a bathroom or two after the heat was off him.

She splashed some cream into her coffee, disgustedly watched it curdle and rise to the surface. "Sour," she said. "Cream's sour. Bat, do you think you could buy that old bag who's going to California some type icebox? I'm tired of stuff spoiling, and warm beer. And when I want a bourbon on the rocks I don't mean diamonds."

"Always griping," Max grumbled. "Quit it, willya?" But he patted her cheek, admitted that she could really cook, and belched to show his happy surfeit.

He was in a good mood, and she took advantage of it. "Another thing," she said. "I want a flock of garden tools. A spade. A pitchfork."

270

"Have a heart, Bebe," Bat flagged her down. "What would a guy living in a trailer want with them things? You want them to think I'm a grave robber?"

"Pruning shears," she ignored him. "Lawn mower. Handsaw. I don't know – lots of things. Maybe I ought to drive in with you and pick them out myself."

Max choked on his coffee and spilled some of it on his white jacket before he could get the cup back to its saucer. His good mood had been completely rubbed out. "Are you crazy or something?" he growled. "Somebody'd recognize that kisser of yours. You're not going nowhere, Bebe, not for one hell of a long time." He got up and went over to the sink, dabbed at the coffee stains with a damp towel.

He was a neat dresser, Maxie was, a mirror of fashion, and a joy to behold. At least he used to be when his tailor, his barber, and his haberdasher were striving to please. As he stood near the sink in the full glare of the oil lamp with the reflector, she observed that he had gone downhill fast. He was frowsy, mussed, not even particularly clean. He didn't look good, and she was going to see an awful lot of him, cooped up here, not even able to go to a movie once in a while to escape his unmanicured hands.

271

He was breathing heavily, looking at her with what was almost hatred. In back of him his shadow on the wall heaved its shoulders. The shadow was huge, towering, as though all the evil in him had burst its bounds and become visible, and for the first time since they had met she was afraid of him. "Okay, Maxie," she said tensely. "We won't discuss the matter any further just now."

"We ain't never going to discuss it," he stated, and threw the wet towel in her face.

The half grown cat lay curled on a pile of weeds Bebe had pulled out of the berry patch. Finished, resting, Bebe stroked the soft grey fur above its belly. "Where did those ribs go, hey?" she whispered. "I can't call you Mr. Bones any more like I did a couple of months ago. You're more like Mr. Butterball."

She yawned, rolled up the jersey sleeves to catch the August sun, and stretched out an arm to pluck a jewel-red berry from one of Grampa's bushes. The dewberry cross miraculously continued to bear like rabbits in the nest of weeds it had taken her eight days to remove. The red juice stained her fingernails, which hadn't been so colored in weeks, not since the nail polish ran out and Bat had refused to buy her any lest his cronies at the store kid the pants off him.

Bat was all right, though. He'd sneaked a trowel to her, a little five-fingered cultivator, small stuff he'd said he was buying for the trailer's windowbox. Max didn't know about that, of course. If he found out, there wasn't much doubt in her mind that he'd beat the tar out of Bat, dependent though he was upon him, lost as he would be without him.

Max, for something that he would have called a reason, had made a big deal out of Bebe's not getting the garden tools she wanted. Maybe it was because of that first night she mentioned them, when he threw the towel at her. He hadn't been satisfied with just throwing it. He'd gone over and picked it off her lap, slapped her cheeks with it until she screamed, and Bat had got up enough nerve to take it from the boss's hand. After that, Bebe hadn't spoken to Max for a whole week and things had never really been the same between them again. Max, in his twisted-up head, must blame everything on the garden tools, and was damned if he would let her have them.

She'd managed pretty well without them. The grass was hayfield deep, but the rose bed was clear and pretty as it used to be, and now the berry patch. She'd ruined every dress she owned in the doing, and was reduced to wearing the cutoff tops of them with boy's jeans, because Bat wouldn't buy girls' clothes without getting the horse laugh. It was a good thing that all the mirrors in the house were old, except the dime-store one above the sink in which you could see only your face. Bebe knew she must look a sight, but she didn't care. She'd never in her life felt better, getting tired from things instead of of them, seeing the farm perk up under her fussing fingers.

She had a relapse, naturally, every time she looked at Max, but she was doing that less and less. He never came outdoors if he could help it, just stayed in the parlor, snoozing, reading the newspapers, or playing solitaire, looking like one of the slugs she found when she turned over rocks.

It wasn't good news he found in the papers. Two people had seen him leave the jewelry store and identified his photographs in the police files. The drowned car had been found near the dunes, and its license plates traced to him. Every fence he had ever used was under surveillance, and the country had been flooded with sketches and descriptions of the stolen articles. Max Swanson was wanted and how, and it was no wonder that he had grown so mean.

She popped another berry into her mouth and ruffled the kitten's fur. "Mr. Butterball," she murmured. "That's who you are."

The emerald-and-diamond bracelet glinted in the sunlight as she took it off. "Would you like a fine collar for your christening, Mr. Butterball?" she offered. "Let's see how it looks. It's only a loan, you understand."

The bracelet fitted the cat's neck loosely and she snapped the catch, hearing what might have been an echo behind her, or the crack of a twig. Without turning she knew what it was. The cat, in a way, knew too – tensing its body, smelling danger. Yet she turned, to see Max half hidden behind a maple tree, glaring at her like a man outraged.

"You crazy?" he muttered, stunned. "You crazy, Bebe? Take that thing off its neck before it runs home and gives me away."

The cat had already begun to scamper off, but it didn't get far – the Luger, which Max had held concealed behind the maple, took care of that.

It was a big gun for such a small target, and the range was deplorably close. Bebe screamed, and screamed, and screamed again until Max's hand against her mouth silenced her. Then she bit the free flesh between his thumb and palm and tasted blood. He jerked his hand away hastily, but she didn't yell any more. She just said, "You crumb! You rotten crumb!"

She walked toward the house the long way, so she wouldn't have to pass Mr. Butterball.

Bat was standing on the doorstep, peering down at the pond. Because she hadn't taken the direct route he didn't see her at first, instead saw Max swaggering up the hill toward him. "Where's Bebe?" Bat called through his cupped hands. "What the hell happened to her? I heard –"

"Here I am," she said. "In back of you."

He turned, with a touching expression of relief. "Are you all right?" he asked. "Did he – I heard a shot, then you screaming."

"I'm all right," she assured him, surprised that it seemed so important to him.

Max rounded the corner of the broken-down porch, puffing a little, the gun still in his hand.

"Got a job for you, Bat," he remarked banteringly. "Little matter of a funeral.

Bebe's the chief mourner. She'll make the arrangements."

He put the gun into its holster and grasped her wrist with the hand that was too holy to touch dead cats.

"Poor Bebe lost her bracelet," he taunted. "She's a pretty careless girl. Get it for her quick, Bat." His tone became serious. "She might catch cold without it."

He cast her arm away roughly and yawned in her face. "Think I'll get some shut-eye before dinner," he said. "What's to eat, Bebe?"

She turned from him sullenly, folding her arms and jutting out her chin. Max went into the house without waiting for an answer.

"What's the rhubarb?" Bat asked.

"He killed the lousy cat," she said dully.

"No kidding?" He seemed dismayed. "I'm sorry, kid, honest I am."

"Sure." Her lip curled. "A fat lot of good that does the cat."

"Well, *I* didn't do it. You needn't get sore at me."

"I'm not sore at you, Bat. As a matter of fact, I'm grateful to you for worrying about me. It was sort of friendly, and the Lord knows I need a friend."

"Well, you got one, pal. Me." He paused. "You want I should bury the cat real nice, put some rocks around the grave or something?"

"Please," she said. "Thanks. He's a little that side of the maple tree." She pointed. "The trowel's in the berry patch."

"Can do." He touched her shoulder lightly, said, "Take care of yourself," and walked away.

It was advice that almost made her laugh as she entered the house and turned left into the kitchen, away from the living room, where Max had already begun to snore. Little good taking care of herself would do with a killer like Max around. The only way she'd been able to live with him was by playing a game of shut-eye of her own, by pretending that he found the taking of life distressing and was a tender guy at heart. People who got in his way when he was pulling a job, according to the rules of his game, plainly got what they asked for, and kind of offended Max by obliging him to do away with them.

Now that she had seen him kill she could no longer kid herself. He hadn't flinched, hadn't looked sorry afterward. The cat represented a menace which he'd averted as calmly and instinctively as a skilled driver turns a steering wheel to avoid a bump in the road. Reflex action. Something threatens you, you kill it.

It could be me, she thought. I could very well be next. I can't run as fast as a cat. Besides, I have no place to run to.

She went to the cabinet to get a few things she needed for supper. Her hand brushed the flour cannister and she remembered the last time she'd used it. She'd spilled some flour on the floor and Mr. Butterball, who had been visiting, sat down in it, leaving the impression of his little round bottom and tail as clear as a footprint. she wished she hadn't remembered that just now, because it made her cry.

She was still crying when Bat came in. He patted her clumsily, then walked to the sink and turned on the water. "I gotta wash up your bracelet before you put it on," he said soberly. "It's –"

"Don't bother," she sobbed. "You could have buried it on the cat for all I care. I'll never wear that rotten thing again."

"Max won't like that," Bat warned. "It's a mighty valuable hunk of junk and he wanted you should have it. He'll think you didn't have no respect for him if you don't wear presents he gives you."

"Respect!" She laughed hysterically. "I *hate* Max, and every filthy thing he ever gave

279

me! I wish to God I could kick him off my farm!"

Her sobs grew louder, drowning out Max's snoring, possibly covering the sound of his footsteps if he should wake and mosey out to the kitchen. Without audible assurance that his boss remained in the parlor, Bat got panicky. "Shut up, Bebe," he said, but not crossly. "I get fed up with Max myself sometimes, but you've got to admit he's a good provider. It'll just mean a row if he hears you talking like this. You don't mean it. It's just that you're kind of stir-crazy, like the rest of us."

He patted her forearm awkwardly as her choking subsided and he could again hear the buzz-saw in the other room. "You know what I wish I could do?" he asked cajolingly. "There's some sort of fair going on in town. They've got a merry-go-round and a Ferris wheel and dolls you throw baseballs at. I wish I could take you. That would cheer –"

"Oh, Bat!" She brightened. "It must be Ellsworth County Fair Week. Honest, would you take me?"

He looked solemn. "You know I can't, Bebe," he reminded her. "I just meant I wished I could. It'd be fun."

"Fun?" she echoed. "It was the most fun I ever had when I was a little girl. I used to go every day and hang around the vegetables my Pop entered, and Grampa's dewberries, and Granny's baked goods. I was so proud of them things I could have died. They were the best, Bat, in every class, the biggest, the juiciest, the tastiest. They took every blue ribbon in sight."

She sighed. "I guess that's why I never wanted to sell the farm. Max thought I should when the lawyer wrote me, but I guess I was still a little proud of the things that had been grown here." Her mouth twisted. "And now, of course, he's glad I held on. Only the farm don't seem the same to me with him on it. I can't feel proud like I used to."

Her forehead puckered, but her eyes were dry and dancing.

"Bat," she implored, "you've just got to take me! You could go shopping in the morning and I'd sneak down the road to meet you. Through the woods. Max would just think I was off weeding or sulking somewheres."

"It's too big a risk, kid. Max would kill me if he found out."

"No, he wouldn't," she insisted. "He needs you."

"Or I'd kill him." His mouth was grim. "I'm not sure which. I don't really know what I'd do if Max got tough with me. He never has."

"He *needs* you, Bat. And I need to get back to the way I felt when I was a little girl, before Maxie came into my life. Will you help me try?" She took his chin in her hands and forced his head around so that he must see the pleading in her eyes.

"Well," he said slowly, and she knew she had won.

It was a bright, spanking day, the kind especially manufactured for Ellsworth County Fair Week. From the top of the Ferris wheel you could see for miles past the hills, and the world seemed very large indeed. Then the cage descended and the world became small, gay, and full of friends who jostled you, and you jostled back, laughing as they laughed. It was terrific not to be afraid, here where there were no Lugers, no hair-triggered tempers, no Maxies.

Sleeping so much during the day, Max was an early riser and she had given him his breakfast before she left. She'd been so disagreeable to him since he shot the cat that he didn't seem to mind when she wandered off afterward with a book. She was reading *Little Women*. Most of the stuff around the farm was pretty longhair, but she sure got a kick out of that Jo. She had parked the book on a birch stump near the road, where she planned to leave Bat's car when they returned.

That would have to be pretty soon, she regretted; the two hours Bat had allotted her were nearly up. He was to look for her near the judges' table in the main tent.

She hoped he'd be late. Judging was just about to begin, and that was what she most wished to see. It was Cakes, Cookies and Doughnuts today; Pies tomorrow. In the old days Granny would have swept the field.

She hurried toward the raised platform in the center of the tent to get a ringside seat, and with a twinge of disappointment saw that Bat was already there. For an instant she considered trying to hide from him, but he saw her too out of the corner of his eye, as men in his trade learn to do. "You had to be ahead of time, didn't you?" she grumbled. "You gonna drag me right away?"

He smiled at her. "Relax, baby," he drawled. "We can give it a whirl for a while." He was holding two sticks of cotton candy. He presented one to her, saying, "Here. Live a little. You been having fun?"

"The best," she said wistfully. She buried her nose in the pink foam, came up for air, laughing. The band at the end of the tent blared a merry dance tune.

"I thought you could hide your face in the candy if you see anybody you know," Bat explained.

"Oh? So that's it." Her eyebrows rose sharply, and the band obliged by shifting to a sour waltz. "You mean you didn't buy it because I might get a bang out of it, but because you thought I needed false whiskers."

Her voice was flat, and so was the cotton candy when she took another bite of it. She tossed it away, half eaten. "The heck with it," she said. "The stuff depresses me. You keep diving in it for a bit of sweetness and it moves away from you. Just like my life, Bat."

The joy had gone out of her, but she felt a little stir of interest as the judges clustered around and plunged a knife into the first chocolate layer cake. A fat lady judge tasted first, chewing like a poker-faced cow. She seemed vaguely familiar in a reminiscent sort of way – not like someone Bebe actually had seen before. Perhaps she was the daughter of an old acquaintance. That was possible. Those judgeships were generally hereditary, and the generation in office eight years ago had been pretty much on its last legs. Old man Judson, for instance, must have been older than Methuselah.

Mr. Judson had been the head judge throughout her childhood – a dear, twinkly little man who made the same joke every year and laughed as hard at it. He would say, delighting Bebe – or, rather, Amantha – that he really should disqualify himself in any class in which Granny Evans was entered, because entries were supposed to be judged on an anonymous basis and he always knew which were hers. He boasted that he could spot Granny's pie crust in the dark, and there was no chance at all of fooling him if the pie happened to be filled with Grampa's dewberries. He'd recognize those big, juicy beauties if he lived to be a hundred and ten.

It apeared that he had a fair chance of reaching that age. For Bebe saw him climb onto the platform, spry as ever, but in time to pass final and inexorable judgment upon the chocolate layer. Fragile as a cobweb, he still had commanding presence and a sizable streak of the actor in him. He twinkled and bowed to the crowd, tasted the cake, smacked his withered lips, and waved at a friend with a bony but sunbrowned hand. Then he sat and waited for the lesser judges to eliminate the entries unworthy of his tastebuds.

He still continued to dominate the scene,

however, his bright-blue eyes casing the audience and finding many friends there. Once his gaze lingered a moment on Bebe and her heart thumped in sudden fear – these old eyes, still keen, might be just the pair to pierce through to some memory of Amantha. She sighed in relief as they moved on to another face.

That would be all she'd need, she reflected, to fix things up good with Maxie. Old man Judson was on speaking terms with just about everybody in town. If he so much as *thought* he had seen Amantha Evans he'd mention it, and the curious would be coming out to the farm in droves. For she was in no doubt as to the kind of reputation she must enjoy in the neighborhood. Granny would have taken care of that, gloating "Like mother, like daughter," clearing her own bloodline of any taint, shooting off her big mouth about Amantha's being the girl friend of some big crook in Chicago, maybe even mentioning Max's name.

She clutched Bat's arm. "Let's get out of here," she urged. "This memory-lane stuff is giving me the creeps."

They were about to anounce the winning chocolate layer, and she was surprised to see Bat react as though she had asked him to leave the ball park when the bases were loaded in the bottom of the ninth. But he didn't put up a fight. He knew they had already stayed overtime and Max might be getting anxious.

Max was anxious, all right. He had hauled that great flabby body of his off the parlor sofa and down to the road. Keeping just within the roadside woods, he'd walked to the point beyond *Little Women* on the birch stump.

Bebe was watching for the stump when she saw Max. At her gasp Bat turned and saw him too, stopping the car with a screech of brakes.

There wasn't anyone else in sight, but she instinctively knew that Max wouldn't pull anything here, where it might at any moment become public. She opened the door. "Going our way?" she asked quaveringly, and moved over to give him room.

He sat there muttering all the way back to the house, all the foul words she had ever heard meaninglessly strung together. Even when the car stopped he didn't move. Nor did the other two for several minutes. Bat was the first to recover and get out of the car. When Bebe started to follow him Max grabbed her thigh, pressing hard with his wide fingertips.

"Max!" she cried involuntarily. "You're hurting me!"

"I'm going to kill you," he announced, quite steadily. "You and your gentleman friend. I'm just making up my mind which gets it first."

She whacked at his fingers, but they only gripped harder. "Let go of me!" she panted. "And shut up with that killing stuff. You got no cause to be sore at Bat. I was just taking a little walk for myself down the road and he found me and brought me home. That's what you'd want him to do, isn't it?"

"You've been gone a pretty long time."

"It was a pretty long walk."

"Yeah?" he derided. "Tell me another."

Bat was methodically taking the packages out of the car, stacking them beside it. His face was flushed, his lips stiff. "How about carrying some of this stuff in, Maxie?" he asked in what didn't seem at all to be his voice. "You can use the practice. If you kill me, you're going to have to run your own errands from now on. And don't forget to drop in at the post office when you're in town. There's a swell picture of you hanging on the wall."

Max's eyes went shrewd. Bebe could almost see the wheels turning as he weighed his need of Bat. But I, she thought, like

288

those poor punks in that war movie, I'm expendable.

"Yes sirree," Bat used the country expression he had picked up, "you've sure been lucky to have me to do your chores, me who always had enough sense not to get his picture taken, whose mother didn't give him a puss that's easy to remember. But if you kill me, pal, you luck's going to run out – fast."

The hand on Bebe's thigh clenched into a fist which Max pounded in emphasis as he asked, "You think I need you? Why, there's twenty guys who'd like to take your place –"

"Yeah?" Bat cut in coolly. "How're you gonna pass the word to them that the job is open? You gonna walk into the railroad station and send a wire? They got a picture of you there, too."

Max spluttered, glowering at his fist as if it symbolized the power that had suddenly deserted him. Then he was like an animal in a trap, flailing out at whatever was nearest to him. What was nearest to him was Bebe. He drove the fist into her ribs like a piston, over and over, while she caught at the steering wheel and tried to pull herself away from him toward the side of the car on which Bat stood.

"No, you don't, sister," Bat said abruptly,

and slammed the door. "I ain't mixing in any family quarrels." With the back of his hand, he smacked her smartly across the mouth. "You caused enough trouble already, wandering down the road."

He picked up a few of the bundles and started for the house, pausing to say to Max, "We ain't gonna let a dame come between us, are we, boss, after all we've been to each other?"

"No," Max answered deliberately. "I guess you're right." He took the Luger from its holster and twirled it around a finger.

Bebe's mouth felt bee-stung. Her eyes weren't working too well, and she was sort of groggy. Once more she tried to scramble out of the car, but Bat had locked the door from the outside. As she fumbled with the catch Max reached over to help her, his arm gliding across her shoulder like a snake.

"Had you scared, baby, didn't I?" he purred. "Well, you had me scared, too, for a minute. If I thought you and Bat were up to any funny business I'd have to kill the both of you. But if you're still my girl, everything's okay. You are my girl, ain't you, Bebe?"

She crouched, not answering him.

"But don't take no more long walks down the road," he advised. "I need you around to cook and take care of a few other little things, see? From now on you don't get out of my sight, except when you're in the kitchen. So behave yourself real good, because Junior and me – " he patted the gun – "will be watching you night and day."

"Better I should be dead," she cracked tartly, meaning it as sarcasm, yet well aware that she might have spoken the truth.

She sat stiff as a corpse in the parlor which had been the setting of all the Evanses' funerals for the last ninety years. Even Mom's. Even that miserable sinner had been brought back for a few grudging words of farewell. And who will say them over me? Bebe wondered.

Not Bat, she reminded herself once again, definitely not Bat. Lately she had begun to think she could count of him, that he was really her friend, but there weren't any real friends in the dog-eat-dog world in which Bat and Maxie lived, into which she had migrated. There was only betrayal, the right hand of friendship swapped for the stab in the back. The worst of it was she had grown so used to their way of thinking that she couldn't feel angry at Bat. To satisfy a whim of hers, he had flirted with death. He'd talked his way out of it this time, but the threat would return if he so much as smiled at her. Considering the dim future that sticking by her presented, she couldn't blame him for sitting firmly in Maxie's corner.

But did he have to seem to enjoy it so much? Playing gin all afternoon with the boss, the Luger on the table between them, for which he reached as readily as Max if she so much as stirred in her chair. Laughing at every nasty crack Max threw her way, trying to reinstate himself solidly, succeeding so well that when she said she would like to pick some dewberries to make a pie for supper Max told him to go along and keep an eye on her.

She got a pail from the kitchen and led the way through the hip-high lawn, past the maple tree where Max had stood when he shot Mr. Butterball. Bat followed so closely she could hear his breathing. When she increased her pace he quickened his, and when she knelt by the first berry bush his shadow fell upon her like a hawk's on baby chickens.

The berries were always at their peak during Fair Week. There was bushel of them at least, and she had a swift remembrance of the bustle of jam-making, the blessed exhaustion that followed it. It would be something for her to do tomorrow, would help get her through the day. She moved to another bush. Bat's shadow following her. "you could help me pick," she complained, "instead of just standing there."

"Haven't you got enough?" He eyed the basket.

"For the pie, yes, but I've got a notion to put up some jelly tomorrow. There's a flock of old jars in the barn. I –"

"Listen to me, Bebe," he silenced her. "Keep your head down and keep picking. He may be watching from the house. Maybe he don't trust me so good as he makes out."

Her hands shook so violently she dropped four out of five berries.

"I've been doing some thinking," Bat went on. "When I talked Max out of killing me this morning I talked myself into something else. I seen that he needs me bad, but that I don't need him at all. I'm gonna blow, Bebe. When I go to the trailer camp tonight, I just ain't coming back."

That will make things real cozy, she thought crazily. Just Maxie and me. And the Luger makes three. "Send me a postcard sometime," she said dryly.

"No. You don't understand. You needn't be here tomorrow to put up no jelly if you come with me. What do you say, kid?"

What *do* you say when a fellow opens the

door of the fiery furnace and asks you to please step out? While waiting for the words, she moved to another bush. Again he followed her, his shadow not seeming oppressive now, but welcome as tree shade.

"How could we do it?" she whispered. "Would it work?"

"Like a charm," he assured her. "You just give him a good dinner and leave the rest to me. When he falls asleep afterward on the sofa, I'll shoot him."

She rocked back on her heels as though he had hit her again. "Oh, no!" she heard herself saying indignantly. "That wouldn't do at all!" A cheap gangster murder in the Evanses' parlor? It was unthinkable. It was bad enough to have Maxie there alive, but to leave him dead on the bloodied horsehair sofa would be the worst insult that could happen to the farm.

"We"d make out fine," Bat promoted. "We'd go to New York. I got connectioins there – bookies, pushers. In a little while I'll be getting you things as good as Maxie ever got you."

She looked up at him, then at the house, seeing the one clearly for the weak guy he was, the other for what it could be if she worked over it, if she swept out the human filthiness that had corrupted it.

She drove her fingers into the earth, scooped up a handful of it, held it out to Bat. "Could you get me anything as good as this?" she asked quietly.

He looked puzzled, and she felt that she owed him at least an explanation.

"I mean," she groped, "I've got something pretty wonderful right here, if I stick with it and find a way to unload our friend Maxie without him shooting me first. There's nice things about you, Bat. There used to be nice things about him. It's just that neither of you would dream of doing an honest day's work in your lives. When I think of how my father worked over this place and what I've let happen to it –"

"It killed him, didn't it?" he challenged. "Your pop died young."

"Not as young as some of your friends, and a whole lot tidier. Besides, you wouldn't want me with you, Bat. I'm not the girl I was, since I came back here. The farm's done something to me."

He seemed stunned. "I'm going anyhow, Bebe," he said stubbornly. "You'll just have to manage somehow with Max, though it don't sound like no clambake." Then he asked the big question: "Or can you think of a better way to get rid of him?"

"It'll come to me." She tried to sound

confident. "The farm won't let nothing terrible happen to me now that I've come home. I've got faith in it. This is where I've got to stay. And it's good earth." She streaked a toe through it. "Stuff will grow here that won't take hold nowhere else. These berries, for instance. Nobody else could get them to –"

She stopped, running smack into a glimmer of hope. It was an outside chance and the odds were long, but it was worth a try. "Bat, honey," she cooed, "would you do me a favor before you go?"

"Maybe," he hedged warily. "I won't rat on Max, if that's what you got in mind. I won't tip the cops off where he is. I'd kill him, but I wouldn't doublecross him."

"It's nothing like that. You'll think I'm nuts, but I'd love to have something from the farm in the Fair this year. If I bake an extra dewberry pie, will you slip it into the judge's table? You may have to swipe an entry card from another pie so things will look legit, but I think you're the boy who can handle it."

He threw back his head and laughed. "This chick is coocoorooney," he told the air. "If that's all you want, and it means so much to you, sure, I'll do it."

She smiled her thanks and hurried toward the house.

It was expecting an awful lot of an aged palate and old memory, but she had to believe in someone, and her money was on old Mr. Judson. She could imagine his thin lips smacking as he recalled Granny's pastry, Grampa's dewberry cross, and the sad thing that happened to the little girl, Amantha, who went to Chicago and fell in with a bad lot.

As she blended the shortening into the flour, she vowed that this would be the most magnificent pie ever turned out in this kitchen. After all, Granny in her maddest moment of creation had never thought of adding an emerald and diamond bracelet.

NEDRA TYRE

The Disappearance of Mrs. Standwick

"Why on earth didn't you tell me I was going to stop over in Richmond?" Ellen Williams asked her travel agent as she picked up her tickets and itinerary for her five-day tour of Colonial Williamsburg.

The agent looked at her in astonishment. For years now Mrs. Williams had been sheeplike in accepting without complaint or comment the trips he had arranged for her. She wasn't like other tourists who badgered him with questions about climate, what to wear, what to buy, how much to tip, telephoning him any hour of the day or night about matters he had already covered fully.

"I met a very nice woman from Richmond when I was in Ireland in June," Ellen Williams continued. "If I'd known I was staying over tomorrow night I'd have planned to see her. It's too late now."

Though exactly how Ellen Williams might have arranged to see Mrs. Standwick, who had seemed to disappear into thin air, was something else again. Mrs. Standwick had not said goodbye, nor had she given Ellen Williams her address. The only reason that Ellen Williams knew she lived in Richmond was a tag on her suitcase printed succinctly STANDWICK, RICHMOND, VIRGINIA.

"I'm sorry," the agent said. "But the inn in Williamsburg didn't have a room for tomorrow night and I couldn't change your transportation, so I got a reservation for you in Richmond. Anyway, I thought you'd like to stop over in Richmond. Lots of people think it has the most beautiful capitol in the country and there are other interesting sights. Besides, it'll make a nice break for you before you go on to Williamsburg. Surely you can telephone your friend when you get to Richmond and explain why you weren't able to give her any warning."

That was an apt suggestion, surely, and Ellen Williams thanked the agent for it. Yes, she would telephone Mrs. Standwick on her arrival.

Ellen Williams said good afternoon to the agent and went home to pack and do all the last-minute things that had to be done before she began her trip the next morning.

She was a reluctant traveler. If she had her way she would never go any farther from her apartment than she could walk. She wanted nothing more in life than to enjoy middle age in her three rooms, devoting her time to her plants, going to the hospital two days a week to do volunteer work, visiting her neighbors, ministering to her cat Thaddeus, of no particular lineage but with very aristocratic airs and tastes. Then when night came and she finished her supper and washed the dishes, she liked to setle down and scare herself to death by reading novels of mystery and suspense.

That simple routine was to Ellen Williams the ideal life.

But her two sons had taken it into their heads that she wanted to travel, that she had an insatiable passion for going places, and every time they saw a travel poster that suggested a new place to visit they made plans for her – usually two long trips each year and additional shorter ones, like the upcoming tour of Williamsburg.

They were the kindest, most generous sons alive. They simply did not realize how they disrupted their mother's life by sending her to the four corners of the earth on independent tours or packaged tours or group tours. Mrs. Anderson down the hall was sweet enough to water Ellen Williams' flowers but she really had no knack for it and half of them died by the time Ellen returned.

Thaddeus the cat was made furious by having to stay at the vet's and it took weeks of cajoling him with special dishes such as lobster and kidneys before he would so much as deign to sit in the same room with her again.

Everything about traveling was much too upsetting, but she couldn't get out of it. Once she had tried to lie herself out of a trip by making a vague complaint about her health, and her sons had promptly sent her off to a famous clinic where all the tedious and exhaustive tests showed that she was in perfect health, and after all that she ended up, as booked, attending every performance of the Salzburg Festival when she didn't even like music.

Well, her sons were wonderful and when they were small they had obeyed her and now she had to obey them. She was proud of their success – Frank was a lawyer and Joseph a banker – and they had both married good-hearted, sensible girls of whom Ellen Williams was very fond. If only her sons would think of something for her to do besides travel! That was their only flaw.

Her flight to Richmond was short and uneventful and the travel agent had known what he was talking about when he recommended the capitol. She couldn't remember having seen a simpler, more pleasing building anywhere. After walking around the capitol grounds she had returned to her hotel in the late afternoon.

The hotel was an old and elegant one and her room was perfectly nice, except that nothing about it suited her. The light was too dim and, besides, the lamp wasn't situated properly for reading. The chair didn't fit her back, the flowers in the wallpaper were purple, the framed engraving of St. John's Church was crooked, and the mirror made her look fat when she weighed only 130 pounds – well, maybe 132.

She was disgruntled and at odds with herself when she thought how nice it would be to see Mrs. Standwick. She riffled through the telephone director. Only one Standwick was listed, thank goodness. It would have been awkward to go down a long list of Standwicks asking for the one who had been in Ireland in June.

She dialed the number. There was no answer. She got up and straightened the engraving of St. John's Church, but it slid right back to its awry position. She tried to make the armchair more comfortable by putting a bed pillow in it, but that didn't work either. She pulled a paperback from her carryall and began to read, only to find herself yawning. She had never in her life yawned over a murder novel. It was time to take herself in hand. So she wrote postcards to her sons and daughters-in-law telling them of her safe arrival, then went to the coffee shop and ordered an omelet and green salad.

When she got back to her room she telephoned the Standwick number again, but there was still no answer. Maybe Mrs. Standwick, poor thing, like Ellen Williams had been sent by relatives on another tour. Ellen Williams looked at herself in the mirror and appeared to have gained ten pounds, in spite of her light supper. She frowned at her appearance and at everything. If only she could be home with Thaddeus and her plants and her bright lamps and her comfortable chairs and a selection of brand-new mystery novels from the public library.

She was one of the luckiest women in the world, yet now she felt like one of the most miserable. She never got into such a mood when she was at home where she belonged. In desperation she left the hotel and window-shopped on Grace and Broad Streets and then she returned to her room and once more dialed the Standwick number. Somehow she hadn't expected an answer, so she was startled when she heard a woman's voice.

"Hello."

"May I speak with Mrs. Standwick, please?"

"This is Mrs. Standwick."

"I hope you're the Mrs. Standwick I know. This is Ellen Williams."

"Who?"

For heaven's sake, Ellen thought, I've never had any trouble with anyone understanding my name before. Ellen is as easy as Mary, and Williams is as simple as Jones or Smith.

"Ellen Williams. I'm at the Adams Hotel briefly and I want to talk with the Mrs. Standwick who was my fellow traveler –"

But Mrs. Standwick did not let her finish. "Yes, yes," she said and then there was a long silence and she said, "I'm afraid you have the wrong number." And abruptly the connection was broken.

Anger made Ellen's hand tremble as she put the telephone back on the hook. She had never been subjected to such unaccountable behavior. the very idea, pretending that Ellen Williams had got a wrong number! Of course that was the Mrs. Standwick she knew. It was Mrs. Standwick's voice and that last sentence gave her away: "I'm afraid you have the wrong number." That was a speech habit of Mrs. Standwick – she often prefaced her statements with "I'm afraid." Ellen Williams remembered so well that she would say, "I'm afraid I'll have to ask you for the butter," or "I'm afraid I'll have to ask you to let me pass." I'm afraid this, I'm afraid that.

Nothing distressed Ellen Williams as much as rudeness. Human beings had to live in the same world, whatever they might think of each other, and they could at least be polite if they had to lie a little. If Mrs. Standwick didn't want to see her she could at least have made a plausible excuse and manged to exchange a few civil words.

Still Ellen must admit that in their short time together she had become very fond of Mrs. Standwick. True, she was a mousy and colorless woman. Come to think of it, Ellen Williams had no idea how old Mrs. Standwick might be. She was the washed-out type that would look about the same whether she was thirty or fifty. Her clothes had no style to them; the material was nice enough, but nothing she wore flattered her and there wasn't enough variety. She had worn one suit and she had only two dresses for dinner. Not that anybody needed many clothes for a five-day tour from Dublin to Cork to Killarney and then back to Dublin.

Ellen thought of Mrs. Standwick's plain, wistful face. No, whatever the reason for Mrs. Standwick's strangeness on the telephone, she wasn't unkind. There was something shy about her – even sad – and she had seemed to depend on Ellen. They hadn't talked much, except to *oh* and *ah* over the Irish scenery, but they always sat together on the bus and at mealtime. Ellen Williams had felt protective toward her, and then on that last morning in Dublin when everyone was saying goodbye, Ellen had tried to find her but she couldn't. Of course it was a time of confusion, with everybody heading in different directions, eager to make travel connections, yet everyone had managed a farewell except Mrs. Standwick.

Ellen Williams had felt sure that Mrs. Standwick had left a mesage for her with someone and that in the hurly-burly of leavetaking it had been forgotten. Ellen had worried about her – well, not really worried, but thought about her on the way home – and then she'd found six of her prettiest African violets dead and Thaddeus sulking even more than usual and the volunteer chairman at the hospital miffed because the substitute volunteer hadn't been conscientious about taking over, so she hadn't got around to writing any letters. And when she had finally settled down, she saw that Mrs. Standwick hadn't written in her address book, though it had been handed round to everyone and all the other tourists' names were there. Moreover, Mrs. Standwick hadn't passed around an address book of her own – at least, not to Ellen Williams.

The faint light in the hotel room seemed to grow dimmer. Shadows lurked in the corners. The night wind stole in and rattled the blinds. Ellen shivered and glanced at the menacing cover on the mystery paperback. Never before had she applied any of her mystery reading to events in real life. Oh, once she had thought how exciting it would be if Mrs. Randolph, who lived on the second floor and was the most ordinary person in the world, turned out to be a double agent, or how exciting it might be if Mr. Watkins, who made a fool of himself in doting over his wife, was secretly poisoning her.

But somehow her feeling about Mrs. Standwick was altogether different. It wasn't vicarious fear. It was real. She sensed that Mrs. Standwick was scared – badly scared. The telephone conversation, if you could call it a conversation, had been odd, to say the least. First she had said yes, she was Mrs.

Standwick, and then in almost the next breath she said that Ellen had the wrong number, and had hung up.

Yes, there was something fishy about it, and if Ellen Williams had been at home she would have gone straight to the police. But she couldn't very well go to the police in Richmond and say she'd telephoned someone and had been told she had a wrong number. That would be ridiculous.

Perhaps there was only some slight misunderstanding, but it would be awkward to make another telephone call so soon to try to clear it up. Whatever the circumstances, she somehow couldn't help feeling that Mrs. Standwick would be glad to see her – after all, they *had* got along so well. In all her years of touring Ellen Williams had never been so drawn to a fellow traveler as she had been to Mrs. Standwick.

There was only one thing to do – to go see for herself. It might be foolish to set out in the dark in a strange city to find someone under such mysterious conditions, but Ellen was lonely and the night was long, and, above all, she felt uneasy about Mrs. Standwick.

Downstairs in the hotel entrance, the doorman pointed in the direction of the street that Ellen inquired about. "It's just a short walk," he said. "About five or six blocks. Go straight down Franklin – your street crosses Franklin."

Ellen Williams set out briskly and traffic soon thinned. She noticed without concern that she was the only pedestrian. She supposed that Richmond had its share of muggings and that she ought not to risk being out alone in the dark, but the air was bracing and the townhouses she passed interested her – they were substantial and well kept, and their interiors – which she glimpsed between the slats of Venetian blinds or half drawn draperies – were colorful and attractive.

Earlier than she expected she reached Mrs. Standwick's street. The house she was seeking was on a corner. It had the same dignity and substance of the other residences she had been admiring and its number was spotlighted in graceful, slender brass figures.

At her touch the iron gate swung open and Ellen Williams quickly covered the short walk and mounted the steep steps of the Georgian house. For an instant she caught her breath, then she pushed the bell and it sounded like an alarm. She started at the commotion she had created in the cold silence.

After a while the front door was opened. Ellen Williams had hoped that Mrs.

Standwick would greet her and invite her inside for a visit, exclaiming in delight over their reunion. Instead, the woman standing there intimidated Ellen. She seemed disdainful in her perfection. She wore an elaborately complicated hairdo and an elegantly simple evening dress. Her throat and left hand were on fire with diamonds.

"Good evening," Ellen said. "I'd like to see Mrs. Standwick, please."

The woman said nothing – she and her diamonds glowered at Ellen Williams.

"Mrs. Standwick does live here, doesn't she?" Ellen Williams' manner was timid and she took a half step in retreat.

A man's voice filled the house, shouting, "Who is it?"

The woman turned and walked down the hall toward the gracefully curved stairway and called up the stairwell in answer to the man. "It's someone who has come to see about a contribution."

That remark astonished Ellen. Her retreat ended. She crossed the threshold and approached the woman. "You've misunderstood me," she said. "I certainly don't want any contribution. I just wanted to say hello to Mrs. Standwick. She and I were on a trip together and I –"

There were heavy footsteps and before

Ellen knew what was happening or could finish what she was saying she was shoved inside a room and the door was closed after her.

"I'll be back in a moment," the woman said through the door.

Ellen glanced around the room. It was large and elegant, its furniture was in the French style, and the brilliant chandelier flashed as blindingly as the woman's diamonds. Ellen Williams sat down on a delicate tapestried settee and squinted against the bright lights.

Time seemed to slacken, and then she decided that it was not so much that time was passing slowly as that a lot of time had passed. Studying her watch, she tried to calculate how long she'd been in the house. She had left the hotel at 7:00. Even though she had sauntered to look at the houses, it couldn't have taken her more than fifteen minutes to reach the Standwick residence.

It was now 7:50. So she had been left alone to cool her heels for more than half an hour. If this was the Richmond brand of Southern hospitality she wanted none of it. She would leave this splendid room immediately and she was tempted to slam the front door behind her.

She grabbed at the slender gold handle of

the door. it did not move. She tried to turn it, first to the right and then to the left. It must be stuck. She pulled and pushed.

The door was locked from the outside.

Ellen looked around frantically for another exit. There was no other door. She walked over to the window and pulled the brocaded draperies apart. Darkness lapped outside the window and as her eyes grew accustomed to that darkness she saw that light from a street lamp faintly illuminated the yard. The ground was too far beneath her to risk jumping.

She went back to the door and beat on it. "Let me out," she yelled. "Let me out at once!"

From somewhere behind her a hand reached out and clutched her. Ellen Williams screamed and turned to find the woman there. A panel had opened beside the fireplace. There had been another door, after all, its outline concealed by the carving of the wainscoting.

Ellen Williams' voice rose in indignation. "What is the meaning of all this? I only wanted to see Mrs. Standwick. She and I were good friends on a tour of Ireland."

The woman ignored what Ellen had said. "Come this way," she ordered. She grasped Ellen Williams by the arm and led her through two unlighted rooms down a narrow passage, and before Ellen Williams was aware of her predicament she was pushed into a small dark room and the door was locked after her.

Everything had happened too quickly. All she could think was that she had been treated like a child who had misbehaved badly and had been shut up in a closet for punishment. For it was a closet to which she had been banished, as she discovered when she reached out to explore her prison and touched various garments hanging from a double row of rods.

She tiptoed and lashed out and came in contact with a shelf crowded with luggage. There must be a light somewhere, but its switch must be outside the locked door – not that a light would do her much good, but she hated the dark.

She groped again. She tapped the wall in every direction, still trying to find a switch, and she cried out in surprise and triumph when she found it and the closet was drowned in light.

Her eyes were dazzled by all the high fashions regimented as to coats, suits, evening dresses, and day clothes. Then Ellen glanced up at the shelf filled with suitcases. One of the cases might as well have shouted

Mrs. Standwick's name. She would have recognized it anywhere – she had helped Mrs. Standwick stow it on the rack in the bus every morning and take it down in the late afternoon during their trip. It was shabby and worn, like all luggage that has undergone the rigors of a bus tour. It was proof that Mrs. Standwick lived here, was somewhere in this house, and that the awful woman who had pushed her into the closet was trying to keep them apart.

The light pained Ellen Williams' eyes. She was tired from her long day and indignant over what had happened, but there was nothing she could do about her plight for the moment. She must try to make herself as comfortable as she could. She must save her strength so that at the next encounter with that woman she could shove instead of being shoved.

Ellen pulled a mink coat from a hanger and spread it on the floor; then she took a sable coat and folded it up for a pillow. She turned off the light and lay down.

Something wakened her. She sat up and wondered where she was. A feeling of panic overtook her as it often did when she was away from home and woke up and tried to decide exactly where she was. The fur beneath her startled her. She extended her arms and the hanging clothes swung out as if to attack her – and then she remembered that she was a prisoner in a closet in Richmond, Virginia.

She scrambled up, turned on the light, and put the fur coats back on their hangers. Her nap had refreshed her and she was ready for action. She intended to scream her head off and to batter at the locked door of the closet until someone came. She tugged at the door and it opened immediately. No doubt that woman was lurking somewhere in the dark, waiting to push Ellen Williams behind another locked door. But Ellen was onto her tricks and ready to give instead of to take – and she intended to find Mrs. Standwick, who had to be somewhere in this strange house.

With resolution, Ellen stalked out of the closet and invaded one luxurious room after the other, calling Mrs. Standwick's name. There was no answer. The house was empty. The elegant woman had left. The man who had shouted from the upstairs had gone. Mrs. Standwick was nowhere in the house.

Ellen Williams left the opulent house with its tomblike silence and walked without fear along the deserted streets. Nothing that might happen to her outside could be as terrifying as what she had already experienced. She was indignant and outraged, and as soon as she could sit down and collect her wits she must decide what to do.

It astonished her to see from the clock in the hotel lobby that it was only 9:00. When she asked for her key, the clerk looked at her with concern. "Are you all right, Mrs. Williams?" he asked. "A woman who didn't give her name telephoned about five minutes ago. She said you had been to her house and seemed upset and she wanted to know if you had got back all right."

Anger like a spasm shook Ellen Williams. Her voice squeaked. "Well, if she calls again, please tell her that I've never felt better in my whole life in spite of the extraordinary welcome she gave me."

When Ellen Williams awoke later than she had intended the next morning, she felt rested and full of purpose. Her duty was clear. Instead of visiting the Valentine Museum, as her typed itinerary prescribed, she intended to see the police. It was the only sensible thing to do. Mrs. Standwick had disappeared and very peculiar things had happened to Ellen when she had made inquiries about her.

316

The police must be informed and she mustn't waste another second. She'd better go to them even before she ate breakfast.

She had just put on her hat and was peering out the window to decide whether to take her umbrella when a knock sounded on her door. Someone called her name. She caught her breath when she opened the door and saw who her visitor was.

Mrs. Standwick stood there, dressed in her neat, nondescript suit. The battered suitcase in her hand reminded Ellen of those mornings in Ireland when Mrs. Standwick had come by her room holding her suitcase exactly like that, ready to set out for their next destination. The anxiety which had troubled Ellen ever since she had attempted to see Mrs. Standwick suddenly left her, and though she was not usually a demonstrative person she embraced Mrs. Standwick warmly.

"I'm so happy to see you," she said. "I've been terribly worried. I was on my way to the police. Oh, I can't tell you how relieved I am to see that you're all right! I didn't know what that terrible woman had done to you."

Mrs. Standwick was so moved by Ellen Williams' welcome that she began to cry. Tears ran down her cheeks. "I'll try to explain," she said. "Excuse me for a minute." From her handbag she withdrew a plain white handkerchief and dabbed at her reddened eyes. Then she picked up her suitcase and went into the bathroom.

Thank heaven she's safe, Ellen thought, and that was all that mattered – though Mrs. Standwick ought to be persuaded to leave that bizarre household where unsuspecting callers were mauled and thrust into closets . . .

Time passsed but Mrs. Standwick did not emerge from the bathroom.

She's disappeared again, Ellen Williams thought wildly. "Are you all right?" she called out.

The bathroom door opened. But Mrs. Standwick did not come out. It was that other woman, heavily made up and dressed in a Chanel suit. Hung across her arm was the same mink coat on which Ellen had dozed in the closet.

"Your Mrs. Standwick doesn't exist any longer," the woman said. "I wanted to tell you last night but I couldn't. I was terrified when you telephoned – my husband was in the library with me and I didn't dare let him know I was talking to someone I'd traveled with in Ireland. He didn't know I'd been there. He thought I'd visited my sister who lives in Italy.

"I mustn't bother you with my problems, but my husband won't give me a divorce and he's pathologically jealous. I'm in love with someone and I had a brief, wonderful meeting with him in Dublin before I took the tour. I dressed for it as I'd like to dress all the time – in plain, comfortable clothes – but my husband insists that I wear high fashion.

"I was so sad over saying goodbye to John and you were so kind to me. There was no way to thank you for your sweetness and I didn't even try. I didn't dare give you my address because my husband reads all my mail and I knew that if you wrote he'd find out that I'd been in Ireland. Last night I locked you up to keep you out of his way until we left for a party. He heard you in the sitting room and that's why I moved you to the closet.

"I sneaked back from the party and unlocked the closet door, but my husband missed me and followed me and I rushed back out at once to keep him from coming inside. So I couldn't apologize to you. The party wasn't over until after two and I didn't want to disturb you then. But the very moment my husband left for his office this morning I came to see you. You must forgive me for everything, Mrs. Williams. You must."

Ellen smiled at the beautiful, troubled woman. Of course she forgave her. But this person was a stranger. The woman Ellen Williams had liked so much had disappeared forever.

ELEANOR SULLIVAN

Something Like Growing Pains

Ralph Boalt came in from putting the car away and found his wife weaving back and forth on her toes, looking through the still unfamiliar kitchen cupboard. "What are you doing?" he inquired, locking the door.

"I'm looking for something to wash this sand out of my mouth."

"Water's good," he suggested, shutting both kitchen windows against the raw sea air and turning to face her. "You look like a sand sculpture. Why don't you go take a bath?"

Outside, the surf splashed methodically, one hefty sigh following fast on another. "Come on," Ralph said, going to the bathroom off the kitchen and turning the squeaky faucets in the tub. "Get the sand off and I'll make you a fire and that silly applejack and grapefruit drink you like."

"Is there any juice left?" Harriet opened the refrigerator door and peered in, rubbing a lock of sand-encrusted brown hair between her fingers. A large can of unsweetened grapefruit juice stood between the bottle of milk and a pickle jar containing one dill pickle sunk in pale-green water. She removed the can of juice and shook it.

"What gets into you at these parties down here?" Ralph called, a deceptive, amused-sounding note in his voice. "You were all over that beach tonight like the sand was stardust. Not that you'll remember it tomorrow."

"I'll remember it," she assured him.

"You'd think you'd remember your first swim in two years, but you don't."

He was referring to the swim she had taken on Sunday with all her clothes on. Harriet ran her finger thoughtfully over a long dark cigarette scar she had already made on the pine-board countertop, then walked to the bathroom, stepping out of her sandals on the way.

Ralph was down on one knee, testing the water with one hand and adjusting the faucets with the other. "You thought you were Esther Williams, for God's sake," he was saying.

"Are you preparing me a bath?" she asked quietly, "or a lecture?"

"Have you got a fresh change?" He dropped a bar of soap and a drying, balled-up facecloth into the water.

"My nightgown is on the back of the bedroom door."

He wheeled the faucets shut, slapped the water, and wiped his hands on a worn towel on the rack. "There you go," he said, leaving her.

She heard him climb the wooden stairs as she shut the door and got out of her scratchy clothes. Stepping into the shallow tepid water and sitting, she frowned as he started to whistle overhead and she wondered why the things she had loved five years before, like his whistling and his good posture and careful manners, drove her wild now.

Shutting her eyes, she sank back, letting the water soak off the sand. She ran her tongue over her teeth, still gritty with sand, stopping at her broken front tooth. She hadn't really stopped being self-conscious about the tooth since she had broken it in a stupid fall after a high-school football game, but she had never had it capped, she didn't know why.

The door opened and Ralph set the pink gown, neatly folded, on the john lid by her head. She quickly closed her eyes again, but he did not leave. He fished for and found the washcloth and knelt by the tub. She sat up and pulled the cloth out of his hand.

"Go away," she said. He stood and wiped

his hand on his corduroy trousers, his face taking on the arrogant expression he used to recoup his dignity, and then left, shutting the door behind him.

"All right," he called in later. "What's keeping you?"

She was sitting with her head forward, her forehead resting on her knees. The room was cold. "I'm, coming."

"Hurry up. You'll catch cold."

The sand on the bottom of the tub was sharp. "All right."

"Don't forget your hair."

"All *right*."

When she joined him in the living room she was wet under the pink-cotton gown and her hair was slicked back and dripping down her collar. He gave it a disapproving glance.

"You told me to soak my head and I did," she explained.

"Have you ever heard of a towel? Your drink's there." He gestured from the flowered sofa where he lay with a glass of whiskey and soda on his chest.

"This?" She lifted a tall glass off the pile of newspapers on the hassock.

"What's wrong with it?"

"It should be pink."

"I can't help that. You told me equal parts

applejack and juice. Does it have to be pink grapefruit or something?"

"Grenadine makes it pink, it's got nothing to do with the grapefruit."

"What possible difference can the color make?"

It's not just to make it pink – it's for flavor. It makes a big difference in the taste." She went to the kitchen, remembering there was no grenadine but pretending to look. In the living room Ralph sang, "'And He walks with me and He talks with me – '"

"'Oh, the Bowery, the Bowery,'" Harriet finished. "'I'll never go there any more.'" She returned to the living room and stretched across the armchair opposite him, swinging her legs over the frayed sailcloth-covered arm so that she too was facing the fire. "No grenadine," she said lifting her glass. "Here's mud in your eye."

"Here's to the kids," he returned solemnly.

"To the kids. Long may they wave goodbye to us as we leave for vacation."

"You haven't missed them for a second, have you?" Ralph said.

"I've missed them all right, don't you worry. I don't *ache* for them. When I start to ache I remind myself how fond Ronnie's grown of whining and Barbara can't ever

325

stop and think before she does anything. I think of the sleepless mornings and the squalor and I know I can survive to the end of the week without too much pain."

"If your life strikes you as squalid don't blame them. You've got the time to teach them manners without any interference from me. I'm on the road five days a week, I'm no distraction."

"You're no *help* either."

"What do you want me to do, find a job in the office? At half the salary?"

"I want you to stop trying to make me feel guilty about enjoying a vacation away from them just because you think *you* should feel guilty because you're *always* away from them." An honest talk can't hurt, she told herself, wanting to run but taking a drink instead.

"You're as truthful with yourself as you've always been," he said, throwing her a quick sinister smile.

"Truth? What's that?" she said lightly, scared, deciding honest talks did hurt. When her friend Bunny's marriage was at the breaking point, Harriet had insisted that if Bunny would only talk it out with Art it would be all right. Communication was the answer. But Art didn't have a hot-potato smile like Ralph's to scare the hell out of

Bunny, that was a big difference. "This is nice," she said, changing her tone. "I should build more fires at home."

"I forbid you to build any fires at home when I'm not there. Just keep your fires confined to the inner woman, please." Forty feet away, outside the window, the tide beat the shore. "I *forbid* you to build a fire in my absence."

"I was a Girl Scout. First-class."

"You'd leave the damper closed or forget to put back the screen or some fool thing. No fires."

"You're a fine one to forbid," she said, lighting a cigarette. "Who left the bottle of gin on the stove last night?"

"*You* did, for God's sake!"

"*I* did!" Who was sitting on that very soda – *sofa* – drinking from that same bottle of gin when I went up to bed?"

"I was. Who got up later in the night after I was in bed and came down for a nip?"

"I came down once, to the *john*. I didn't see that bottle again until I got up this morning, *hours* before you did, and there it was, smack on the open pilot. If I hadn't thought fast and grabbed a pot holder, I might have burned my hand off. We're lucky it didn't explode!"

He swung his feet to the floor and went

purposefully to the kitchen, returning with an almost empty bottle of gin. "How come when I went up to bed this bottle was more than half full?"

"Have you ever heard of evaporation?"

"I don't buy that."

"Will you buy the possibility that you could be mistaken about how much you left?"

"I'm sold on the fact that you left it on the stove. I put it on the counter here when I went to bed."

"You're a dream," she said softly into the fireplace.

He slammed the bottle down on the table near the porch door and threw himself back on the sofa.

"I myself –" she began.

"I *myself,*" he repeated scornfully.

"I myself *personally* say it was an accident, no harm done, let's forget it."

"Easy for *you,*" he told the ceiling.

Why did I marry him? she asked herself, taking more of the drink and regarding him across the woven-straw rug. His mouth was a dry line and the planes of his nose were hard and sharp even in the artificial light. Why did *he* marry *me?* What made us think we could be happy?

They had left home early Saturday

morning in the company car, leaving the children with Harriet's mother, who had convinced them they needed a vacation by themselves in a rented cottage on the Connecticut shore, where they had friends. Ralph had insisted on driving the whole way, declaring, *"No*body's got that much insurance" when she asked to take the wheel.

The drive had been the best part of the vacation – the only good part, in fact – the lush gren country leading to the shoreline, the blood-red barns and antique shops and the proud little restaurant where they had stopped for lunch.

For a few brief hours she had thought that her mother was right and that the vacation might be the answer to the last few demoralizing years. But they had done nothing but drink and fight since the Longmires' beer party on Saturday night. Their arrival there, and seeing Steve and Judy Longmire and other old friends jubilant and tanned, was the last good moment she could recall. They had stayed until the party went dry and on Sunday had got straight out of bed and gone to another party, a clambake on the beach, very little of which (including her first swim in two years) she could remember...

"Do you think you're a better person for this marriage?" Ralph asked.

"I'm not a compulsive cleaner any more."

"That's because you'd rather booze with the neighbors than stay home and clean, it has nothing to do with me, or the children."

"I only drink with you."

"That's a feeble lie."

"I'm sorry you think so."

"*Some*thing's occupying your time besides the children. Or some*body.* "

"I'm not a kaffee-klatscher."

"I believe you."

She drew herself up straighter to look at him, the applejack doing its work at the pit of her stomach. "Let's not start with the really damaging words now, please."

"No, but what can I believe? Yours is a deceitful nature."

She ignored his meaning. "You've got a nerve. The gay deceiver himself."

"Are we coming to Grace Ordway?"

"You lead the way every time."

"I might deceive you but Grace Ordway wouldn't."

"There's only one thing honest about Grace Ordway and that's her being so honestly ugly. In that department she's very honest."

"She has beautiful teeth."

"So you've said. You've also said she is quote salty gal unquote."

"I was entitled to Grace Ordway."

"I used to think I was something of a salty girl myself."

"I was entitled to Grace Ordway."

"Go to heaven."

"When a man finds his wife was committed to a mental institution before she married him and didn't think to mention it, he's got a right to react when he finds out."

"I was an outpatient. Just a little crackers for a short time. Something like growing pains, the doctor said."

"You're on the records for extensive psychotherapy, that's all I know. Plus two shock treatments."

A wide blue flame wrapped itself around the front log. the room was warm and the slipcover wet from her hair. She drained her glass, forbidding herself to cry. "You may recall –" She reached down and returned the empty glass to the floor. "You may recall a conversation before we were married in which you explained to me the wisdom of two people keeping certain aspects of their past a secret."

"A mental breakdown wasn't the kind of thing meant."

"How did I know you were protecting yourself from your raunchy past?"

He went to the fireplace, moved the screen to the side, and stoked the fire.

"Let it die," she said.

He continued to prod the logs, creating sparks. "I wish I could forget it," he said finally, "but I can't."

"You can though," she insisted, "if you don't make a memorandum of it."

He replaced the poker and the screen and brought his empty glass to the kitchen, leaving behind an offensive smell of perspiration, like scalded chicken soup. Harriet sat watching the flame flick shadows on the walls and furniture, hearing the ocean play its steady rhythm against the beach.

"Are you going to bed?" she asked as he started back through the room toward the stairs.

"What does it look like?"

"I didn't hear you brush your teeth."

He started up the stairs.

"Is it such a crime that I was sick, Ralph?"

"I couldn't have cared less that you were sick," he answered, out of sight, his climbing a tired scrape on the uncarpeted stairs. "The crime is that you didn't tell me."

"*Why?*"

It was a whisper she decided he hadn't heard when finally he answered from the top of the dark stairwell.

"Because you didn't trust me to understand, you destructive, insensitive foul-up of a broad, how many times do I have to tell you?"

She heard him undress, shut the bedroom window, and climb into the creaking bed. Her empty glass was a disappointment but she resolved not to mix another drink. The ship's-bell clock on the mantel chimed eleven. Crossing to the sofa she plumped up the dry pillows and lay on her side, breathing the fragrant wood-smoke and wondering where the sweet peace of sleeping with Ralph had gone.

The clock sounding midnight roused her and she sat up, her head aching loosely. She walked stiffly to the bathroom for an aspirin and washed her face, noticing as she did that her nightgown was inside out. She took it off, turned it right side out, and slipped it on again. She took a second aspirin and sprayed the mud out of the bottom of the tub down the drain. In the kitchen she rinsed the glasses, filled the ice-cube tray, and put out the light.

Back in the living room she knelt on the sofa, holding the curtain aside to look out. It was too dark to see the surf and she rose and unbolted the door, walking out onto the sandy porch and down the stairs in her bare feet.

Billions of stars swept in brilliant arcs through the black sky. The air was spicy with smoke from the chimneys along the beach. Lowering herself onto the steps she sat facing the sea, the breeze stirring the still-damp ends of her hair.

Her mother hadn't liked or trusted Ralph and had fought the idea of her marrying him. But convinced the marriage was inevitable, she had made Harriet promise not to tell him about the breakdown, persuading her that he would plague her with it afterward when they quarreled and eventually it would ruin the marriage.

Would he have done that if he had known from the start? Harriet's head still ached as she climbed back up the porch stairs and went inside, locking the door behind her. She would never know.

Except for the sigh of the ocean, Ralph's light snoring from the upstairs, and the mouselike sounds in the fireplace the cottage was very quiet. The almost empty bottle of gin on the table caught her eye and she brought it to the darkened kitchen, draining it on the way. Placing it on top of the trash barrel by the sink, she then walked with interest to the stove.

334

In the small hole in the center of the stove the tiny flame of the pilot light burned steadily. Harriet turned on the gas under each of the four burners, slowly, one at a time, then lit all four, increasing and diminishing the intensity of their flames before extinguishing them again.

She went to the narrow linen closet by the bathroom door and felt around the upper shelves for the two army blankets they had brought with them for the beach. Leaving one on a chair by the table, she placed the other across the floor by the back door, pushing its thickness snugly against the threshold. She checked the windows to make sure they were fully shut and returned to the stove where she blew out the pilot light on the top of the stove and then the second one inside the oven. Finally, turning all the gas jets full twist, she moved to the living room, sensing the whisper of the escaping gas behind her, and tucked the second blanket neatly against the floor by the porch door.

There was an old *Life* on the table she didn't remember having seen and she browsed through it standing, dusting sand from one foot with the sole of the other. Then she flipped the last page and stood a while, absently patting her hair, which was now completely dry, before starting for the stairs.

Halfway across the room she hesitated a few seconds longer to stare at the embers, touching the lukewarm screen with her fingers. She wished she could have built more fires for the children. Well, they would be all right. They could remain with her mother. Her mother was still young. They would be no better and no worse off with her.

With a last look at the small sealed-off room she started up to the bedroom and her husband, who would probably, as was his habit these days, turn his back to her when she climbed in beside him.

LOUIS BROMFIELD
The Wedding Dress

Zenobia White is dead! This morning as I came down to breakfast I saw through the tall window that overlooks the meadows the figure of Jabez Torrence, who lives on the river farm, coming up the lane from the highroad. He was running, and when he saw me he cried out in a loud voice, "Zenobia White is dead!"

And then he fell silent, embarrassed, speechless, as if he understood at once how silly it was to be excited over the death of a queer old maid who had lived long past her time – an old woman who had lived almost a century.

"Zenobia White is dead!"

Something had gone out of our world... the world of Jabez and me and all the county. Who could say what it was?

She had been dead for three days, said Jabez. No one would have found her in her little house among the bushes if her dogs had not set up a mournful unbroken howling. Jabez' father had walked in through the

337

thicket surrounding her house. "Even the birds," said Jabez, "were still." He walked through the chickens and dogs and cats up to the door, and knocked. But there was only silence, as there had been only silence on one lonely night more than seventy years before. Inside on her bed Zenobia White lay dead. She was dressed in a wedding gown of white silk, with the veil of a bride covering her immensely old and wrinkled face. The stuff of the dress was so old that it had turned yellow. It must have been made eighty years ago.

So something had gone out of our world, and Jabez, in his bewilderment, knew it as well as I. We should never see Zenobia White again, walking down the highroad with the long train of her yellow taffeta dress trailing in the white dust, a basket over one arm, her lace mitts adjusted neatly, the plumes in her big hat waving in the breeze ... Zenobia White, walking down the white highroad, very tall and straight and proud for such an immensely old woman, her black eyes flashing proudly beneath the little veil of black lace that hung from her queer bedraggled bonnet ... Zenobia White, immensely fierce and old, dressed always in yellow taffeta like Sarah Bernhardt in the picture by Carolus Duran ... Zenobia White, followed by a whole procession of cats.

Far down the valley beyond the figure of Jabez I could see the little house surrounded by bushes. I could even see for a moment a glimpse of the old white horse which Zenobia had raised from a colt and which had never known harness or saddle... the old white horse which lived inside her garden and attacked any intruder with bared teeth and unshod hoofs... the old white horse which this morning had *not* attacked Jabez' father. This morning, when Zenobia White lay dead in her wedding dress, he stood sadly, waiting... The garden was full of birds, orioles and wrens and cardinals and a great number of dogs – queer, yellow mongrel dogs, unwanted by anyone, which had come to live with old Zenobia. And cats too, scores of them, which prowled in peace beside the dogs.

Zenobia White, with a thousand stories clinging to her memory! The story of the night when robbers evaded the old white horse and tortured Zenobia by baking her feet in her own oven! But she had not told them where her money was. They had gone away when she fainted, defeated. And after that Zenobia's proud walk carried the hint of a limp...

But she belonged to my grandfather's day

– a tall, handsome girl of twenty who sat a horse like an Amazon and was courted by half the men of the county. But even in those days she had lived alone in the cottage. The mother of Zenobia White had been an Indian woman, an Iroquois princess, who died soon after she was born. At twenty she was an orphan.

Zenobia White at twenty, living alone in the days when prowlers and renegade Indians infested the county. But Zenobia, young and beautiful, had stayed in the little house by the river, alone, armed with her father's pistols.

"But Zenobia," my grandfather used to say, "could look out for herself." He knew, perhaps, because he was one of those who admired her.

But Zenobia loved, with all the fierceness in her black eyes, young McDougal, red-haired and fiery tempered, the fastest runner in all the county. And she was to marry him. They went in the long, still summer evenings to ride the tangled trails of the wild countryside. And they quarreled, for they were both of high tempers. And one night, two days before they were to be married, my grandfather, returning from the mill, saw them come home. They had quarreled, and Zenobia rode a little ahead of her lover, flushed and angry and handsome. And when they reached the cottage she turned in alone, without a word... My grandfather says she was a beautiful woman.

And then (my grandfather said) Zenobia had gone into the house, and after bolting the doors and windows of the lonely house against intruders sat down to read her Bible and pray that her fierce spirit might be subdued. She sat reading thus until long after midnight... in a tiny house set in a clearing pressed upon by the great trees of the forest. And presently, as Zenobia read, the sound of footsteps stole in upon her consciousness – faint and confused in the rustling of the lilacs – the sound of footsteps – the footsteps of one or perhaps of many men.

Zenobia put out the flame of the single mutton tallow candle and sat listening, listening to the sounds in the garden, the sound of the owls and of the wind rising over the river. And slowly, when the sounds persisted, she took her father's pistol and, raising it, fired through the door, to frighten the ghostly intruders. The sound of a shot and then a silence while Zenobia stood there in the darkness with the smoking pistol in her hand, waiting – waiting!

There was only silence. They had gone

away. There was nothing but the sighing of the wind and the faint hooting of the owls ...

And in the morning (my grandfather said) Zenobia was awakened by the brilliant spring sun streaming in at the window and by the happy clamor of the thrushes and cardinals in the garden. The sunlight fell upon the wedding dress that lay spread out over the chair at her side. And when she had dressed and gone downstairs (she was singing, she told my grandfather) she unbolted the doors and windows one by one until she came to the last, which opened into the garden. And there, full in the path, face downward, his red hair flaming in the sunlight, lay Jock McDougal – dead – with a bullet through his heart.

I looked up and saw the figure of Jabez, sitting now under a tree in the lane, still puzzling. We shall never again see Zenobia White with the procession of cats at her heels, her yellow taffeta trailing the white dust. Zenobia White is dead. She is being buried tomorrow in her wedding dress.

SHIRLEY JACKSON
This Is the Life

"Honey," Mrs. Wilson said uneasily, "are you *sure* you'll be all right?"

"Sure," said Joseph. He backed away quickly as she bent to kiss him again. "Listen, *Mother,*" he said. "Everybody's *looking.*"

"I'm still not sure but what someone ought to go with him," said his mother. "Are you *sure* he'll be all right?" she said to her husband.

"Who, Joe?" said Mr. Wilson. "He'll be fine, won't you, son?"

"Sure," said Joseph.

"A boy nine years old ought to be able to travel by himself," said Mr. Wilson, in the patient tone of one who has been saying these same words over and over for several days.

Mrs. Wilson looked up at the train, as one who estimates the probable strength of an enemy. "But suppose something should *happen?*" she asked.

"Look, Helen," her husband said, "the train's going to leave in about four minutes.

His bag is already on the train, Helen. It's on the seat where he's going to be sitting from now until he gets to Perryton. I have spoken to the porter and I have given the porter a couple of dollars, and the porter has promised to keep an eye on him and see that he gets off the train with his bag when the train stops at Perryton. He is nine years old, Helen, and he knows his name and where he's going and where he's supposed to get off. And Grandpop is going to meet him and will telephone you the minute they get to Grandpop's house. And the porter –"

"I know," said Mrs. Wilson, "but are you sure he'll be all *right?*"

Mr. Wilson and Joseph looked at one another briefly and then away.

Mrs. Wilson took advantage of Joseph's momentary lapse of awareness to put her arm around his shoulders and kiss him again, although he managed to move almost in time and her kiss landed somewhere on the top of his head.

"Mother," Joseph said ominously.

"Don't want anything to happen to my little boy," Mrs. Wilson said, with a brave smile.

"Mother, for heaven's *sake,*" said Joseph. "I better get on the train," he said to his father.

344

"Good idea," said his father.

"'Bye, Mother," Joseph said, backing toward the train door; he took a swift look up and down the platform, and then reached up to his mother and gave her a rapid kiss on the cheek. "Take care of yourself," he said.

"Don't forget to telephone the minute you get there," his mother said. "Write me every day, and tell Grandma you're supposed to brush your teeth every night. And if the weather turns cool–"

"Sure," Joseph said. "Sure, Mother."

"So long, son," said his father.

"So long, Dad," Joseph said. Solemnly they shook hands. "Take care of yourself," Joseph said.

"Have a good time."

As Joseph climbed up the steps to the train he could hear his mother, saying, "And telephone us when you get there and be careful –"

"Goodbye, goodbye," he said, and went into the train. He had been located by his father in a double seat at the end of the car and, once settled, he turned as a matter of duty to the window. His father, with an unmanly look of concern, waved to him and nodded violently, as though to indicate that everything was going to be all right, that they had pulled it off beautifully, but his mother, twisting her fingers nervously, came close to the window of the train, and, fortunately unheard by the people within, but probably clearly audible to everyone for miles without, gave him at what appeared to be some length an account of how she had changed her mind and was probably going to come with him after all.

Joseph nodded and smiled and waved and shrugged to indicate that he could not hear, but his mother went on talking, now and then glancing nervously at the front of the train as though afraid that the engine might start and take Joseph before she had made herself absolutely sure that he was going to be all right. Joseph, who felt with some justice that in the past few days his mother had told him every conceivable pertinent fact about his traveling alone to his grandfather's and her worries about same, was able to make out such statements as, "Be careful," and, "Telephone us the minute you get there," and, "Don't forget to write."

Then the train stirred, and hesitated, and moved slightly again, and Joseph backed away from the window, still waving and smiling. He was positive that what his mother was saying as the train pulled out was, "Are you *sure* you'll be all right?" She blew a kiss to him as the train started, and he ducked.

Surveying his prospects as the train took him slowly away from his mother and father, he was pleased. The journey should take only a little over three hours, and he knew the name of the station and had his ticket safely in his jacket pocket. Although he had been reluctant to yield in any fashion to his mother's misgivings, he had checked several times, secretly, to make sure the ticket was safe.

He had half a dozen comic books – a luxury he was not ordinarily allowed – and a chocolate bar. He had his suitcase and his cap, and he had seen personally to the packing of his first baseman's mitt. He had a dollar bill in the pocket of his pants, because his mother thought he should have some money in case – possibilities which had concretely occurred to her – of a train wreck (although his father had pointed out that in the case of a major disaster the victims were not expected to pay their own expenses, at least not before their families had been notified) or perhaps in the case of some vital expense to which his grandfather's income would not be adequate.

His father had thought that Joe ought to

347

have a little money by him in case he wanted to buy anything, and because a man ought not to travel unless he had money in his pocket. "Might pick up a girl on the train and want to buy her lunch," his father had said jovially.

His mother, regarding her husband thoughtfully, had remarked, "Let's hope *Joseph* doesn't do things like that," and Joe and his father had winked at one another. So, regarding his comic books and his suitcase and his ticket and his chocolate bar, and feeling the imperceptible but emphatic presence of the dollar bill in his pocket, Joe leaned back against the soft seat, looked briefly out the window at the houses now moving steadily past, and said to himself, "This is the life, boy."

Before indulging in the several glories of comic books and chocolate bar he spent a moment or so watching the houses of his home town disappear beyond the train. Ahead of him, at his grandfather's farm, lay a summer of cows and horses and probable wrestling matches in the grass; behind him lay school and its infinite irritations, and his mother and father. He wondered briefly if his mother was still looking after the train and telling him to write, and then largely he forgot her.

With a sigh of pure pleasure, he leaned back and selected a comic book, one which dealt with the completely realistic adventures of a powerful magician among hostile African tribes. This *is* the life, boy, he told himself again, and glanced again out the window to see a boy about his own age sitting on a fence watching the train go by.

For a minute Joseph thought of waving down to the boy, but decided that it was beneath his dignity as a traveler. Moreover, the boy on the fence was wearing a dirty sweatshirt which made Joe move uneasily under his stiff collar and suit jacket and think longingly of the comfortable old shirt with the insignia *Brooklyn Dodgers* in his suitcase. Then, just as the traitorous idea of changing on the train occurred to him, and of arriving at his grandfather's not in his good suit became a possibility, all sensible thought was driven from his mind by a cruel and unnecessary blow. Someone sat down next to him, breathing heavily, and from the quick flash of perfume and the movement of cloth which could only be a dress rustling, Joe realized with a strong sense of injustice that his paradise had been invaded by some woman.

"Is this seat taken?" she asked.

Joe refused to recognize her existence by

turning his head to look at her, but he told her sullenly, "No, it's not." Not taken, he was thinking, what did she think *I* was sitting here for? Aren't there enough old seats in the train she could go and sit in without taking mine?

He seemed to lose himself in contemplation of the scenery beyond the train window, but secretly he was wishing direly that the woman would suddenly discover she had forgotten her suitcase or find out she had no ticket or remember that she had left the bathtub running at home – anything to get her off the train at the first station and out of Joe's way.

"You going far?"

Talking, too, Joe thought; she has to take my seat and then she goes and talks my ear off, darn old pest. "Yeah," he said. "Perryton."

"What's your name?"

Joe, from long experience, could have answered all her questions in one sentence, he was so familiar with the series – I'm nine years old, I'm in the fifth grade, and, no, I don't like school, and if you want to know what I learn in school it's nothing because I don't like school and I do like movies, and I'm going to my grandfather's house, and more than anything else I hate women who come and sit beside me and ask me silly questions and if my mother didn't keep after me all the time about my manners I'd probably gather my things together and move to another seat.

"What's your name, little boy?"

Little boy, Joe told himself bitterly; on top of everything else, little boy.

"Joe," he said.

"How old are you?"

He lifted his eyes wearily and regarded the conductor entering the car; it was surely too much to hope that this female plague had forgotten her ticket, but could it be remotely possible that she was on the wrong train?

"Got your ticket, Joe?" the woman asked.

"Sure," said Joe. "Have you?"

She laughed and said – apparently addressing the conductor, since her voice was not at this moment the voice women use in addressing a little boy but the voice which goes with speaking to conductors and taxi drivers and sales clerks, "I'm afraid I haven't got a ticket, I had no time to get one."

"Where you going?" said the conductor.

Would they put her off the train? For the first time Joe turned and looked at her, eagerly and with hope. Would they possibly, hopefully, desperately, put her off the train? "I'm going to Perryton," she said, and Joe's

351

convictions about the generally weak-minded attitudes of the adult world were all confirmed; the conductor tore a slip from a pad he carried, punched a hole in it, and told the woman, "Two seventy-three." While she was searching her pocketbook for her money – if she knew she was going to have to buy a ticket, Joe thought disgustedly, whyn't she have her money ready? – the conductor took Joe's ticket and grinned at him. "Your boy got *his* ticket all right," he pointed out.

The woman smiled. "He got to the station ahead of me," she said.

The conductor gave her her change, and went on down the car. "That was funny, when he thought you were my little boy," the woman said.

"Yeah," said Joe.

"What're you reading?"

Wearily Joe put his comic book down. "Comic," he said.

"Interesting?"

"Yeah," said Joe.

"Say, look at the policeman," the woman said.

Joe looked where she was pointing and saw – he would not have believed this, since he knew perfectly well that most women couldn't tell the difference between a policeman and a mailman – that it was undeniably a policeman, and that he was regarding the occupants of the car very much as though there might be a murderer or an international jewel thief riding calmly along on the train. Then, after surveying the car for a moment, he came a few steps forward to the last seat, where Joe and the woman were sitting.

"Name?" he said sternly to the woman.

"Mrs. John Aldridge, officer," said the woman promptly. "And this is my little boy Joseph."

"Hi, Joe," said the policeman.

Joe, speechless, stared at the policeman and nodded dumbly.

"Where'd you get on?" the policeman asked the woman.

"Ashville," she said.

"See anything of a woman about your height and build, wearing a fur jacket, getting on the train at Ashville?"

"I don't think so," said the woman. "Why?"

"Wanted," said the policeman tersely.

"Keep your eyes open," he told Joe. "Might get a reward."

He passed on down the car and stopped occasionally to speak to women who seemed to be alone. Then the door at the far end of the car closed behind him and Joe turned and took a deep look at the woman sitting beside him. "What'd you do?" he asked.

"Stole some money," said the woman, and grinned.

Joe grinned back. If he had been sorely pressed, he might in all his experience until now have been able to identify only his mother as a woman both pretty and lovable. In this case, however – and perhaps it was enhanced by a sort of outlaw glory – he found the woman sitting next to him much more attractive than he had before supposed. She looked nice, she had soft hair, she had a pleasant smile and not a lot of lipstick and stuff on, and her fur jacket was rich and soft against Joe's hand. Moreover, Joe knew absolutely when she grinned at him that there weren't going to be any more questions about people's ages and whether they liked school, and he found himself grinning back at her in quite a friendly manner.

"They gonna catch you?" he asked.

"Sure," said the woman. "Pretty soon now. But it was worth it."

"Why?" Joe asked. Crime, he well knew, did not pay.

"See," said the woman. "I wanted to spend about two weeks having a good time there in Ashville. I wanted this coat, see?

354

And I wanted just to buy a lot of clothes and things."

"So?" said Joe.

"So I took the money from the old tightwad I worked for and I went off to Ashville and bought some clothes and went to a lot of movies and things and had a fine time."

"Sort of vacation," Joe said.

"Sure," the woman said. "I knew all the time they'd catch me, of course. For one thing, I always knew I had to come home again. But it was worth it!"

"How much?" said Joe.

"Two thousand dollars," said the woman.

"Boy!" said Joe.

They settled back comfortably. Joe, without more than a moment's pause to think, offered the woman his comic book about the African headhunters, and when the policeman came back through the car, eyeing them sharply, they were leaning back shoulder to shoulder, the woman apparently deep in African adventure, Joe engrossed in the adventures of a flying newspaper reporter who solved vicious gang murders.

"How's your book, Ma?" Joe said loudly as the policeman passed, and the woman laughed and said, "Fine, fine."

As the door closed behind the policeman,

the woman said softly, "I wonder how long I can keep out of their way."

"You can't keep it up forever," Joe pointed out.

"No," said the woman. "But I'd like to go back by myself and give them what's left of the money. I had a good time."

"Seems to me," Joe said, "that if it's the first time you did anything like this, they probably wouldn't punish you so much."

"I'm not ever going to do it again," the woman said. "I mean, you sort of build up all your life for one real good time like this, and then you can take your punishment and not mind it so much."

"I don't know," Joe said reluctantly, various small sins of his own with regard to matches and his father's cigarettes and other people's lunch boxes crossing his mind. "It seems to me that even if you do think *now* that you'll never do it again, sometimes – well, sometimes, you do it anyway." He thought. "I always *say* I'll never do it again, though."

"Well, if you do it again," the woman pointed out, "you get punished twice as bad the next time."

Joe grinned. "I took a dime out of my mother's pocketbook once," he said. "But I'll never do that again."

"Same thing I did," said the woman.

Joe shook his head. "If the policemen plan to spank you the way my father spanked me –"

They were companionably silent for a while, and then the woman said, "Say, Joe, are you hungry? Let's go into the dining car."

"I'm supposed to stay here," Joe said.

"But I can't go without you," the woman said. "They think I'm all right because the woman they want wouldn't be traveling with her little boy."

"Stop calling me your little boy," Joe said.

"Why?"

"Call me your son or something," Joe said. "No more little-boy stuff."

"Right," said the woman. "Anyway, I'm sure your mother wouldn't mind if you went into the dining car with *me.*"

"I bet," Joe said, but he got up and followed the woman out of the car and down through the next car. People glanced up at them as they passed and then away again, and Joe thought triumphantly that they would sure stare harder if they knew that this innocent-looking woman and her son were outsmarting the cops every step they took.

They found a table in the dining car and

sat down. The woman took up the menu and said, "What'll you have, Joe?"

Blissfully, Joe regarded the woman, the waiters moving quickly back and forth, the shining silverware, the white tablecloth and napkins.

"Hamburger?" said the woman. "Spaghetti? Or would you rather just have two or three desserts?"

Joe stared. "You mean, just blueberry pie with ice cream and a hot fudge sundae?" he asked. "Like that?"

"Sure," said the woman. "Might as well celebrate one last time."

"When I took that dime out of my mother's pocketbook," Joe told her, "I spent a nickel on gum and a nickel on candy."

"Tell me," said the woman, leaning forward earnestly, "the candy and gum – was it all right? I mean, the same as usual?"

Joe shook his head. "I was so afraid someone would see me," he said, "I ate all the candy in two mouthfuls standing on the street and was scared to open the gum at all."

The woman nodded. "That's why I'm going back so soon, I guess," she said, and sighed.

"Well," said Joe practically, "might as well have blueberry pie first, anyway."

They ate their lunch peacefully, discussing

baseball and television and what Joe wanted to be when he grew up. Once the policeman passed through the car and nodded to them cheerfully, and the waiter opened his eyes wide and laughed when Joe decided to polish off his lunch with a piece of watermelon. When they had finished and the woman had paid the check, they found that they were due in Perryton in fifteen minutes, and they hurried back to their seat to gather together Joe's belongings.

"Thank you very much for the nice lunch," Joe said to the woman as they sat down again, and congratulated himself upon remembering to say it.

"Nothing at all," the woman said. "Aren't you my little boy?"

"Watch that little-boy stuff," Joe said warningly, and she said, "I mean, aren't you my son?"

The porter who had been delegated to keep an eye on Joe opened the car door and put his head in. He smiled reassuringly at Joe and said, "Five minutes to your station, son."

"Thanks," said Joe. He turned to the woman. "Maybe," he said urgently, "if you tell them you're *really* sorry –"

"Wouldn't do at all," said the woman. "I really had a fine time."

"I guess so," Joe said. "But you won't do it again."

"Well, I knew when I started I'd be punished sooner or later."

"Yeah," Joe said. "You can't get out of it now."

The train pulled slowly to a stop and Joe leaned toward the window to see if his grandfather was waiting.

"We better not get off together," the woman said. "It might worry your grandpa to see you with a stranger."

"I guess so," said Joe. He stood up and took hold of his suitcase. "Goodbye, then," he said reluctantly.

"Goodbye, Joe," said the woman. "Thanks."

"Right," said Joe, and as the train stopped he opened the door and went out onto the steps. The porter helped him to get down with his suitcase and Joe turned to see his grandfather coming down the platform.

"Hello, fellow," said his grandfather. "So you made it."

"Sure," said Joe. "No trick at all."

"Never thought you wouldn't," said his grandfather. "Your mother wants you to –"

"Telephone as soon as I get here," Joe said. "I know."

360

"Come along, then," his grandfather said. "Grandma's waiting at home."

He led Joe to the parking lot and helped him and his suitcase into the car. As his grandfather got into the front seat beside him, Joe turned and looked back at the train and saw the woman walking down the platform with the policeman holding her arm. Joe leaned out of the car and waved violently. "So long," he called.

"So long, Joe," the woman called back, waving.

"It's a shame the cops had to get her, after all," Joe remarked to his grandfather.

His grandfather laughed. "You read too many comic books, fellow," he said. "Everyone with a policeman isn't being arrested – he's probably her brother or something."

"Yeah," said Joe.

"Have a good trip?" his grandfather asked. "Anything interesting happen?"

Joe thought. "Saw a boy sitting on a fence," he said. "I didn't wave to him, though."

361

KATHRYN GOTTLIEB
The Gun

I was sweating. The month was July, the city
was New York, the air-conditioner in the
office of the Consulate of the African
Republic of Matanzia was noisy and blew hot
air at me, and the news was bad. "They've
held back the cash," said Joseph Arundu.
"You'll have to forget the job." He shook his
head. "I regret it exceedingly."

"*You* regret it!"

He looked at me gravely from the far side
of the mahogany desk. "We do, you know.
We need you."

"Oh, look, what the hell – I mean, I'm
sorry, forgive me, but what am I supposed
to do? On the basis of our contract I
terminated my job, I gave up my lease." I
was trying to keep the anger out of my voice,
which left the whine in. "I gave up my
women," I said lightening it. I wanted the
job badly. I am a civil engineer, the job was
water-resources development. I liked
Arundu and the others of his countrymen I
had talked to some months before, and I

wanted to go to Africa. I had been looking forward to it the way one looks forward to a new life. "What do you want me to do?"

Arundu was a big man, handsome and somber. He was wearing a white robe of some kind and a small Nehru-type hat with bits of mirror glass set in around the edge. Outside of that he was just like you and me, only more interesting.

"Wait for us," he said. "In three months we'll have the funds to get started. I'm sure of it. The Bank has promised." He shook his head and looked at me with a small smile. "It is only at the last minute that the Bank advised us of the delay. Red tape. Red tape! You have this also in your country? Look." He leaned forward confidentially. "Do you want me to settle your contract?" He looked me sturdily in the eye. "We're broke. I can offer you a lifetime supply of coconuts."

Go fight City Hall. "I'll wait," I said. "I'll wait."

And that was the beginning. If the International Bank for Development had come through with the cash on schedule, I wouldn't be writing now from this place of confinement.

I'd said I'd wait, but meanwhile I had to live. I called my old friend Tom Stanley who is president of a small upstate outfit called

363

Paleotronics. Tom said he could fit me into a temporary slot in Engineering and so I shortly found myself up in Elsinore, a small town forty miles west of Albany, New York, and a long way from Africa – but now, in July, just as hot.

Elsinore is the kind of town where if you want to stay overnight you have to buy a house; so Tom and his wife Jane made room for me in their own split-level for a week and then Jane found me a place of my own, primitive quarters in the gatehouse of a boarded-up estate just outside the town, northwest of the plant. There I lived happily on delicatessen, reading Joseph Conrad, and stayed away from the Stanleys. I saw no one else, formed no ties, worked some evenings on stuff I brought back from the office – they were busy there at Paleotronics, expanding into bankruptcy – and wandered in the summer nights through the rankly over-grown and scented garden and thought of Africa.

So far so good.

One night – I had worked late, it was after seven – I stopped at Pete's Delicatessen, bought a half pound of ham, two rolls, and a six-pack, put the package on the car seat, then sat there with the car keys in my hand, watching the late July sunlight blasting down

Main Street which runs west and uphill at that point, and watching, listening to, and inhaling the traffic, which is heavy – there's a lot of trucking along this route. I was tired. Hot, tired, bored, edgy, worried, and critical.

I watched the poor skinny high-school girls and their poor skinny little mothers walking down the street with their lifelike faces, and then I scowled at a car that pulled into the space ahead of me. I disaprove of sloppy driving, and this car stopped well short of the curb, its tail sticking out into traffic just enough to annoy. The driver, a woman, got out slowly, no hurry, and walked over to the parking meter, a straight-backed, idle walk with a lot of don't-care in it.

My first sight of Kay Bannerman. I watched her with idle dislike. She was tall, looked about twenty-seven, and cared little for the opinion of humanity, being washed but not, I think, combed. Her hair, a kind of dull brownish-gold, was yanked back from her face and held by a barrette at the nape of her neck. She was wearing a limp garment made in two pieces that failed to meet in the middle, washed out and worn out; she needed starch, or embroidery, or a collar and tie.

I stared at her as she fumbled in her purse for a coin to put in the meter. She had a firm

365

profile, high cheekbones, and a human-looking mouth. She wasn't wearing any make-up. She caught my glance and looked at me with hatred. She was beautiful. She gave up on the coin hunt and sauntered away from the meter. Violation, it said.

I watched until the screen door of the delicatessen, slamming behind her, made her invisible. The sun was hot, the fumes were shortening my life, and the noise offended my ears. I drove home. The ham was sweating and the beer was warm. I kept thinking of her. I didn't know at the time either her name or what it was she had against the world.

I soon enough found out both.

The Stanleys gave a cocktail party. There must have been forty people jammed into the little recreation room I had slept in that first week. I was in a friendly mood, glad to see people for a change. I hadn't really seen anyone to talk to outside the Paleotronics office and I hadn't heard a word from the Africans. I was beginning to worry and I was glad of the distraction. I got there pretty much on time and found the place already jammed with the prompt.

I had a couple of drinks and talked to various people and then through a momentary clearing in the crowd I saw a tall girl standing at the end of the room. She was alone. Her back was to the rest of us and she was staring at a picture on the wall. I had a vision of sweated ham and blinding sun that came and went like an aberration before I recognized the back in the black dress. Under that dress was the thin white waist I know so well that dwelled between the top and bottom of that unspeakable two-piece.

I elbowed my way across the room, saying sorry, sorry, and when I got near her I saw that the hair was piled on top of her head this time and held in a sort of French knot by, I think, the same barrette. The hair was the dark gold I remembered and strands had come unfastened or had never been fastened and were straggling down the back of a really beautiful neck. I came up even with her and she never looked around at me until I said hello.

Then her eyes looked right at mine. They were a dark shade of blue and set in deep, nicely spaced sockets. She had a somber expression that reminded me of Joseph Arundu's. A lot of people are finding the world heavy going these days.

She spoke. "You," she said.

I acknowledged it. Would she like a drink?

She would.

"I plowed my way to the bar and back again and we drank our drinks together. People left a little space around us.

"Tell me," she said. She looked amused. "Where you come from, are there women?"

"Cleveland. Yes."

"Delicatessens?"

"The world's best. Why?"

"Then how is it you never saw a woman walk into a delicatessen before?"

"I stared at you," I said. I felt the color come up in my face. "If you don't want to be looked at, then don't go out like that."

The faint smile faded. "Like what?"

"That thing you were wearing," I said. "That garment. Like the things you see flapping on lines in people's yards on country roads when you're driving by at high speed. It forces people to look at you. It – " (I was groping for words, or for a thought) "it forces intimacy. And don't go around with hair straggling down your neck."

Her hand went up to smooth back her hair and my stomach gave a lurch. She was wearing a wedding band. I'm not a poacher. But now it was too late.

She saw the movement of my eyes. "Dead," she said. "He's dead. Lying in the cold, cold ground."

368

"That's not nice," I said. "To talk like that."

"You wanted to know." And then – "I'm going. I have to go home." She looked around, stooped, and put her glass down on the floor next to the wall out of the way because there was no other place, and then she was forcing her way out through the people who were looking at her oddly and I stood there saying to myself. Let it end, let it end now, and then I found myself walking down the room after her and it took time because the people had come together in her wake and when I got to the end of the room she was walking out the door.

"Don't go," I called after her. I didn't even know her name. Behind me someone tittered. A knot of people came between us and when I got to the door she was gone. I stood outside on the flat stone step. The night was warm and the air was moving softly. Out on the street a motor was spinning and not catching. The battery had run down. I didn't want a woman. I didn't want to want a woman. I didn't want to care about anyone. This was not the time in my life for it, for ties and bondage, for the Tom-and-Jane life, for nine-to-five. *After* Africa.

Silence in the street. Then she came

walking back over the lawn. When she came up to me I caught her wrist. She said, "I think I must have left the radio on."

"I'll take you home."

She looked dismayed. "You mustn't leave the party. You mustn't leave here with me."

"The party's all right. I'll come back and say good night. Come on."

"But my car –"

"I'll call a garage. Don't worry. All right?"

She told me her name was Kay Bannerman, and where she lived.

Her house was out in the same direction as mine, but not so far. It was an old-fashioned-looking place, almost a mile beyond the last split-level and with falow fields on either side of it; waiting for the developers, growing weeds and money. I turned off the engine and we listened to the summer evening. The tree frogs were making a lot of sound. I leaned back against the window at my left and looked at her. She stared straight ahead. Her profile was beautiful and strong, her expression vulnerable and sad. After a long time I got out of the car and went around and opened the door on her side. She got out and stood facing me. The street light was shining on her face. She was very beautiful, like Ingrid Bergman on the late-late TV movies. I wanted to touch her face in the lamplight, but I folded my arms. "Look," I'm going to Africa."

"Don't be angry," she said. She was smiling faintly. "I'm not going to stop you." She turned away from me and went up the path to her front door. I stood where I was and watched until she opened her door and I saw a light go on behind it as it closed.

I went back to the Stanleys' and said good night and thank you. I picked up a lot of sideways looks there, including one from my host. I went back to the gatehouse and spent a sleepless night, my haven destroyed. At three in the morning I turned on the light and picked up Mr. Conrad's book, since that gentleman spoke to my condition.

The next morning at Paleotronics, George Russell who had been at the Stanleys' party stopped at my desk, smiled unpleasantly, and passed on without comment. Russell is a man with transparent red hair and a badly assembled face – he has thin lips that don't appear to meet at the corners, and yet they must.

I left promptly at five and drove directly to her house. As I drew near, looking across the open fields I saw her working in the garden beyond. Even at that distance I had no doubt it was Kay; she was dressed in coveralls and her hair was tucked up under a railroad cap, but her bearing was distinctive. She was picking something and putting it in a basket. I drove up the weed-grown driveway, stopped behind the house, and got out. She turned and came up to me, not hurrying. The vegetable patch was a good distance behind the house, maybe 300 feet. She was carrying a small basket of tomatoes under one arm and holding onto a bunch of rooted cuttings of some kind. Chrysanthemums. A sharp end-of-summer smell wafted off them.

"Come onto the porch," she said. She sounded as though she had expected to see me there.

We sat on the wooden steps leading up from the garden to the kitchen porch. The paint was peeling from the steps. "Isn't it lonely here for you?" I wanted to ask, but I kept silent. I was afraid she would think I wanted to take advantage of her loneliness and I didn't want her to think a wrong thing of me. What I felt for her had to do with herself and not with her being alone.

She took off the railroad cap and loosened her hair. Her fingers left tracks of topsoil on her forehead. I felt that I knew her very well – as parker, shopper, drinker, digger – yet didn't understand her at all. "It's hard to know you," I said.

She made a face. "I'm simple," she said. "Either silent or shouting. Look, I've got to get these in the ground." She showed me the chrysanthemum sections. "Maybe later, when the sun's gone down. I'm late with them. I should have divided them a month ago. Wait here." She got down from the steps, then disappeared around the corner of the house for a few moments, and came back empty-handed. "I've put them in the shade."

The back of the house faced west. The hot late sunlight was pouring across the garden and into our faces. A rough-barked oak grew just beyond the steps, high-limbed and choked with dead wood. The shade fell on the driveway and beyond. I squinted up into the tree. "You want to get those dead limbs out of there," I told her. "It's bad for the tree. Don't you know anything about trees? You could get some of that lumber on your head someday."

She didn't answer. A squirrel was posted out on the end of one of the dead limbs. Very pretty. "Oh, for God's sake," I said.

"What?"

"Nothing. Those are nice-looking tomatoes you've got there."

She looked pleased. "They're good. It's a new variety from the Ag Station up here. It's just got a number, no name yet. They're meaty and the plants don't wilt. We used to grow Rutgers but they weren't always good. A friend of mine with the College gave me the plants." I felt jealous of the friend with the College and the we who used to grow Rutgers. Both.

"It must be lonely for you here," I said.

She got to her feet. "I really must get those sections in the ground."

"That's stupid, to put them in now. You don't want the sun on them. Can't we talk for a little while longer?"

"All right," she said. But she didn't sit down again.

"Have you lived here long?"

"In this house? Five years. Six. We started those chrysanthemums from seed. Hardly anyone bothers to do that any more. But you really ought to see them. A lot of singles, but all colors. All the colors you can imagine. And every plant is different.

We were standing very close. I was astonished to see tears come into her eyes. "And I intend to see them in bloom again. I'm staying. They all thought I'd be out of here a long time ago. But I'm not going to leave until I'm ready. Not a minute before.

I'm going to plant them, pinch them, water them, weed them, and pick them. By the middle of October they'll be finished. Hard frost. Then I'll leave."

"Where will you go?" I asked her. I was dismayed that she was going and that made no sense, because by the fall I would have gone a lot farther myself. Remember Africa.

"I don't know where I'll go. But," she said again. "I'm no going to leave until I'm ready."

Pariah. I remembered her standing alone at Tom's party.

I gestured at the garden. "He died, you said."

She nodded. "Oh yes," she said. "He died."

Well, how? I wondered. It was no long respectable illness. All the vigorous gardening. And he must have been, probably was, young. Drink? An accident? Maybe she was driving. Maybe that was it. "How did he die?"

Her voice was matter-of-fact. She was back on familiar ground. "I shot him."

Then she turned and walked up the kitchen steps, quickly but not running. The door slammed behind her. The basket of tomatoes was lying on the step in the sun. I left it there and drove home.

I kept away the next day and the next day and the one after that. Then I went back. I drove into the driveway. The weeds seemed taller to me, like a threat. She was sitting on the back steps staring out across the garden. She got to her feet as I walked to her. I took her hand. We didn't say anything. After a while she said, "Come into the house. I'll fix you something to drink."

After that time I went to her every evening directly from the office. Sometimes I took her out to dinner at a place I found up the road near Tompkinsville where we didn't run into anyone she knew. More and more often she cooked something or threw a salad together, or I picked up cold cuts or a couple of steaks. The tomatoes from the Ag Station seeds were very good – tasty and solid. In the evenings we weeded the garden or sat on the back-porch steps and talked, or were quiet. Sometimes we went in the house. I was in love with her.

I liked the quiet times best. I liked to watch her work in the kitchen or in her garden. She had a quiet, put-together way of moving. I liked to look at the back of her neck and the slope of her shoulders and the arms and the back, and the narrow long waist and round hips. I remembered my first sight of her, walking into the little store and the screen door closing behind her.

"I can't believe there was a time I didn't know you," I said. It was a wrong kind of thing to say under the circumstances. Cruel, even. The time when I wasn't going to know her was going to start again very soon. And I said other things like that.

She never answered directly but she'd look as though I'd given her some secret drink of intoxicating power. Something in her eyes and in the set of her mouth would change. I didn't say it to make the effect. I'd hear myself saying the injudicious things, as if the truth were compelled out of me. And all the time the end of summer was coming and I lived one day at a time.

She talked to me freely about killing her husband. Matter-of-fact, sitting across from me at the kitchen table, telling me about it in a steady voice, getting it out of the way. It had been, she said, an accident. He had liked to hunt. She had not, but she had gone with him, on occasion, anyway. "I'm companionable," she explained to me, smiling a little, smoothing back her hair with her strong, long-fingered hand – a gesture I got to be familiar with. She was silent a lot, she told me. But companionable. It was not a mean silence, just her nature.

The shotgun that killed him had been returned to her by the police. If I cared to see it I could look up to the bend in the stairway, just crane around from where I sat. I didn't have to. I had seen the gunrack on the landing when I came in; it was a funny old house, full of nooks and angles and useless space. The stair landing was visible from the kitchen.

"Look at it and know it," she insisted. "It's the middle one. Otherwise, you'll be wondering and sneaking looks." I looked. I didn't expect to feel anything about it and oddly it gave me a jolt. The middle one; she had taken it in her hands and killed a man with it, a man who had slept with her. I turned back to her, meeting her eyes with conscious effort.

"There," she said to me, "that's over with." She told me the rest of it. He had died here, in the kitchen. "Where you're sitting," she said. He had asked her to bring him the gun. She sounded like a child reciting something learned by rote. "I sound like a parrot," she said at the end. "I've told it over and over. But that is what happened."

There had, of course, been an inquiry, of a fairly extensive nature. Their friends had stood by her; they had been well liked as a

378

couple. "People liked Dick better than they liked me," she said. "I seem cold, or stand-offish. I'm not really. But I seem so. Dick was the hearty type. We knew a lot of people. You met some of them at Tom and Jane's. Those two are still kind to me. They are the only ones. But everyone stood by me when Dick died. It was important that they did. There were no witnesses, after all, to the shooting. The police relied on what they could find out about me, my character, about my relationship with Dick. The gun was in my hands when he was shot. I told them so. I was bringing it to him and I tripped over a torn edge of the linoleum."

I looked, involuntarily, downward.

"I kept meaning to have it fixed. But I tripped, so that I fell against the table, and the gun went off, and Dick fell over, very slowly. It was like slow motion, the whole thing, or something happening in a dream. It seemed to me at any moment of its happening that I could have stopped it or made something else happen, but it kept happening. There was nothing I could do, I was off balance, and I suppose it all took just a few seconds, really."

"But I don't understand about everyone," I said. "The people in town, I mean. Your friends. What's gone wrong?" I was remembering George Russell, the leers, the suggestive glances, the silences, the odd looks on the night of Tom's party. And I seemed to have been ringed with a peculiar atmosphere ever since that night. It was a small town and I was sure that everyone who knew me, and a lot of people who didn't, knew where I spent my time.

"They testified, you see, that Dick and I were happy. That they knew us very well, and that I couldn't conceivably, in their view, have wished to kill Dick, or even to hurt him. Then when it was all over, the inquiry closed and the gun back in this house, they turned their backs on me."

"Why?"

She shrugged. "Because they all lied. Out of kindness to me, or maybe they were squeamish. Maybe they didn't want the trial and the publicity and all that. I don't know people's motives. Maybe they didn't want me to die or spend a lot of years in prison because of something they said or guessed. We quarreled, you see, the two of us. Like cat and dog. Everybody knew it. It was an ugly habit we had got into. And it had been going on for, I don't know, three years.

"We had our first public quarrel, and after that we never seemed able to get back on common ground. Sometimes I think Dick hated me. I'm not an easy person and we were too different. We never should have married each other. We'd have had good marriages, I think, with other people. Dick's temper got worse and worse. Twice, two different times, he hit me. In front of people. I don't know how much longer we could have gone on together. I don't believe in divorce, really."

She paused, and sighed. Those eyes, in their beautiful deep sockets, were downcast. She was staring at the table. "So you see, they lied for me. And they all believe that I killed him. Which I did. But they think I wanted him to die. Or killed him in a fit of temper. They think I murdered him. If they had just turned their backs on me," she said with a sort of sad intensity, "it wouldn't be so painful. But they –"

"What? What has everyone done to you?"

She raised her eyebrows, then smiled. "Just that. Turned their backs. That's all. It's enough, really. It's been very difficult for me here. I feel like the leper with his little bell."

"Lonely."

"No. I'm not lonely. I'm alone. I don't want to be with them. Come on." She jumped to her feet. "I'm hungry. Would you like something cold? Or steak? Steak and salad?"

"But all that gardening?" I said. I was bewildered. "I thought you must have been very happy. People that gardened together."

She laughed. "It was the only time we didn't quarrel. Gardening together. We were tired and our hands were full and we worked side by side. It was the only good thing. Wait until you see Dick's chrysanthemums. He was a wonderful gardener."

"I'll be gone by then," I said. I hated Dick.

She stood very still, upright, by the sink. "Don't say that," she said. "I don't want to know that."

A couple of nights later I said to her, "But why do they hate you? You're not hateful. Do they really think you meant to kill him?"

"Do they? I don't know. Do they think so? Do you think so? After the hearing, when everything was quiet again, a couple of the men thought I must be lonely. You know? And I wasn't, not for them. So they all turned against me. First one, then another, then everybody."

That conversation took place on a Monday night. The next day George Russell caught up with me at the water cooler and said something filthy about Kay. I punched him in the mouth. I didn't know I'd done it until I saw the blood well up from his lip. I looked at my knuckles. They were white and turning red. He smiled at me with his mouth wet and red as though he'd scored a point.

"You're a pair," he said. "You're a pair."

Before the day ended, Tom Stanley called me into his office. I apologized for the business at the water cooler. "Why don't you stay away from her?" he asked me. "It's none of my business what you do, but she's bad news, believe me."

"I don't believe you," I said.

But all the same. I was full of unease, and anger, and distrust. It seemed to build inside me as time went on.

We were, it should be plain, in the midst of a love affair. There seemed to be no way I could put a stop to it. I lived for the time of day when I could be with her. She asked nothing of me, and never said, even, will I see you again? She was steady and loving and I couldn't believe she had killed in anger. Yet, under the steadiness I began to sense that she knew they all had got to me. She grew sad as time went on. Withdrawn. Not passing moods; something barely felt, but always there.

August was ending, and I would soon be

hearing from the Africans. We never spoke of it directly. But she spoke about the future once or twice – not ours, not mine, just her own. When the garden was finished in the late fall she would shut up the house and go away.

"What will you do?" I asked her.

"I don't know. I used to do editorial work. But I feel as though that was in another age. I don't want to do editorial work. I wish I could just be someone's gardener. I just don't know. My mind hurts."

But often she shook off the mood and was gay and lovely and amusing. I loved to watch her being domestic, fixing things at the kitchen sink. I couldn't imagine being with any other woman. She was quick-tempered, I found, as I have always been, and we began to quarrel over little things, things that don't matter, always ending in laughter and lovemaking.

The summer wore on. The earliest of the chrysanthemums began to bloom. The house became like my own house, familiar in all ways: its chipped paint, a loose banister I had nailed into place. I was always conscious of the gunrack and its contents. It seemed remarkable to me that the police had brought back that shotgun. And yet, why not? It belonged to the Bannermans and it had been involved in an accident. Just that. When I stood beside the refrigerator and turned a certain way I could see it there on the landing and my eyes were drawn to it.

One evening – it was the start of Labor Day weekend – she noticed me staring at it.

"I've used it since, you know," she said.

"Used it!"

"There were rabbits in the garden. I tried everything to make them stay away. They were destroying the last of Dick's garden. There was a little Redbud tree, a variety he had rooted. They ate it to the ground. It seemed too bad. I felt that enough of him had been destroyed," she said passionately. "I couldn't stand it about his flowers and things. I know what you think of me. Don't think I don't know what goes on in your mind. But I couldn't stand it about the rabbits. I went out there and I shot at them, not to kill them but to frighten them away. Not just once" – she had turned to face me directly, her eyes intent, holding mine – "not just once. On three separate successive evenings. They they stayed away."

That night we made love like strangers.

Then, just a week later, I had to say the thing we had both been waiting for. Usually she was outside, working in the garden or sitting on the steps, just waiting for me, when

I drove in. This time she was in the kitchen and I walked in and sat down at the table where her husband used to sit. I remember looking down at my hands clasped on my knees, my arms, bare in the heat, tanned, the hair bleached with the sun. I felt the news was printed on my forehead. She had been standing at the sink, cutting a stalk of celery into bits. She turned around, the knife in her hand, and looked at me without saying a word.

"They called me today," I said. "They want me out there by the first of October."

She kept staring at me like a blind woman, but a blind woman who saw everything. Then she dropped the knife, not on the counter but on the floor, and came to where I sat and dropped to her knees and put her arms around my legs. She crouched there for minutes, her face buried in the cuff of my trousers. Then she looked up at me. Her eyes were dry. I felt the tears start in my own. "No," she said.

"I have to go."

"Please." Her voice broke. She caught her bottom lip between her teeth. But she didn't cry.

I stood up and pulled her gently to her feet. I put my arms around her and she stayed quite still in my embrace. After a while she put my arms away from her and moved back to the sink. Her face was pale and almost without expression. She stooped and picked up the knife and straightened again, put back the hair from her forehead, every line of her body, every gesture and movement so known to me.

"I can't let you go," she said. As I came to her she shook her head. "No," she said. "Don't touch me. I've got to think. You know, I know what we'll do. We'll eat. Then I'll think. I'll think later." She sounded as simple as a child, a child in pain and determined not to show it. She turned back to the sink and started to cut the celery again. Now she was crying.

"Do you think I want to leave you?" Do you? Do you?" I was hoarse.

She turned to face me again. "I don't know."

"Kay, I have to go. Try to understand. It's something I *have to do*. I promised this to myself. I gave up a good job for this and I got rid of everything that mattered to me and every *one* that mattered to me. I have to explore the world a little and explore myself. This is the time of my life when that's the thing I *have* to do. Now. *This* time. The time isn't going to come again. Kay, *I have to do it.*"

387

I was terrified I wouldn't be able to leave her; not that she could make me stay but that *I* wouldn't go. "I have to do it," I said again. "Do you think I want to go now? Do you think I want to leave you?"

"I don't know," she repeated, shaking her head. "I just don't know. I only know if it were myself, I could never leave you. How can we leave each other?" She made a small gesture of asking, or of despair. She was still holding the knife. "Do you love me?" She sounded shy.

"Yes, I love you."

"Then how can I let you go? How can I?"

Suddenly I couldn't stand it any more. "Will you stop that! Will you? Will you? I was shouting. "And will you put down that damn knife!" Her head came up and her mouth opened. She looked as if I'd struck her. She fumbled behind her for the counter, and put the knife on it, without even turning around.

I hated what I was doing. I hated myself for it. I hated her for standing in my way. I hated her because I loved her. I was standing with my back to the refrigerator. I wrenched my eyes away from her and my glance fell on the gunrack. "Get that damned thing out of the house!" I shouted. I raced up the stairs after it. The case was unlocked. I grabbed

388

the middle gun out of the rack and tramped back into the kitchen with it.

"You must be crazy to keep this in the house," I shouted at her. "You have no feelings. None at all. If you had any feelings you couldn't have this gun in the house."

I flung open the screen door and walked heavily out onto the back porch. The sun was still in the sky, warm and golden, much farther to the south than when we had first stood here together. How many times we had stood or sat together on these steps, time after time, before love and after love, in the beneficience of the summer evenings. I looked at the gun in my hand as though a stranger had put it there. I was bitterly ashamed. I heard her open the kitchen door behind me and I turned. She was calm, not crying.

"I must have been out of my mind," I said.

"No," she said. "It's difficult, that's all. My situation. And you going away. The whole thing is difficult. I shouldn't have tried to keep you. I swore to myself that I wouldn't stand in your way when the time came. I'm sorry. I really am."

"But I love you."

She smiled a soft and gentle smile – the calm after the storm. "You'd better put down the gun," she said. "I think it's loaded."

I set it down hastily, propped in the angle of the porch railing and the top step. I smiled back at her. Some kind of madness seemed to have passed. The gun was simply an instrument for frightening rabbits. I trusted her absolutely. And I never loved her more than in that moment.

"I'll get on with dinner," she said, and turned back to the kitchen. At the screen door she hesitated. "Pick us some tomatoes?" she asked me. "Pick two. No, three. And make sure they're ripe."

Tomatoes. At the far end of the garden. Three hundred feet in a straight line – and the loaded gun between us.

I didn't trust her after all.

But I loved her and I had hurt her enough. And I am, though this would not have occurred to anyone, a gentleman. "All right," I said.

I walked down the steps, leaving the gun where it stood. To have moved it would have been to destroy her. When I had gone a dozen paces into the garden I turned and looked behind me, because she hadn't gone into the kitchen. I should have heard the door. She was still standing there, her back against the door, looking after me.

I turned and walked on, stiff-legged as though I were forcing my way through water. I didn't want to move but I had to keep going. The tomatoes were still fifty yards away and maybe farther than that, maybe on the other side of eternity.

I plowed on, fighting the undertow. I passed a small clump of chrysanthemums starting to show color, and I thought of the man whose flowers they were. Helpless to stop myself, I turned once again and looked back at her.

She still stood there, looking after me. In the oak beside the porch two squirrels spiraled up and down the trunk, hell-bent for happiness. She saw me look at them, and I think she laughed. Then she turned and opened the scren door and walked into the kitchen. the door slammed behind her and the shotgun toppled over and I flung myself to the ground.

There was a great bloody gully across my thigh, nothing to inconvenience me, and a scattering of lesser wounds from the ankles on up. The pattern, Kay said admiringly in the hospital, reminded her of the way one is supposed to scatter crocus bulbs.

I have now been confined in this place for two weeks. My bags are packed for Africa –

391

Kay packed them – and her bags are packed for Africa; all the summer clothing she could buy in the local stores. Tomorrow morning I'll get out of this place and on Friday morning we will get married, the Stanleys in attendance. Then we will drive down to the city and that night we will fly to Matanzia together. Being, both of us, incapable of looking after our own selves, we are going to look after each other. Put another way, the battle between us has only begun, and will now be carried on at infinite length and in a hotter climate.

HOLLY ROTH
They Didn't Deserve Her Death

"There – " Ben Parkins said, presumably to
his wife and mother, although he seemed to
be addressing the car's windshield – "is
Sitges." He waved his hand in a try at lordly
contempt. "On your right, *the* golf course.
On your left, *the* hotel. Ahead, *the* Mediter-
anean." His constant state of half suppressed
fury rode volcanically beneath the word, and
the theatrical sweep of his arm missed its intent
and resembled a swing at an unseen enemy.

Huddled in the corner behind him, trying
to escape the wind off the sea and her own
frightening exhaustion, his mother thought
tiredly that his fury was aggravated by the
fact that he could not face its cause. At least,
she presumed he did not admit it, even to
himself. Although it was quite possible that
Alice, who was stupid, avaricious, and
entirely without emotion or subtlety, might
have brought it crashingly home to him. Yes,
it was quite possible that Alice had so often
said to him, "Why doesn't your mother die,

393

for goodness' sakes?" that he had come to acknowledge the hope. For his sake, she hoped that it wasn't true. It would be a terrible thing to live with.

He said, "Of course, down that street on our left there is undoubtedly a village – couple of crummy *bodegas*, a few dirty cafés."

Mrs. Parkins said nothing. She had been far too tired to drive the twenty miles to Sitges, but if she had asked to be left in bed in the hotel in Barcelona, Ben would have refused to make the excursion.

Alice spoke up in the flat nasal voice that – for Mrs. Parkins, at least – would have canceled out her beauty if her facial expressions hadn't already negated it. She had two expressions, blankness and the cupidity that occasionally displaced it. Alice said, "For goodness' sakes, let's get out and stretch."

Ben turned his profile toward the rear of the car. "Mother?"

"Please" – Mrs. Parkins tried to keep the pleading note out of her voice – "you two take a walk. I am enjoying just sitting here."

She thought he would refuse, but instead he threw his door so wide that the hinges squealed in protest.

When she was alone, a particle of peace descended on Mrs. Parkins. She slid lower in her seat and let her head drop back against the upholstery. She was a tiny woman and her frailness made her seem even smaller.

She could see no way out. She would give them the money if she could, but John had left her only the income; the principal would go to Ben when she died. There was enough income, it seemed to her to support a dozen people, but Alice's demands more than equaled those of a dozen people. She supposed that, in addition, Ben was deeply in debt. On his "expectations," she thought, was a distaste that had nothing personal in it; it was simply a self-destroying way for a man to exist. She hadn't wanted to come to Spain, and the doctor, after a horrified look at the electrocardiogram, had thrown up his hands in despair. But Alice wanted to make the trip and Ben, with that remnant of conscience that made everything so much worse for the three of them, refused to leave unless Mother would go too. "After alll, it's Mother's money."

Those bitter revelations of how he was being eaten up inside always wrung her heart.

She wished she *would die*... Then a moment's revolt flooded over her. They didn't deserve her death; she could not believe that God's world was so ordered that the wicked and the greedy and the heartless would prosper.

She felt a stab in her side; it crescendoed. She slid still lower and gave in to the wave of pain. There seemed to be a hope of peace just over the crest.

Alice draped her magnificent figure on the low sea wall, looking out at the rippling Mediterranean with enormous eyes of a glowing purple that rivaled the amethyst of the beautiful sea, and said, "For goodness' sakes, why won't your mother *die?*"

"Alice!" Ben choked, and then grew red as the volcano seething within him threatened to erupt.

She turned the blank purple eyes on him. "Ben, be sensible. She's old, and if you don't pay some of those bills soon, you're going to be in trouble. Can't you borrow some money?"

"I have borrowed, as you well know." She shrugged and looked back at the sea. "And I'll tell you something else." He hesitated; if Alice ever got the idea that hanging on wasn't going to pay, she would leave him instantly. But fury drove him on. "I haven't been able to borrow from – reputable places, like banks, because I have no collateral. So the rates are enormous – just plain usury. If

396

I don't pay up soon – in a year at the outside – the interest is going to eat up the principle. The money will all be owed before we get it, or damn near."

The sensuous figure turned away from the sea and swayed in his direction. "Ben," Alice whispered huskily, "couldn't we – *do* something?"

For a split second his body matched the motion of hers, and then he flung himself violently backward. "Alice, for God's sake!" He stamped toward the car, blindly, like an enraged bull.

Alice followed him. Her face showed no more thought or emotion than usual, but the edge of a decision had started forming in her little mind. She had noticed lately that a tiny bulge was growing around her waist: she had better get on with this business before it was too late.

She arrived at the car's side a minute after Ben. "Where's your mother, for goodness' sakes? I want to go."

"She's here." Ben's face was pressed against the rear window and his voice had an oddly choked quality. "She's on the floor."

"The *floor?* For goodness' – " Alice's voice disappeared.

Ben opened the door and bent over. After a minute he straightened, closed the door, and turned around. There were tears in his eyes. "Get in the car." He stepped in on his side and stared through the windshield. He continued to stare for a minute or so after Alice was seated. She didn't rush him; everything would be all right now. She had no decisions to make. She could relax and be glad that the six years hadn't been wasted.

Ben said, "This is a one-horse town. Probably has one cop, who's also chief of police and coroner. If they *have* coroners. If we get involved here, heaven alone knows what'll happen. Might even be accused of murder."

"Any doctor will know –"

"Yeah, but I don't think any doctor will know whether she died now or thirty minutes from now. For that matter, she could have slipped down like that while we were driving and we might not have known it for an hour."

"So?"

"So we're going to drive back to Barcelona and straight to the American consulate." He put the car in gear. "Fast. Hold tight."

The curbs of the narrow Calle Junqueras were, as usual, parked in with cilialike regularity and completeness. Ben found a place in the Plaza Urquinaona, jerked the car's nose in at the required angle, leaped out, and was halfway to the corner before Alice caught up with him.

"Ben," she said, "wait. Shouldn't you – Won't someone see her?"

"I pulled the lap robe over her back in Sitges. And she was very – very small." He grasped Alice's arm a little too tightly. "Come on."

The consul wasn't in but the woman assistant they were referred to was pleasant, sympathetic, and obviously capable. Ben assessed her and then told the flat, exact truth.

When he had finished she said soberly. "May I extend my sympathy? You must be –" She dropped it there and became briskly businesslike. "Your handling of the situation was exactly right. I shudder to think of the insanities you'd have been subjected to, especially since you don't speak Spanish. We'll go to the police right now. With me along, at least they won't hold you interminably. But even in Barcelona –" She waved a hand, as if the explanation was beyond the realm of words.

"Even in Barcelona?" Ben insisted. He had a sense of foreboding. Why? He hadn't done anything to – He shuddered.

The woman looked at him with a mis-understanding sympathy. "It's all right," she said reassuringly. "It's just that they're not very efficient. Lately we've had to deal with a number of thefts, for instance, and not a single thing has been recovered. Infuriating. Well –"

In the cramped elevator Ben looked at Alice's face and wished she would show – something. The intelligent woman was standing so inescapably near. But then the emotion Alice would display if she were capable –

Outside they walked quickly to the corner, and when they had rounded it and taken a few steps Ben stopped abruptly. Then he ran. The two women caught up with him. He looked up from the empty space at the curb with equally empty eyes.

The woman understood instantly. "The car was here? What about the keys?"

"I was in a hurry."

"Of course. Well, I'm afraid –" She paused. "We'll report it immediately. But there have been a half dozen cars stolen lately and not one was recovered. In this case, they – the thieves – will look in the back and then they'll undoubtedly panic and – and do a very thorough job of disposing –" Her voice trailed away. The city squealed and screeched and surged around them, but they were removed from it, caught in an odd silence.

Alice hadn't spoken since they entered the consulate building. Now she said, "But what will happen?"

"Why, we'll go to the police –"

"No, I mean how do we prove – What happens to her effects?"

"Oh." The woman swung around to face Alice. "I am a lawyer," she said. "I can assure you there's no need to worry about that. There will be a legal acceptance of death in five years' time. Then her heirs will be – rewarded."

No female's attitude had ever interested Alice. Damn! she thought with enormous bitterness. She had never disliked the old lady, but for a vicious moment she wondered if this outcome would have pleased – or seemed right to – Mrs. Parkins. Well, that didn't matter now. Alice was thirty, but there was that little bulge around her waist. She had no choice but to try all over, and quickly.

Ben read her mind as easily as if the thoughts were reflected in her still face. So that was that. He had a strange feeling of peace. His mother had never really preached at him, but when he was a boy she used to speak, with obvious belief, of God's justice.

AVRAM DAVIDSON
"Thou Still Unravished Bride"

It used to be said, in some circles, that "a lady" had her name in the newspapers exactly three times: when she was born, when she was married, and when she was buried. It was never altogether true, for "a lady" was entitled to be mentioned when she became a mother, too.

Of course, there are ladies who, even today, are not likely to be seen in the public print at all. This is not because they are hyper-ladylike; it is because they live in large cities and are obscure – and poor. Sally Benner was certainly a lady of this class. And yet she received attention enough in the newspapers because – it appeared – she was not going to be married, and perhaps not buried, either.

Mrs. Benner heard Sally stirring at six in the morning. At seven Sally started to get up, but her mother pushed her back. "There's plenty of time," Mrs. Benner said. "You didn't get to bed till late, and you need your rest. I'll tell you when to get up." So the young woman said, "Yes, mother."

She was a very obedient daughter. That was what made it all so odd.

At eight Mrs. Benner let her get up. Sally took a shower and came down to breakfast, kissed her father, kissed her mother. The two women clung to one another, shed a few tears. Old Joe Benner looked up from his coffee and waffles and growled a bit. "Women," he said, addressing the canary. "The way they cry about weddings makes you wonder why they bother about 'em at all."

"You shut up," said his wife, without malice. "You were so pale at your own wedding that the minister didn't know whether to marry you or bury you." And she gave a little whimper of laughter.

"I've often wished it was the last," Joe said – and pretended to duck as Mrs. Benner game him a light smack on the cheek with her hand. "That's for being so fresh," she said. He captured his wife's hand and held onto it and told Sally that he hoped she'd be as happy with her Bob as he and her mother had been with each other.

That was the way the start of the day went. No sparkling dialogue, exactly, no dramatics. The Benners were respectable working-class

403

people. They had four children. The other girl, Jeannie, the eldest, had been married off long enough ago for Mr. B. (he said) to recoup his fortunes for the wedding of his youngest.

There was going to be a reception at the church, then a family supper at Leary's Restaurant, then a big reception (with dancing) at Anderson Hall. After that, the newlyweds would take off on their honeymoon at – but of course no one presumably knew where that was to be except Sally and Bob. Mrs. Mantin, Sally's mother-in-law-to-be, had thrown out some pretty strong hints that *Someone* ought to know where (meaning *She* ought to).

"Suppose an emergency of some sort comes up?" Mrs. Mantin had asked her son more than once, with a snivel standing by in case her son – whom she was now about to Lose Forever – should talk sharply to her.

"Keep the old man out of the bottle and there won't be no emergency," Bob said. But he told her after a while that his older brother Eddie was privy to the secret, and she had to be content with that.

After Sally went in to dress and her mother attacked the dishes and her father (he had his own plumbing business) prepared to just step around and check up on the arrangements, Mrs. Benner remarked, "Well, never let it be said again in my presence that the Lord don't answer prayers. How many years I been praying for Sally to find a nice fellow!"

"He took his time, though, didn't he? Seeing how Bob lives right down the block here. But," Mr. Benner hastened, as Peg Benner turned on him ready for battle, "I'm not complaining. Long as they're suited, *I'm* suited." But he didn't get off that easily; his wife let him know that it was seldom enough that *he* went to church, and it wasn't *him* who had the heartbreak all these years waiting and watching and worrying, and it was all for the best because early marriages weren't near as likely to last.

After he left, his married daughter Jeannie came over, and so did their two daughters-in-law, and so did Sally's best friend, and also Mrs. Benner's sister Emma. They examined the bridal gown and the guest list and the presents and they hugged Sally and started crying a litle, to warm up for the evening. Suddenly it was ten o'clock and they looked up as the church clock started chiming and there was Sally, dressed to go out.

"And where do you think *you're* going?" Aunt Emma demanded in a mock-ferocious tone. "You better behave – you're not too big to be hit, you know!"

Sally said she was just going out to pick up a few things at the store. She was a tall, quiet girl – pink and slow and sweet. The failure of the male race to snap her up years ago had long been held against it by all distaff branches of the Benner family.

"What things?" demanded Aunt Emma. "What could you buy that ain't been bought already?"

Her best friend said she'd go with Sally. Her sister Jeannie said to wait just a minute, she'd drive them down. But Sally, for all her quiet and obedience, had a mind of her own. She said, "No, I'll just go by myself."

"Ah, let her go," said her mother. "Let her get a breath of fresh air and take a little walk. Here's the whole lot of us jabbering away – let the girl alone." She waved at her daughter, who waved back as she walked off down the street.

It was lined with two-story wooden houses; they were set right next to one another. They were all kind of on the small side, but each had a back yard, a tree and a little garden and some potted plants, and some had a swing on the porch and stained glass in the front door. It was a comfortable neighborhood, a quiet one, known to even the older generation from childhood. It was safe, it was home.

"Listen here, Peg," Aunt Emma demanded. "I wanna see that seating list. If you've put me and Sam next to Maymie Johnson like you did at *Jeannie's wedding* –"

Mrs. Benner gave the sigh of one who had – or as nearly as makes no difference – married off her last child, a daughter aged thirty, and for whom life holds no further problems, and she said to her sister, "Oh, if you didn't have sumpthing to complain about, Emma, I honestly believe you'd *die*. Maymie Johnson, poor thing, hasn't set foot out of her house in *munce.* " Emma said, No! and asked what was wrong, and Mrs. Benner said, Well, she had like what they use to call dropsy, but nowadays the doctors gave it another name.

Sally rounded the corner and came face to face with Bob Mantin, on his way back from the barber shop with his brother Eddie. She said, "Oh!" and blushed. Eddie cried, "Hey, you ain't supposed to see your bride the day of the wedding, it's bad luck!" and he playfully put his hand over Bob's eyes.

Bob pushed aside the hand. He and Sally gazed at each other. Neither, it seemed, could think of anything to say. Finally Eddie asked Sally where she was going and she said to the store to get a few things. He said, "Oh."

Bob broke the silence at last. "Well, I'll, uh, see you tonight, honey."

Sally nodded and they parted.

"So I said to her, 'Well, it's up to them, Mrs. Mantin,' I said. 'Joe and me, we put it up to them,' I said. 'We let them choose. Do you want a big wedding or would you rather have the money to buy furniture?' we asked them. and they talked it over and the decision was entirely theirs. 'I know it's very nice of you and Bob's father to move all your things off of the second floor and put in a kitchen and all,' I said. 'But if they want to buy furniture, I mean such expensive furniture, that they have to do it on time, why that's up to them,' I said. 'That's up to *them.*'" Mrs. Benner's sister, her older daughter, her daughters-in-law, and her younger daughter's girl friend all listened to Mrs. Benner and nodded. Occasionally they punctuated her recital with Believe *Me* or *I'll* say and Imagine *That!*

And then the church clock began to chime eleven. The expression on Mrs. Benner's face (at once combative and self-excusing)

408

changed immediately. "Why, what's happened to Sally?" she exclaimed.

At first her emotion was one of mere affectionate annoyance. By half past eleven she had begun to feel vexed. By twelve she was experiencing a definite anxiety. Jeannie got into her car and went to look for her sister. Mrs. Benner got on the telephone and began calling places where it was possible Sally might have stopped off, to get so engrossed in conversation as to forget this was her wedding day. The girl friend (a thin girl named Agnes with a skin condition, who had – after the first outburst of joyful congratulations – begun to moan that after the wedding Sally wouldn't want her around any more) left to call on a few people who had no telephone. One of the sisters-in-law went around the corner to Mr. Benner's shop, as his line was busy.

"What's he doing there, anyway, so long?" fretted his wife. "He should of been back here long ago – hello, Sadie? Peg. Is Sally there? Oh... Well, *was*, she there? This morning, I mean. She wasn't? All right, Sadie, I'll see you this – no, no, it's all right, I just thought she might of dropped by. Tonight, then, Sadie. 'Bye."

And so it went. Sally hadn't been to anybody's house, even the Mantins'. Bob's brother Eddie answered the phone. He told of their having met on her way to "the store." When? Oh – a little after ten. No, she didn't say which store. "Should I tell Bob? I mean, I will right now if you want me to, but – I mean, she'll prob'ly turn up any minute now, so why get him nervous for nothing? But if you want me to –" Mrs. Benner said, No, he was right, there was no point in getting Bob upset, too.

By half past one they had canvassed all the stores in the neighborhood. The only one where Sally had been seen was Felber's Pharmacy. She had bought some things, the druggist said, at about ten or fifteen minutes after ten. She had seemed okay. When Mr. Felber said to her, handing over the package (cosmetics, hairpins, chewing gum), "Well, today's the big day, eh, Sally?" she had smiled and said, "I'm so happy, Mr. Felber." He had wished her all the luck in the world.

Now it was half past two. Suddenly Aunt Emma, who had been saying, "Oh, I wouldn't *worry*, Peg, she's prob'ly just wandering around in a kind of sky-blue-pink daze" – Aunt Emma suddenly burst into tears and said, "Well, I don't care what *anybody* says: *I* think we oughta call the *police!*"

And all the women broke down and began to wail, and so Mr. Benner found them when he returned. And after he got them quieted down, that was what he did. He phoned the police.

The wedding was called off, but quite a number of guests turned up anyway – some because they hadn't got the word, others because they thought Sally might turn up in time for the wedding to take place, after all. Naturally, they all made their way to the house; and the police decided not to turn them away because – who knows – one of them might know something that would shed light on the matter.

But no one knew anything.

Late that night Detectives Bonn and Steinberg were talking about it with Captain Foley. "Everybody says the same thing," Bonn observed. "She was a nice, sweet, quiet girl. She was a homebody. She's had not broken engagements, no troublesome ex-boy friends. She never even went steady before. So far as anybody knows, the girl was perfectly happy with the marriage. Except for the fiancé, his brother, and the druggist, though, nobody seems to have seen her once she left the old lady's sight."

Steinberg took up the tale. "The fiancé

seems to be okay. Nobody knows anything against him, and even if they did he's been with some member of his own family all day long – brother, mother, father. *He* says she *couldn't* run off by herself. Crying like a baby, the guy was. At the same time he doesn't want to admit she maybe met with foul play. So he says it's got to be amnesia."

Bonn was dark and thin, Steinberg was red-haired and stocky. Captain Foley, who was pale and bald, asked, "What about the druggist? And don't give me that line. He sold her vanishing cream."

Bonn said, "Well, as a matter of fact, Captain, he did. Vanishing cream, face powder, deodorant, hairpins – and a pack of chewing gum."

Foley shook his head. "That don't sound like no suicide to me. I know, I know – people have committed suicide on the eves of their weddings before. But a girl who's going to kill herself don't buy deodorants and chewing gum. Even if the river *is* only five blocks away, I'm not buying suicide. No, either she made a voluntary disappearance – in which case she ought to have her butt smacked, not letting the family know – or else it was foul play. And if she was attacked, she's most likely dead by now. They've been

412

through every empty building in the neighborhood?"

"Not only in the neighborhood, but in that whole section of the city," said Steinberg. "How could she be the victim of violence in broad daylight, at ten o'clock in the morning, in a place where everybody knew her?" But Captain Foley said the violence needn't have occurred in the neighborhood. A car pulls up to the curb, a guy offers her a ride, she gets in – what's to notice? And then the car drives off. She wasn't the kind of girl to accept a ride from a stranger? Then maybe it wasn't a stranger.

The story was in the morning papers, and the usual crowd had gathered – or rather, was circulating; the police wouldn't let them stay near the Benners' house. Mrs. Benner was in her room, having failed to fight off the effects of a sedative the doctor made her take. Joe Benner and Bob, red-eyed, were sitting together in the kitchen drinking black coffee.

"It was amnesia," Bob repeated for the thousandth time. "She wouldn't run off. Not Sally. Her picture's in the papers, somebody's bound to see her."

"Sure," Sally's father repeated, his face reflecting no such optimism. "Sure."

413

Bonn and Steinberg mingled with the crowd. They looked and listened.

"They ought to call in the FBI."

"Can't do that unless there's evidence of a kidnaping."

"They ought to drag the river."

"Evidence – whadayacall evidence?"

"They must of had a quarrel. Don't tell *me*. They had a lover's tiff, and the boy friend's ashamed to say."

"They oughta drag the river."

"My cousin he run out on his own wedding once. But a guy, that's a different thing. Know what I mean?"

The next day Mrs. Benner went on television and appealed to her daughter to return home or – if for any reason she was unwilling to do this – at least to communicate with her family. For the afternoon and evening news she was joined by Bob Mantin. He begged Sally's forgiveness if he had offended her in any way. He asked only that she notify them if she was all right. The minister of the Benners' church issued a statement.

But no one heard a word from her. The usual flow of evil communications began, by mail and phone. Sally's body was in an alley on the other side of town. Sally was being held for ransom. A woman had seen her from

414

the window of a bus in another state; she was coming out of a bar.

"Speaking of bars," suggested Bonn, "let's circulate in a few of them. For all I know the girl is what they say she is, but maybe she isn't. If there's any dirt, you hear it over the bar." Steinberg nodded.

Perhaps it is because Americans have guilt feelings about drinking during daylight hours that almost all bars are dark and dim. When the first place fell into focus after the bright street, the detective partners observed that there was a moderate gathering in the bat-cavern. An elderly woman with wild white hair and a cracked-enamel face was crooning into her beer, "I don't care, you go ahead'n laugh if you wahnoo, but I say, in my opinion, all these young girls disappearing: it's the white slave trade. What I think."

"Naa," said a sharp-looking young man a few stools down. "That's all a thinga the past. No mystery in *my* opinion. Girl changed her mind. Woman's privulidge, is'n it, Mabel? And she's afraida go home."

The man to his right met this suggestion with such an insufferable smirk that the sharp-looking fellow was nettled. "All right, Oscar," he said, "whadda *you* think?"

"I think they oughta drag the river," said Oscar. Bonn looked up. He saw out of the

415

corner of his eye that his partner had caught it, to.

"Weren't you over by the Benners' place yesterday?" Steinberg asked Oscar.

Oscar said, Yeah, he'd went over to take a look. But the cops kept moving everybody on.

"*You* saw that, did'n ya? Howdaya like that? 'Move along, keep moving,'" he mimicked. "No wonder they ain't found nothing out yet. Waste all their time like that."

Bonn said, "Yeah, well, I heard you make the observation at that time that they ought to drag the river."

"And I *still* say it."

Mabel ordered another beer. The sharp-looking man took a look at Bonn, observed Steinberg, affected a startled glance at the clock, and was suddenly gone. Steinberg moved into his place. "Well, now, Oscar, that's a long, long river," he said. "Where do you think they ought to start dragging? Because unless they pick the right spot, they could spend a year and not find anything. Where would you imagine is the best place?"

Oscar studied his face in the mirror. Bonn moved in from the other side. "From the Point, maybe?" Bonn suggested. Oscar snorted. Bonn, seemingly offended, said, "What's the matter with the Point?"

Steinberg said, "Well, where then? Come on, Oscar. I'm really interested."

"You guys reporters or sumpthing?"

Bonn nodded. Oscar brightened, turned to face him.

"No kidding?" he exclaimed. "You writing up this story?"

"I've got my car outside," Bonn said. "Why don't we take a ride down by the river?" Oscar thought that was a fine idea. He and Bonn went out.

Steinberg said to the bartender, "And who might that guy be?"

The bartender shrugged. "One of the old man Portlin's nephews. Old lady died maybe a month back. Portlin don't like to live alone so he invites Oscar to move in with him. What does Oscar do? Well, matter of fack, I don't b'lieve he does *anything*. Except play cards, drink beer, and watch the TV. And shoot off his big mouth, like for instance just now."

There were parks along the river, wastes, factories, and docks, some of them abandoned. Bonn and Oscar Portlin walked along one of the docks. "Look how dangerous it is," said Oscar. "Girl could of come down for a walk, tripped, and – zing! – in she goes. See what I mean? Maybe hit her head going over. Then she wouldn't come up or yell for help or nothing. You hadda lotta experience with incidents like that. Whadda *you* think?"

It was a pleasant day, the breeze whipping the water lightly. Sea gulls swooped and skimmed low, creeing to one another. Out in the river a tug passed slowly by with a string of barges. "I think," said Bonn, after a pause, "that it sounds very possible. I think we ought to tell the police. Oscar's reply to this was a short, blunt syllable. "Don't like the police much, huh?" Oscar's lip went *psshh!* "They give you a hard time? A bum rap, maybe?"

That did it. "Boy, you can say that again!" Oscar burst out. His rather nondescript face darkened.

Sympathetically, Bonn asked what the rap was. "Off the record, of course."

Oscar smirked. "Off the record? Statchatory Rape. It was a bum rap. She *said* she was eighteen. How was *I* supposed to know? She was a tramp, anyway. Everybody knew that."

Bonn said, gee, that was too bad. But he still thought they ought to see the cops.

When Oscar still demurred, Bonn took out

his badge. Then – in silence – they went back to his car.

"She was always such a *good* baby," said Mrs. Benner in a tear-choked voice to a lady reporter. "See this picture here. When she was only eight months old –" She showed the reporter photos and locks of hair and letters and school books – her daughter's life from infancy to womanhood.

What did Sally like to read when she was young? the lady reporter asked.

"Poetry," said Mrs. Benner. "She always liked high-class poetry." She blew her nose. "This little book here, now, she bought this with her own money." Mrs. Benner belonged to a class and generation which did not buy books; that fact alone would have served to grace the small volume even if it were not hallowed by having belonged to her missing daughter.

"It's the poems of John Keats. She always used to say to me, 'Oh, Mama, they're so beautiful!' She particularly liked this one – I know the name the minute I see it. Oh. Here. This one." She moistened her lips and prepared to read, following the line with her finger.

" '*Thou still unravished bride of quietness...*' "

419

Her voice was measured and proud. As the meaning of what she had just read penetrated her awareness, she looked up at the reporter, then over at her daughter's picture on the piano. Then she raised her hands and screamed, and dropped her face into her hands and cried again and again in her grief and fear and anguish.

"All right," said Steinberg, "so it was a bum rap, she was a tramp, she said she was eighteen. So let's forget that one. What else you been sent up on? We'll find out soon enough."

Oscar mumbled that he was never convicted of anything else.

"So you weren't convicted. What were you tried for besides this one? Nothing? Sure? Okay. Ever charged with anything else? What were you charged with?"

The man looked around the small cubicle. He tried to smirk again, but failed. "Ah, that was a bum rap, too. Wouldn't even press charges."

"What was it?"

Oscar swallowed, took another long look around. Then, not meeting anyone's eyes, he said loudly, "Rape. But she did'n' even press the charge!"

Bonn said. "What makes you so sure the

girl's in the river? Did you put her there?"

"No. Naa. I never even seen her."

"You kept saying the police ought to drag the river," Steinberg hammered away. "Why? You put her in the river, didn't you? She resisted you and you killed her. Isn't that what happened?"

"Or maybe," Bonn suggested persuasively, "it was an accident. You didn't mean to kill her. So maybe you made a pass – what the hell, it could happen to anybody. Only she was a dumb kid, she got scared. . ."

Oscar nodded slowly, his lips beginning to settle into their habitual smirk.

Bonn went on, "She started to run, tripped on that rotten old dock, fell and hit her head. Maybe it was like that, huh? It could've happened to anybody. Why don't you tell us, kid? Then we can wrap this up, you cop a plea, get a few months which you can do them standing on your head. Give us the details, that's all we want. We find the body, settle the whole matter. Let's have the story. The stenographer takes it down, we order in some lunch – you hungry, huh? – we get some steak and some French fries –"

The smirk was in full reign now. Oscar shook his head, slowly, admiringly. "I got to hand it to you," he said. "Boy, you must have eyes in the back of your head. Yeah,

421

that's just how it happened. She trips and falls and hits her head. I feel for the pulse – there's no pulse. The dame's dead. So, I mean, I panicked. I figured, who'd believe me? With my record. You know what I mean? So I threw her in the river." He looked up at the two detectives.

Bonn asked, very softly, "Where did you throw her in? Right where you showed us?" Oscar nodded. Bonn's sigh was echoed by Steinberg. For a minute no one spoke. then Bonn said, "Well, I better go tell them so they can start dragging. And then I guess the family has to be told. Okay, Steinberg, you get the truth out of this monkey –"

"But I told you the truth," Oscar protested. He was bewildered; the tone of the last remark had frightened him. "That's just how it happened, like you said. 'Accident.'"

His face bleak, the officer said, "That story wouldn't convince my six-year-old daughter, and she still believes in Santa Claus. You know what I think of when I meet characters like you? Suppose when *she* grows up –" Abruptly he turned and said, "Take care of him, Steinberg," and walked out.

Bonn drove his car three times around the block where the Benners lived. Finally he parked and started up the steps. "They ought to have the police chaplains take care of things like this," he muttered. His finger hesitated on the bell. A noise, a babble of voices, that he had unconsciously assumed was a neighbor's television, was coming from the Benner home.

He tried the door. It was open. He walked in.

The apartment was crowded, everyone shouting and crying and laughing. *Hysteria!* he thought. *It's finally hit them!* Mrs. Benner and a young woman were sobbing and clutching each other, rocking back and forth. Bonn turned to old Joe Benner, who was crying, tears running down his face. "Mr. Benner," he began.

"Oh, Lord, the police!" someone said. "We didn't tell the police!"

"Tell us *what?*" Bonn demanded. And then they all started yelling at once and Mrs. Benner released the young woman, who turned around to face him – and he saw that it was her daughter Sally.

Bonn sat down abruptly.

"Oh, I feel so ashamed," Sally said, starting to cry again.

Bob Mantin hugged her and sniffled, "Never mind, honey – never mind, honey."

"Why?" asked the detective. "Why did you do it, Miss Benner? Where were you?"

"Oh, it was such a silly thing – I'm so ashamed. It was just this awful impulse. It started in the drugstore when Mr. Felber said, 'Well, today's the big day,' and I said, 'I'm so happy, Mr. Felber.' And then I got outside and it was like I heard another person saying, 'Are you *really* happy? Do you *really* love him?' And I said to myself, Gee, I don't know! I really don't know. Maybe I don't love him. Maybe I was only desperate because here I am thirty years old and no one else ever asked me to marry him. And I thought, Oh, wouldn't it be terrible to get married if I wasn't sure? I was like in a daze. So I got on the bus and rode to the station and I took this train to Chicago. And when I got there, I read in the papers about how nobody knew what had happened to me, so I just took the train back. Oh, I feel so ashamed! I'm sorry if I caused you any trouble."

The detective stared at her. She didn't look very bright, but even so – "You just took the train back," he repeated. "You didn't even bother about a phone call or telegram! No, sis, you didn't give us any trouble. You only had every police officer on the force working overtime for four days, that's all! You only –"

But he was interrupted. A fat woman in

eyeglasses (Aunt Emma) said, "Well, aren't you the brave one, yelling at this poor little girl! I s'pose you're disappointed she isn't dead, huh?"

Bonn stared at her. "Well, excuse me, lady," he said. "But that's just exactly what I did think, and you know why? Because some psycho down at the jail just confessed killing her and dumping her body in the river!" And Bonn snatched the telephone and dialed headquarters. "Steinberg? Listen, this is all for nothing. Call off dragging the river –"

His partner said, "What do you mean, call it off? Where are you? At the Benners? Better bring one of them down to identify the body."

Bonn said, "*What* body?"

Steinberg said "The *girl's* body. They found it first thing. She was right where he dumped her in, poor kid. Her dress was snagged on a spike, that's why the body didn't come up. Bring one of them down to identify her. Better make it the brother-in-law."

Bonn hung up, feeling that he needed time to set Steinberg straight. All he could do was look at Sally Benner and tell himself that her disappearance had not been all for nothing, after all.

425

KELLY H. BLAU

"What Have You Been Doing All Day?"

With the early-morning sun pouring onto the pitted formica table she could almost pretend the prison didn't exist except as part of her imagination, that the wide ever-lengthening bars pressing across her bare arms and down the floor really were the shadowed panes of a plain kitchen window in a plain tract house. Soon her mother would call to her, "Shirley! Shirley! Do hurry, dear, or you'll be late for school!"

She smiled, remembering the elastic grip of bobbysox around her trim ankles and the scratchy wool of a bright plaid skirt against her young thighs; but instead of shiny brown loafers a pair of misshapen tennis shoes now flopped on her feet beneath the scarred chair, and the plaid skirt of memory was a wilted cotton shift that sagged limply between her knees.

The coffee in the heavy mug before her was bitter from having been reheated from the night before. Its taste reminded her that

426

her mother would not be calling her, that another day in this prison sentence was about to begin. Oh, they came to visit, her mother and the others. The girls, their hair fixed differently now, and the boys too – only now without the football uniforms that had made them so exciting. They smiled and smiled at her and she had to grin back until her mouth ached.

"You look so well, Shirley!" they said. Inanities dropped with the aggravation of a leaky faucet until she finally stopped her gay pretension and convinced them to go drivel elsewhere. But now, at least, there was a moment of peace, a pinpoint of quiet before the harassment began again.

As always, without enough warning, the alarm rang. Her teeth clenched and she had to remind herself to be careful not to ruin the orthodonture Daddy had paid for. Oh, God! That screeching bell! She could not ignore it. She washed her cup at the sink and filled a pail. The floor must be scrubbed first. It must shine and gleam so that you could eat from it, they said. The Man liked it that way. If it didn't glow he would look at her with a slight twist of his cruel mouth and say, "Well, Shirley, what have you been doing all day?"

Push the mop. Wring it out. The women

on television did it. Push it until the floor is spotless. Intermittently the bell rang. It would continue to ring until it was obeyed. Another order, another question. What have you been doing all morning? You are expected to participate! You must! Chain yourself to the oven until your face is raw from the heat and bake cookies and cakes until you retch with the sick sweetness. Jab your fingers with a thousand needles until your blood splotches over the stiff denim of unending piles of tattered dungarees that must be mended. Set up the padded board and iron, Shirley. Wrinkles and creases are forbidden here. It doesn't matter if your knees have locked in an agony of exhaustion. Everything must be cleaned and pressed. It's your duty, Shirley.

Dear Lord, I'm too young to be here!

Far away, the wailing began. Low, keening, rising now to the pitch of an air-raid siren. Come! Obey me!

But the floor must shine first! Hurry! Push the filthy mop for one last sweep, then put it away and answer the screaming.

The room now, and the screaming muffled not at all by the closed door. Open it, Shirley. It doesn't look like a cell. There are bright curtains and a brightly colored rug. On the bed the guard with the baby face that she sees in her dreams. So sweet, that face; her young heart had taken to it from the beginning and loved it. She had thought that here, at last, was the one who would comfort her in this place, perhaps even be her escape. But behind the child features was a meanness that delighted in thinking of ways to debase her. Bathe me, slave! Feed me and never act as though you do not enjoy every second.

Mutely she did the baby's bidding until he was content at last. His fondness for the bottle was a weakness she had quickly learned to use. With the warm liquid soothing his belly, he stared drunkenly from her to the ceiling and back again as he cooed unintelligible nonsense. She felt the bile rise in her throat at his helplessness, knowing he would demand again and again and that she must answer. His gurgling laugh pursued her down the hall.

Back to the safety of the kitchen now that he was satisfied. Perhaps she could steal a cup of tea before they remembered her. Just a tiny minute of respite. She waited for the water to boil and idled quietly to the window. The world was out there. Occasionally she had been able to see the normal people – calm, happy, everyday people who didn't know and couldn't understand the woman held prisoner in this place. Today there was only an old man walking a black dog. The animal strained and pulled against the leash. Poor beast, I know what you are feeling. The horrible choking stoppage of your throat so that you must gag or die as you fight to be free.

Oh, help me! *Help me!* I don't belong here! I'm innocent! No one told me!

The silent screaming echoed through her skull and her arm lifted to crash through the glass. Call the man! Free the dog! *Free me!* But the old man was gone and the whistling demand of the teapot made her cringe as she ran to obey it.

The hot tea burned her throat as she gulped it down and the sudden memory of her first cup of coffee made the prison place disappear. It had been after the junior prom. She and Buck had gone to an all-night diner for coffee and she had felt too grown up to tell him that her parents had never let her drink coffee before. It had seared tears into her eyes that night.

She could still feel the prickle of the tulle bodice of the pink dress on her arms. Oh, it had been lovely to be sixteen! Her hair had curled along her shoulders and brushed against the orchid pinned there. She had been the only girl at the prom with an orchid. But then Buck would do anything for her.

430

She had been such a popular girl. Every boy there had wanted to dance with her. Even the seniors and Peggy MacCracken's cousin who was already in college had waited on line. The music had played on and on but her legs were strong and firm and tireless beneath the wispy bouffant skirt. Music swirled again across her mind, her eyes closed, and her tight-lipped mouth eased into a smile.

Noise again. A banging, crashing, thudding of boots and the raucous laughter of the two jailers broke into her reverie. They burst into the kitchen shouting for food and tracking layers of mud across the floor. "Hey! Don'tcha know it's time to *eat!*" She poured the tea down the sink and quietly began making sandwiches, hiding tears of frustration at the soiled floor.

They took their places at the table, ignoring her as she moved about the kitchen, noticing her only when something more was required. It became a game to see how much they could spill. Milk from the carton poured across the formica, seeping into the cracks and dropping in slow motion onto the floor. She felt her anger rise but bit her tongue. It would never do to speak out. Soon they would be gone, back to whatever they did, and she would be left with the floor to clean

431

again, and the dishes, the windows, the beds – the beds, oh, Lord, the *beds!* It was so late and the beds weren't made!

The dirty spaghetti strands of the mop snatching at the remains of the lunch reminded her of a bedraggled pompon. Hers had been purple and orange. It had rustled like maple leaves in her upraised hands as she had jumped – laughing, crying in excitement over the touchdowns, goading the team on with a voice that became hoarse. Her legs had kicked, drawing the attention of the bench boys with their giant shoulders, their helmets on their knees as they knelt in homage to the contest on the field.

The door slammed and she jumped guiltily, banging her shin against a cupboard door. The Man merely passed through without looking at her.

He came after dark, the eternal briefcase clutched in his hand and his suit still immaculate. Did he ever really work or did he come only to torment? He glanced around the kitchen, his face a mask of supercilious contempt.

Once, when she had first come here, he had not mocked her. He had been kind and gentle, even eager to help her. But she had been pretty then. Now his eyes, when he saw her at all, held only ridicule or boredom and

432

his mind had thoughts only for the outside people – those important people who gave him his power to rule this place and the money to keep it running smoothly. The money was very important. He said so. She knew each time the raises came because then he would smile and be happy and things were almost as they had been in the beginning. For a while. Then he would begin to crave more power or decide his domain should be larger, more modern – and the bars would slam down again.

She held her breath, but this time he didn't ask the question. Her mind did it for him. Shirley, what have you been doing all day?" Doing all day? All day? Another day passed, time going, creeping away from her.

"It's raining again," he said, glancing at the patches of wet his feet had left on the floor. Then he was gone.

Bed at last. Lights out and beautiful soft darkness. The blanket chaffed at her chin and it was good to feel the realness of it. But it wasn't over. There was a sound and the Man was there standing beside her bed in the dark. He came to her often and once more her teeth clenched in agony. Not now, not again. She must not cry out. She must not! She lay and forced her mind back to fall afternoons and spring evenings, to pompons and corsages.

This is not me! This is *not* me! The words reverberated through her head. I can't stand this! No more! I do not belong here! Oh, sweet heaven, what would my mother say if she could see this, know what they are doing to me here? She didn't know it would be like this when she let him take me. I have to get out! I must go back where I belong, now, before it's too late.

She slipped from the bed and crept to the kitchen. There were no bars now, no locked doors. They trusted her, these omnipotent jailers. She giggled with teenaged glee as she slipped through the passageway into the dimness of the kitchen.

It was late. The rain was streaming in sheets across the roadway when the Man's mother drove past the house on her way home from a bridge party. She could see the lights blazing from the kitchen through the blur of the windshield and decided to stop. One of the boys must be sick. Certainly there was trouble of some kind. Buck and Shirley were always in bed by ten-thirty. Buck insisted on it.

The only sound in the kitchen was the dull splat of rain on the roof, and the rest of the house seemed as dark as the sky outside. The fluorescent glow of the overhead fixture spotlighted the litter of old high-school yearbooks and yellowed dance programs on the kitchen table. Happy dancing couples stared at her from a page dusted with the powder of a presed orchid. Cheerleaders arched in the contortions of pre-game frenzy and orderly rows of self-conscious faces grinned from beneath the faded, scribbled verses across dog-eared pages.

Whorls of dried mud marched haphazardly across the floor and the cutlery drawer beside the stove hung precariously on its hinges. Some of the knives had fallen to the floor to gleam dully in the silence.

Poor Buck. He deserved better than Shirley. The way she had let herself go! The horrible frumpy clothes she wore, and hiding – yes, *hiding* in the house all the time! You couldn't talk to her. She just sat twisting her red hands and staring at you like an imprisoned animal. It was ridiculous. You could hardly call Buck's lovely house a prison!

She pursed her lips, feeling a little silly. They'd obviously just forgotten to turn off the light in the kitchen. But she would just tiptoe down the hall and make absolutely sure everything was all right –

Buck was lying on his bed, blood oozing into the blanket twisted about his waist and blackening the lavender sheet beneath him. The two older boys were sprawled across the bunk beds, grotesque in the feeble glow of the night light. She didn't stop to look at the baby. She couldn't bear to go into the nursery room.

Neighbors called the police. They were frightened of the mad woman, grovelling in the rainsoaked lawn and screaming what sounded like "Shirley! Shirley! Oh, my God, where are you, Shirley?"

It was probably just a bunch of kids. The officers from the patrol car pulled on slickers and ran into the shelter of the stadium. Wouldn't you know the high-school janitor would start hearing noises in the middle of the downpour? The officers plodded up the ramp and looked out at the field where the white-chalk marking had begun to fade in the wet.

Shirley was marching in front of the home bleachers, her arms raised in a victory sign. The officers moved closer. Her face glistened in the glare of their flashlights. The lights wavered down over a faded flannel night-gown, plastered against her thin body by the rain.

As they watched, the woman suddenly crouched against the ground in a graceless squat, then rose into the air, arms and legs thrown out in spreadeagled abandon. Her voice rose over the drumming of the rain – a young, exuberant, exhilarated voice.

"Yea Team! Yea! Yea! Yea!"

EDWARD D. HOCH
The Way Out

Joyce Ireland first noticed the man in the elevator on a rainy Tuesday in October. Perhaps she noticed him because they were the only two without raincoats. She didn't need one for her daily trip to the bank on the first floor, and seeing him coatless she guessed he too much be on business inside the building.

He was a tall man, not handsome, with black bushy eyebrows that one noticed before anything else. Joyce came, in fact, to think of him as "the man with the eyebrows" when she saw him again on the same elevator two days later. She would have guessed his age at about thirty-five, though he could have been older, and she noticed at once that he wore no wedding ring. At twenty-eight, Joyce Ireland was a girl who noticed things like that.

She had lived alone in a little downtown apartment since the death of her mother the year before. It was a lonely sort of existence, which made her long for the faraway places

438

she'd never be able to see on the take-home pay she received from Worldwide Finance Company. In October, with another winter on the way, she had the distinct feeling that life was passing her by. Perhaps it was her looks that were against her. She'd never been pretty, and with the coming of the miniskirt even her unattractive knees were now revealed to the world.

That was why she began to notice the man with the bushy eyebrows. When he got into the elevator behind her for the third time in a week, she had the wild thought that he was trying to pick her up – a shy lover who had seen her on the street and followed her to the office. Now he'd present himself for her approval and she would get away from Worldwide Finance forever.

That was her first thought. The second one was that he was going to rob her.

Joyce made the trip from Worldwide to the ground-floor bank every afternoon at the same time – just a few minutes before the 3:00 closing. She always carried a large brown envelope filled with the checks and cash they'd taken in since the previous afternoon. Because of the nature of its business, most payments to Worldwide Finance were in cash – very few Worldwide

439

customers had checking accounts. The afternoon trip to the bank was a ritual dating from the days when a girl might carry a few hundred dollars down in the elevator with her. Now, with business increasing steadily, Joyce sometimes had as much as $5,000 in the bulky envelope, especially late in the week when their customers came in faithfully with their pay envelopes.

This day, a Friday, she'd made out the deposit herself, and she knew she carried $4,355 in cash and a number of checks. She clutched the envelope a little tighter but of course the man with the bushy eyebrows did nothing. There were three other men in the elevator, and they rode all the way down. Perhaps, she decided, the man was waiting for a day when he was alone with her to grab the money and run.

Though nothing happened on Friday she thought about the man all weekend, and she decided finally that he *was* a thief. There was no doubt about it in her mind. At one point, on Saturday night, she was in the act of phoning her boss, Mr. Melrose, to tell him but then she hung up. He'd think she was foolish, or ask why she hadn't told him sooner. Mr. Melrose was like that.

Besides, what did she owe the company? Not much for a measly $87.50 a week. Not when she was secretary and part-time bookkeeper and hadn't had a raise in three years. She was thinking about that last part when the idea came to her – slowly at first, in bits and pieces like a jigsaw puzzle. Suppose, just suppose, there was a robbery and the bandit got away with the money.

But suppose, she went on in her mind, the bandit lost the money too. Suppose she – Joyce Ireland – ended up with the four or five thousand dollars. Who would be the loser? Not Worldwide Finance – they were insured against robbery. Certianly not the bandit, who didn't deserve the money in the first place. It would be hers, all hers, like finding it in the street, like inheriting it from a rich uncle she'd never known.

With all that money she could travel to Florida or California, buy a new car and a whole new wardrobe that would make men notice her at last. She could leave the dingy apartment where she was wasting her life away – leave and be free.

On Sunday night, as the last piece of her plan clicked into place, Joyce decided to steal the bank deposit.

The man with the bushy eyebrows did not appear on Monday or Tuesday, and for a time she began to think it had been her imagination, that he never had planned to rob her in the elevator. She became nervous and irritable at work as she waited for the man with the eyebrows to reappear, and one day even Mr. Melrose was moved to comment on her mood.

"What's the matter, Joyce?" he asked after one of her outbursts. "Have a fight with your boy friend?"

She wanted to tell him that his remark showed how little he knew about her private life, but she held her tongue. " I just have a little headache," she answered finally. "It's nothing."

Mr. Melrose was big and jolly and red-faced and most customers seemed to like him. Sometimes they liked him even after he'd sent collectors to their homes or started garnisheeing their salaries.

"Take the rest of the afternoon off if you'd like," he suggested with rare benevolence. "Tuesday's always pretty slow."

"Thanks, but I'll be all right."

Nothing happened on Wednesday either, and she took to watching for the bushy-eyebrowed man on her lunch hour, hoping to see him somewhere on the street. But he didn't reappear.

By Thursday she was about to abandon the careful preparations she'd been making each day and forget the whole thing.

But it was the fifteenth of October, and the first and fifteenth brought even more payments than the usual payday. By noon there were people lined up with their payment books and their money, and by 2:30 Mr. Melrose was out of his office asking the other girl, "How much cash have we taken in so far today, Sue?"

The girl, a dumb brunette Joyce despised, looked at the column and replied, "Just $5,275, Mr. Melrose."

He nodded. "Joyce, you'd better go down with it now. I don't like that much cash in the office."

She nodded and picked up the big handbag she'd bought only a few days earlier. Then she waited while the brunette stuffed the money, checks, and deposit slips into the familiar brown envelope. "Here you are," Sue said finally, handing it over.

Joyce took the envelope and her bag and left the office, walking down the hall to the elevator as she had so many times before. As she stood alone waiting for the elevator to reach her floor, she'd half forgotten about the man with the bushy eyebrows. It wasn't until she stepped into the car that he suddenly

443

appeared and hurried in behind her. She felt her heart begin to thump with excitement.

There was only one other passenger in the elevator, an elderly woman who would be no protection at all. If he was ever going to do it this would be the day. She clutched the fat brown envelope closer.

The elevator made no other stops as it dropped steadily toward the ground floor. Just the three of them, silent passengers in a sealed world. Joyce waited.

The man shifted his feet a little and cleared his throat. The elderly woman simply waited. The elevator bumped to a stop on the ground floor and the doors slid open. There was the busy lobby, the bank – and nothing had happened.

The man smiled and allowed the elderly woman to step out. Joyce started to follow, and then he clipped her on the jaw with his fist.

It happened so fast she had no time to think. She fell sprawling out of the elevator as he snatched the brown envelope from her suddenly limp hands. He was running, the elderly woman was screaming, and hands were grasping at Joyce.

"You all right, lady?"

She tried to talk, to wipe the blur from her eyes, and she couldn't. For a moment she

444

thought her jaw was broken, but then words came. "Money – he took the money –"

"Don't worry, lady. They'll get him."

She put a hand to her jaw, feeling for the first time the beginning of a dull throbbing pain. Her next thought was for her handbag, and she clutched it to her. "It was the bank deposit," she managed to say as two men helped her to her feet. "He got away with it all."

A policeman came into the lobby, apparently summoned from traffic duty. "You all right – not hurt?"

"He – he hit me on the jaw, but I don't think it's broken."

"The guy got away, but there's an alarm out for him. What did he look like?"

"Tall, bushy eyebrows, black hair. About thirty-five."

"Ever see him before?"

"I –" She hesitated only an instant. "No, not that I remember."

He was writing it all down. "How much money did he get?"

"Over five thousand. I forget the exact amount."

"We'd better go up to your office," he said, taking her arm.

Upstairs, Mr. Melrose went into a state of panic. He barely asked how Joyce was feeling before he started pacing the office floor and wringing his hands. "What will they say in New York?" he mumbled. Worldwide Finance's home office was located there. "They'll think I don't know how to manage this place. They'll ask why I trusted so much money to an office girl."

"There was nothing I could do, Mr. Melrose! He took me so by surprise!" Her jaw was beginning to swell now, and she resented his attitude. It only justified in her mind what she had done.

The policeman took down the exact amount of the loss and went away. the brunette followed Joyce into the restroom and tried to soothe her, applying a cold towel to her swollen jaw. Finally, when she was alone, Joyce stole a glance into her large handbag. The original brown envelope with its $5,275 deposit nestled safely in the bottom, hidden beneath cigarettes, Kleenex, and a key case.

She smiled as she imagined the robber's face when he opened the envelope he had taken and found all those neatly cut pieces of newspaper.

Joyce spent the evening in her apartment, nursing her throbbing jaw with cold compreses. She'd counted the money as soon as she arrived home, and now she had it safely hidden inside a sealed plastic pouch in the bathroom toilet tank. It would be best, she knew, to keep it hidden for a time before spending any of it. No need to flaunt it immediately and attract suspicion. She knew there was always the possibility the robber would be caught and tell the police about the cut-up newspapers, but then it would still be only his word against hers. She was certain no one in the office had seen her make the switch in envelopes as she stepped into the hall. She'd been practising it every day that week without being detected.

The robbery rated a brief mention on the local news broadcast that evening, and the following day there was a half column story buried on a back page of the paper. Loan offices and finance companies were being held up nearly every week and there were no unusual angles to this one, not from the paper's point of view.

Joyce sighed over her coffee and decided to call in sick. It was a Friday and she felt like having the weekend to herself. Her jaw still ached and Mr. Melrose expressed no surprise when she told him she'd be staying home till Monday. "Take care of yourself," he managed to say. "You're more important than the money."

He must have almost choked on that line, she thought as she hung up.

She spent the rest of the day relaxing and treating her jaw, which seemed a bit better in the afternoon. The swelling had gone down, and a couple of aspirins relieved the ache. She was even thinking about going out to a movie or phoning a girl friend when the doorbell rang.

"Yes?" she spoke through the intercom.

"Police, Miss Ireland. We have a few more questions."

She sighed and pushed the buzzer, releasing the lock of the front door. In a few moments there was a knock on her apartment door and she opened it without hesitation.

She gasped and tried to slam it shut but he was too fast for her. It was the man with the eyebrows. His foot in the door, he shoved her back. She opened her mouth to scream and he quickly covered her mouth with a dirty sweating palm.

"No more, little lady, or I'll break that jaw for good!" She struggled, trying to get free, biting, clawing, but he held her fast. "I want the money. I came for the money and I want it. Where is it?"

She moaned under his hand and he took it away slowly. " No tricks now!"

"I – my arm!"

"I said no tricks if you know what's good for you. Now where's the money?"

The pain in her arm was excruciating but somehow she had to bluff him. "Didn't you get enough yesterday?"

He gave her a violent push that sent her flying across the room to land on the sofa. She turned and twisted, sucking in her breath for a scream – and she saw his knife.

He held it loosely in one hand, moving it just enough to catch the glimmers of afternoon sunlight through her window. "I'd hate to cut you up, little lady. You know what I got yesterday. Newspapers! Somebody took the money and it could only be you. I'm damned if I'm going to run from the cops for a job I didn't pull!"

"If there was no money in the envelope I'm as surprised as you are," she said, trying to keep her voice calm. "I didn't make up the deposit – the other girl did."

She started to rise from the sofa but he took a step forward and she changed her mind. Now that she had a good look at him, he wasn't nearly as dangerous as he'd been in those first moments. He still wasn't good-looking, but the bushy eyebrows helped to accent his deep brown eyes. His jaw was set and firm, the jaw of a fighter. "Cut the stalling and tell me where it is," he said, but his voice was just a bit softer, and the knife, still in his hand, was not quite so menacing.

"I saw you in the elevator," she managed to say. "Last week. I didn't tell the police that."

"Why not?"

"I don't know."

"Because you were planning to steal the money yourself, that's why."

She didn't answer that. Instead, she asked, "What made you pick on me?"

He shrugged. "I saw *you* in the elevator." Then, his eyes hardening a bit, he said, "Let's cut the talk now. Give me the money."

"I don't have it. The other girl must have switched envelopes."

"For what reason? So the bank would get cut-up newspaper?" He was growing impatient, and the knife moved upward.

Staring at it, Joyce knew she had only two real choices – give him the money and see her dream collapse, or risk the chance that he might kill her. Once she gave him the money she couldn't tell the police without implicating herself. He had her in much the same position she imagined him to be in. So it was give him the money or – a flash of inspiration! – offer him more money!

"What if I could get even more for you?"

she asked softly. "Would you let me keep some then?"

"More? What do you mean, more?"

"If I took more from the office. If I took another bank deposit and just ran with it."

"And have the cops after you?"

"What choice do I have? If I give you the money, I've got nothing."

He frowned down at her, not fully understanding. "You're a stupid broad, you know that? The cops would grab you in no time."

"Look, I'm offering you a deal. Take it or leave it."

"Spell it out."

"I'll get an even larger amount of money for you. And you let me keep what I already have."

"When?"

"Monday. As soon as the office opens."

He hesitated, but she could see he was thinking it over. "How do I know I can trust you?"

"What can I do? Tell the police and implicate myself? If I tell them I'll lose the money anyway. It would be the same as giving it to you."

"Show me the money," he said quietly after a moment.

"You'll take it."

He put away the knife. "If I'm trusting you, I should get some trust in return."

She saw that she had no choice, not if she wanted him to go along with her plan. She stood up and led the way into the bathroom. "Remember, there's much more I can get. If you slug me again and take this, you'll lose the larger amount."

"I undedrstand." He stood away from her, aware of her suspicions. His eyes widened a bit as she lifted off the top of the toilet tank. "Say, you're a real pro, aren't you?"

She unsealed the plastic wrapping and showed him the money. "Here it is, and here it stays."

He thought about that. "If it stays, then I stay, too. I have to protect my investment."

"You can't stay in this apartment all weekend."

"Why not? It's one place the cops won't be looking for me."

She had to admit the accuracy of his statement. "But what if some friends of mine come by? What if –?"

"Tell 'em you're sick, like you told the office. Tell 'em your jaw hurts." He grinned a little as he said it.

"It does hurt!"

He sat down, making himself at home. "I'm sorry about that, but it had to be done."

452

When she grasped that he really was going to stay, her mind was awash with possibilities. She imagined herself assaulted, or murdered in her bed. From there it was not too difficult to imagine herself running away with this wild, untamed man. "I don't even know your name," she said.

"It's Dave. That's as much as you need to know."

"Mine's Joyce. Joyce Ireland."

"I saw it in the papers."

She was nervous with him, as nervous as a girl on her first date. "Do you want – can I get you a drink?"

"Sure, why not? It's going to be a long weekend, baby."

They had a drink and then, because it was nearly time to eat, she took out two steaks she'd been saving for a special occasion. "You haven't told me anything about yourself," she said. "Where you come from, what you do."

He shrugged. "I was in the Army for a while. When I got out a friend and I stole a car. I ended up with a year in jail, and I guess that fixed my life. I've been running and robbing ever since."

"But – but you're so well dressed!"

"It's all an act. When you're trying to get

453

close enough to ladies to snatch their bank deposits, you don't dress like a bum."

They had another drink after dinner, and she talked about herself – about her mother and her childhood and the lonely life she'd led till now. "I suppose that's why I wanted the money," she said. "Once I guessed you were going to steal it I wanted it for myself. I imagined all the glamorous places it could take me."

"Where's that?"

"Oh, Miami or Las Vegas or maybe even Paris."

"You got big ideas."

"You have to have in this world, I guess, because everybody else does. Until this week I thought I'd be spending my whole life at Worldwide, working for Mr. Melrose."

She expected him to ask to share her bed that night, but he curled up instead on the living-room sofa. She could hear his snoring through the bedroom door before she finally dropped off herself.

On Saturday she had to go grocery shopping, and she asked if he would accompany her. He debated for a few moments and then shook his head. Too risky. She was surprised he trusted her to go out alone, but then she remembered the money was still in the tank. She was the one who must trust him.

But he was there when she got back, watching a college football game on television. She went to the bathroom and checked the money, and that was there too. She had trusted him and he had trusted her. Perhaps it was the start of something.

"You don't talk much about yourself," she said that evening while they were eating.

"You'd be bored with it."

"No. No, I wouldn't." She looked away, and when he didn't answer she said, "You know the first thing I noticed about you?"

"What?"

"Your eyebrows." She laughed and he laughed too – and he leaned forward to kiss her.

On Sunday afternoon she teased him into driving to the zoo with her. But he watched the animals with such studied detachment she knew he was thinking of his time in prison. The afternoon was not a success. When they got back to the apartment he was anxious to talk about the plans for the following day.

"How much money can you get on a Monday?"

"Collections and payments won't be too

455

large, but we might easily have a couple of thousand left over from late Friday business. Mr. Melrose always insists on depositing before three o'clock, even on the days when the bank is open later. He keeps what's left over in the office safe."

"So how much?"

She sighed. "Maybe six thousand or so."

"Will he know you took it?"

"Probably. Especially when I don't show up for work on Tuesday. I'll take the bank deposit down and just keep going. With the other money it'll give us more than ten thousand, Dave."

He averted his eyes. "You wouldn't like running with me."

"Why not?"

"Because I'm no good. I'm a crook."

"I guess after last Thursday I'm a crook too."

They sat up late Sunday night, watching an old movie on television. In the morning she packed a small suitcase, taking her two favorite dresses and the few items that would be important to a new life. That was all.

He drove the car downtown and she sat by his side, increasingly nervous. "I'll have to get us another car," he said. "This one will be hot."

"You mean steal one?"

"Why not?"

"I wish you wouldn't."

"You're stealing, aren't you?"

She tried to explain. "But it's just from Mr. Melrose and the company. In a way they owe it to me."

The money – the $5,275 – was in its brown envelope on the seat between them. She was sliding out when she decided to leave it there. It was too late to stop trusting him now. "I'll be down a little before three," she said. "Be ready."

"Don't worry, I'll be waiting."

She stood at the curb and watched him drive away, and somehow it all seemed right.

Mr. Melrose welcomed her with a smile and words of sympathy. The brunette, Sue, muttered something and bent her head over a ledger. Joyce went to her desk and began opening the morning mail. Before long it had settled down to be a day like any other Monday.

At 2:30 she totaled up the bank deposit and announced, "there's almost five thousand, Mr. Melrose – $4,934."

"Good," he said. "Joyce, I've decided to go down to the bank with you for a few days – just as a safety measure."

Her stomach turned and she had to steady

457

herself against the desk. "That's hardly necessary, Mr. Melrose. The robber's not likely to try it again so soon."

"No, but another one might. No sense taking any more chances. I'll go with you."

They walked out to the elevator and waited in silence. Her mind was whirling as she tried to think of a way out. Dave would have the car by now. He'd be waiting for her. She had to shake free of Mr. Melrose and take the money with her. Otherwise Dave would think he'd been double-crossed and take off with the original loot. And she'd be left with nothing.

The elevator arrived, empty. As she and Mr. Melrose rode down in silence, her eyes darted about the closed car, looking for a sign that would tell her the way out.

The indicator light went from 3 to 2 to 1, and then the car stopped with a little bump. She looked at the light and saw a B under the 1, and knew what she had to do. Mr. Melrose was not gentleman enough to let her out first. As he stepped out of the car she quickly pressed the B and the *Door Close* button and prayed. "Hey! Joyce! What –" His voice was silenced by the closed elevator door and she was dropping to the basement. Fast! Fast! Every second counted!

She'd been there only once before, looking

for an old filing cabinet, but she remembered her way. She was suddenly like a child, running in the near-darkness between piles of dusty boxes, finding her way out. It was the way out of all her past, her childhood and mother and self. The only way out.

Then she was free, breaking into the sunlit alley, running toward the street. She was right on schedule, and she was sure Dave would be waiting. They were a team, a pair, suited to each other.

He reached over to open the door for her. It was a tan Chevy, last year's model, and she didn't ask where he'd found it. "I was beginning to get worried," he said.

"Mr. Melrose came down with me. I had to ditch him."

"Then he's wise?"

She nodded. "He's wise now."

He wheeled the car around a corner. "Well, how much is there?"

"Almost five thousand."

"Good." She placed the envelope on the seat between them and his hand closed over it possessively.

"Dave?"

"Yes?"

"Where are we going now? Someplace far away?"

"I know a motel about twenty miles from here. We can hole up there for the night."

"The police will be looking for me."

"Hell, yes!"

"But I still feel good, Dave. It's what I wanted to do." She stared straight ahead, through the spotted windshield. "I don't mind about Mr. Melrose. Or any of it."

They were at the motel before 5:00, and he booked a single room for the night. She walked around a bit, not wanting quite yet the confinement of the room, and stood for a time at the edge of the empty swimming pool, imagining all the other pools there would be, in Florida or Mexico or California.

Then she went back to the room and found him just hanging up the telephone. "Who were you talking to?" she asked.

"Nobody. Room service."

"Oh."

After a half hour no one had come, and she thought he'd better call again. Then she suddenly rolled over on the bed. "Dave?"

"What?"

"Do motels like this have room service?"

"Sure, why not? You think I was lying to you?"

"Dave."

"Hell, what now?"

460

"Dave, why were you so certain I'd taken the money and not Sue, the bookkeeper?"

"I told you. We went all through that."

"How did you know I was at home Friday? You said I'd called in sick, but I never said it. Dave, how did you *know?*"

"What is this, anyway?"

Her stomach was churning again. She was off the bed, panicky, knowing only that something was terribly wrong. She ran to the door and flung it open, she had to get out of here – and there was Sue from the office, facing her, smiling.

She thought she screamed then, but she couldn't be sure. She only saw Dave's fist coming at her once more, and felt its jarring thud against her jaw. She toppled over, hitting the floor hard, but she didn't lose consciousness.

Joyce saw them embrace. Then Dave handed Sue the two packets of money and she stuffed them into her pocketbook. And suddenly they were gone. Together.

Joyce stayed on the floor for a long time without moving. When she finally got to her feet, her jaw was aching even worse than it had on Thursday. She sat on the edge of the bed and tried to think, but she couldn't. Later, much later, she reached for the telephone and dialed the police.

461

ANTHONY BLOOMFIELD
Just Like the Old Days

Fifteen years I hadn't been back, knocking sixteen. They'd rebuilt the railway station. The center I could scarcely recognize, it was all a pedestrian district now. From the taxi I looked down Castlegate, where The Black Swan used to be, and there was just this arcade of fancy shops.

I'd been booked in a hotel out beyond the Botanic Gardens, just off a new road. Standard modern sort of place, they're all alike, anonymous.

A sandwich and a pint, that did me for lunch. Then I got another taxi to the plant. It was in an industrial area, where the workmen's homes used to be.

It could have been a sticky session. After all, I'd come down to tell them it wasn't good enough, all these delays, they better sort themselves out. But he was sensible about it, the works manager, didn't try to shuffle the responsibility.

And he had his problems too: the papers he showed me - well, I had to admit our

Head Office wasn't altogether blameless. He asked me out to dinner.

I went back to the hotel, had a shower, and changed my shirt. Before I went out I phoned Mave at home. She put the kids on. Gary was in a hurry to get back to the telly, but Fiona rambled away.

"I really miss you, Daddy... What are you going to bring me back, Daddy" She'd have gone on all night if Mave had let her. I told Mave I couldn't promise for sure, but I'd try to get back late tomorrow.

Be good, she said. If you can't be good be careful.

You know me, I said, Old Faithful. She went ha-ha, but she knew I meant it.

We had dinner at the Royal, of course. It had been toned up since my day, not that in those days I was what you might call an habitué. After a couple of drinks in the cocktail bar I ordered lobster bisque and *filet de boeuf Stroganoff*. We had a bottle of Beaujolais with it, vintage.

He was a pleasant chap, the works manager. Not local. When I told him I'd been born and raised here, he asked me if I ever regretted having left. Frankly no, I told him, of course the place has changed.

He suggested we go on to a club. I knew

463

what that meant, strippers and gambling. That's not my scene at all. So then he insisted on driving me back, and out of courtesy I took him to the bar for a couple of brandies.

It might have been the brandies, but when I got to my room I wasn't a bit sleepy.

I switched on the telly, but there was something wrong with the picture and it was too late to make a fuss. I hadn't got a paper. There was a Bible, of course, or the phonebooks.

This plant manager, when I told him I'd lived here till I was close on 30, he'd asked me if I still had any friends in the town. Any old flames – wink-wink, nudge-nudge. I told him – it was true – I'd lost touch. I didn't mention Henry.

To a certain degree I suppose Henry had been in a corner of my mind, so to speak, ever since I got here. Ever since this trip was fixed up, for that matter. Now, for want of anything better, I got out the phonebook. There was one Henry Butterworth and two H. G. Butterworths.

After I'd left we'd corresponded for a time, then sent Christmas cards for a few years, but none of these addresses rang a bell. Of course, for all I knew, he might have left the district, too.

Without really thinking, I dialed the Henry Butterworth number. He turned out to be a retired schoolmaster. I apologized and rang off.

Then I started to dial one of the others, but I put back the receiver without completing the number. I suddenly wondered: do I really want to speak to Henry? Do I want to see him? So much water under the bridge, what would we have in common any more?

I'm not used to a big meal at night; because of the kids we normally have high tea. That's probably why, when I got into bed and put out the light, my brain was still hyperactive. I kept remembering the old days with Henry, however hard I tried to alter the direction of my thoughts.

When I got to sleep at last I had these horrible dreams. Something terrible kept happening to Fiona, over and over. It was a bit like watching the telly: I was detached, I couldn't influence the course of events, and I didn't feel very much. Except at the end of each episode, when it happened, an empty sensation as Fiona seemed to disintegrate before my eyes. Henry didn't appear in the dreams, as a participant I mean, but when I woke up I had this powerful impression of him, as if he'd been a kind of invisible presence throughout.

Next day at the plant things didn't go so well. The works manager, he seemed to be presuming on the strength of our social evening. I had to pull rank. Anyway, came four o'clock it became clear I'd need another day. I rang the hotel, then I rang home to tell Mave, but she wasn't in. She'd be fetching Gary from school, I supposed.

I think the manager expected me to reciprocate his hospitality, but one night out, that was enough for me. Back at the hotel I'd got the same room. I didn't bother to change clothes, I might go to the bar for a beer, then I'd have supper sent up.

I rang home again, and I couldn't understand it at first, there was no answer. Mave was always home at this time, so I had a little panic. Then I remembered she'd said, since I'd be away, she'd take the kids to see her mother. It was funny I hadn't remembered her telling me. I thought of phoning her mother's, but they were probably on their way back by now.

I dialed the desk to tell them about the TV. They said the engineer had gone off duty, but they'd try to find someone to fix it.

I didn't particularly feel like a drink just yet. They hadn't sounded very hopeful about the TV. The room, its impersonality, suddenly depressed me.

On an impulse I got out the directory and dialed the number   I'd started to dial the night before.

"Hullo, Henry," I said when he answered. I recognized his voice straight off. "Long time no see."

"Curly!" he said. "That's Curly," using the nickname no one had used for fifteen years. "Where are you?"

I told him. I told him what I was doing here.

We only spoke for a couple of minutes. He took it for granted, since I was in town, that we were going to meet. He lived on the outskirts now, but he could be here in half an hour.

"All right," I said. "Where?"

"The Mucky Duck, of course. Where else?"

"The Mucky Duck?" I repeated.

"The Black Swan, Curly. Surely you remember."

I remembered. I also remembered when I'd passed in the taxi that it had disappeared.

"No," said Henry, "it's still there. You'll

find it. It's changed, of course, but it's still there ..."

The Mucky Duck had certainly changed. It used to be a dingy, smoky tavern, not rowdy – not often – but always busy, with a rough disreputable clientele. Now it was colored lights, carpets, and piped music, and a few couples on their way to the pictures. All they'd kept was the name.

Henry was changed, too. And yet, somehow, he hadn't – not in the way the Mucky Duck had. He looked older, naturally. His hair was receding, and he was wearing glasses which he hadn't before. But he had the same way of speaking, even to the same expressions, and the same mannerisms I remembered. He was the same old Henry. After a couple of drinks the fifteen years faded away. It was just like the old days. In the old days we always used to start in The Mucky Duck.

"Right then," said Henry. We'd downed our second pints. "Onward Christian soldiers."

That's what he always used to say. Outside it was just growing dark. "Where are we heading?" I asked.

He looked at me quizzically. "Where did we always go?"

He meant The Markets. "Hasn't it all been flattened?" I said.

"Not entirely," said Henry. "You'll still recognize the old stamping grounds."

We walked through the center, past the Law Courts and the Town Hall. It was all dead as mutton. Back of Woolworth's we dropped into another pub to sustain ourselves on the way. It was part of the pattern, the old pattern.

Like any old friends meeting after all that while, we brought each other up to date. I told Henry about my job, and about Mave and Gary and Fiona. Henry had never married. He was still working for the same printing company, a little higher up the ladder now, that's all.

I wanted to ask him if he had any regrets about not having a family, about not having moved on. But I didn't. I suppose I thought it might have sounded patronizing. As it was, everything was easy between us, unembarrassed.

Opposite the castle neither of us had to say anything. We crossed the road to go into The Hole in the Wall. It was almost empty, but then it never had been a very popular pub, for some reason. It was just the first you came to on the edge of The Markets. From there we went on to The Fox and Goose. It was Scotches by now, that was the old pattern, too.

The Markets, between the castle and the canal, is the oldest part of the city. Narrow streets and alleys and stone steps, with a pub on almost every corner. It was because it was so ancient, I suppose, they hadn't pulled it down, there'd be preservation orders. Most of the slummy tenements were gone though, and quite a few of the pubs were boarded up. "You still come down here much?" I asked Henry.

"From time to time," he said. "Not so often as we used to. It's not the same fun on your own."

In The Nag's Head I remembered I hadn't phoned Mave. There was a pay phone by the Gents, but there must have been something wrong with it, I couldn't get through. The Nag's Head is in the heart of The Markets. It's a singing pub, and it was pretty lively. "Just like the old days," said Henry.

"It's just like the old days, eh, Curly?" he said again, taking my arm as we crossed Watergate. "Had some times, didn't we, the two of us, in The Markets in the old days."

"Fifteen years ago," I said.

"That's right," said Henry. "Of course, times have changed."

We were heading for The Volunteer, it was taken for granted. That's where we always ended up, at The Volunteer. "And we're fifteen years older," said Henry. "With age one becomes more discreet." He pressed my arm.

I didn't answer him. I knew what he was getting at, of course, but there was no reason to talk about it. Some things are better left unspoken.

Henry seemed to sense my feelings: he started asking me about Gary and Fiona, my plans for their education, and so on. He sounded genuinely interested.

We came to the square, just up from the canal. Even in the old days this part had been "redeveloped." The Volunteer stood on the far corner, just where it used to be, a barn of a place, a Victorian gin palace. Across the square was the Palais de Danse. I remembered when they'd opened it, in the Fifties. It was a big success. Now, though, something was wrong, there were no lights on. Then I read the poster over the doors, advertising a used-car auction.

Henry had followed my gaze. "the Palais closed five or six years back, he said. "They're going to pull it down and build a multistory carpark." We started across the square. "There's a disco down the

471

street, that's where the kids go nowadays."

The Volunteer hadn't changed much inside. It was my round, I got doubles again. I'd been mixing them on an empty stomach, but I was still *compos mentis.* All the kids from the disco, of course, they were dressed differently and had different hair styles and makeup and so on, but it was just the same as when they used to come in from the Palais. I felt confused, it was so much the same. The jukebox was deafening. There was suddenly a fresh influx, and four girls came and sat at a table close to where we stood.

"What's that?" I couldn't hear what Henry was saying to me. I was looking at the girls at the table.

"I said," Henry said, "how many was it altogether?"

"How many what?" They were real slags, the four girls, plain as old boots. Otherwise, of course, they'd have collected some boys by now.

"Was it six or seven, curly?"

"It was six," I said. "You can't count the other one, that was an accident."

"Right," said Henry. "Call that one an accident. Then it was six, I agree. It was six we did, the two of us." He turned away from me and shouted to the barman. It was getting near to closing time and they were frantically busy.

When Henry got the drinks he gave me both glasses to hold and pushed his way through the pack to the Gents. I moved away from the bar to a less hectic spot and put the glasses on a ledge. Some things are best left unspoken. It was the drink that had loosened my tongue. The drink and the atmosphere, the sense, so to speak, of *déjà vu*. But I blamed Henry for bringing up the subject.

He came back from the Gents. Where we were standing now, we were in line with the door. Some people were leaving, others pushing in for a last drink. "It must be, let's think, best part of a year since I was down here last," Henry said. "It's not the same fun on your own."

I seemed to recall he'd said that before, but I couldn't be certain. Truth to tell, the drink was getting to me finally. I'm not used to it, we don't drink at home unless we're entertaining. And Mave doesn't care for pubs. I remembered I hadn't phoned Mave. I didn't believe she'd be seriously worried. I hadn't said I'd definitely be back tonight. All the same, it depressed me not having spoken to her. When I'm away I always try to phone her once a day. Henry nudged me. "See what I see," he said.

It didn't register, straight off. I looked at Henry, blinking there behind his glasses. The thing about Henry – he hadn't really changed – he looked so inoffensive, so negligible. He jerked his head toward the door.

Couldn't have been more than fourteen or fifteen, and she showed it. They'd never have served her at the bar. She stood just inside the door, peering through the crowd. She was wearing narrow slacks and a white blouse. There was almost nothing of her, like a reed.

"Target for tonight," Henry said, and I laughed. It used to be another of his catch-phrases, like "Onward Christian Soldiers." I didn't like it, but I laughed. After a small pause Henry laughed too.

Quite a pretty little face, with her mouth painted bright red and soft brown hair halfway down her back. She plucked up her courage and came in. I supposed she was from the disco, she'd lost her friends, perhaps her boyfriend, judging from the anxious look on her face. She came right past us, squeezing through spaces that weren't there. She was teetering on those crazy wedge-soled shoes.

Then a gang of sailors lurched in, in their Navy uniforms. They were all fairly drunk.

One of them, he couldn't stand unsupported. Straight away they started larking with the four girls at the table.

The bell rang for final orders. It was my round so, though I didn't particularly want another, I asked Henry. He wasn't fussy, he said, he'd make his last. The reed-girl went out again, she hadn't found her boyfriend. At the far end of the bar a bit of a scuffle broke out, there was the sound of breaking glass, but they're used to that sort of thing in The Volunteer, and it didn't amount to much. When the barmen pulled down the shutters, Henry said, "The guillotine descends."

We went out onto the pavement. The pattern was you stood talking for a few minutes as the crowd started drifting away. In a doorway oppposite I thought I saw a white blouse, but I didn't say anything. One of the sailors was being sick against the wall. It was a mild night, smooth and misty, the sort of night I somehow associated with the old days. the fresh air was reviving me, I was enjoying it again, the nostalgia, so to speak.

"Curly," said Henry, "night's candles are burnt out," and we started across the square. The white blouse was gone from the doorway. We took the steps down by the side of the church. There were still a good few people about, mostly, you could tell, heading home from the pubs. At the bottom we turned toward the canal.

"It was six," said Henry, "we did together. And I'm not counting that redhead. What would you reckon the score stands at now?"

I didn't take it in. Perhaps I refused to take it in.

"Six in seven years. There's been another fifteen years," Henry reminded me. "Of course, I don't come down here as often as in the old days. As I say, it's not so much fun on your own." He looked at me inquiringly. "You don't care to hazard a guess, then." I just shook my head.

You see, it had never occurred to me he'd gone on with it. Gone on with it alone. So far as I was concerned, it was so much a thing of the past, it belonged to fifteen years ago. I almost never thought about it. I had almost forgotten them. All except, for some strange reason, the little redhead, and she was an accident, we never even laid a finger on her.

We'd reached the canal by now. I was in a daze. It's shattering, having something like that dragged up, that's been buried for fifteen years. I was a different person then. Henry, I felt – well, I felt he should have grown out of it, too.

We'd lost the other drinkers when we'd

started along the canal. The path used to be made of cinders, but now it was concreted over. As well as our own steps, I could hear, ahead of us, a clack-clack-clack, like someone chopping wood. Then, where the path passed the old brickworks, I saw her white blouse.

Henry, I realized, must have spotted her all the time. He reached into his jacket pocket. I knew what for without seeing it. It was like one of those dreams that keep repeating themselves, so you know what's coming in advance. He'd taken off his glasses, I hadn't previously noticed. His hand glittered.

We were walking more quickly than she was on those ridiculous shoes. She didn't start to run until we were less than fifty feet behind. By a strange coincidence it was just about here, running toward the tunnel, that the redheaded girl had slipped in the water.

In the darkness of the tunnel the white blouse stood out brightly, like a signal. Almost as soon as she'd started to run, her shoes must have come off – there was no more clack-clack-clack.

Henry was running a little ahead of me. Out of the tunnel, without stopping, he held out his hand, offering the loop of wire.

What I should have done, but you don't think, I should have taken the wire from him and thrown it away. In the water. I suppose I couldn't believe it, that this was really happening. Not, so to speak, in the present.

When I didn't take the wire, Henry gave a sort of grin. He was glad. We used to take turn-about, one holding her, the other tightening the loop round her neck. It was more exciting if you were the one with the wire.

We were only gaining slowly, the reed-girl could run. Though when we'd get to her, all skin and bones, she would be almost too easy. I remember that's what I thought, I couldn't help myself.

We were twenty feet behind. There was a scrapyard, and ahead another bridge. A voice called out "Jenny!" I think the caller must have been standing on the bridge.

He yelled her name again. "Jenny!" It might have been her lost boyfriend, there's no way of telling.

Henry stopped dead and I almost bumped into him. The man had come down off the bridge, and she ran into his arms. He was looking at us over the top of her head.

Without undue haste we turned and started walking back. The full enormity, it was just beginning to hit me. Henry put his glasses on again and dropped the wire back in his pocket. "Better luck next time," he said, with a little smile.

JOYCE HARRINGTON

The Tomato Man's Daughter

The River Man sat on the deck of his houseboat sipping a cold beer. While he sipped, he watched the Tomato Man's daughter.

Elva Mildrum moved up and down the long green lanes of the tomato vines, sometimes stooping, sometimes stretching, always filling her bushel basket with bright red fruit. She was a tiny one, the Tomato Man's daughter, but golden pretty and a hard worker to boot.

The River Man licked his lips and popped the top off another beer from the cooler at his side. The river lapped tiredly against the sides of the houseboat and the high white ball of the sun sucked the juice out of all the earth. Nothing moved, except Elva steadfastly picking tomatoes, and the endless hordes of mosquitoes that had to move or die.

"Hey, Elva! Come on down!" The River Man called across the grass slope that lay between the houeboat and the tomato fields.

Elva parted the dark green leaves of the tomato vines, saw him, and waved. The River Man pulled his sticky T-shirt away from his broad freckled chest. The shirt was stained gray with sweat, and sweat ran out of the gray stubble of his crewcut and down the creases of his square red face.

"Come on down, honey," he called again and waved a beer can temptingly in her direction.

Elva shimmered through the fence of staked-up tomato vines. On small bare feet she floated down the slope toward the houseboat. She carried a ripe tomato in each hand.

Like a fairy princess, thought the River Man. Just like a dream fairy princess. Sweet dear Jesus! He wiped sweat from his forehead with the back of his hairy freckled arm.

Elva climbed the narrow board that served as a gangplank. She stood before him and held out a tomato.

"Eat it. It's good," she said.

"Thank you kindly, Elva. I will." He took the tomato from her hand. "Will you set yourself down?"

"Pa sees me here he'll whip me," she stated sadly.

"Where is your mean old daddy?"

"Gone to Columbus. Told me to don't ever do anything but pick tomatoes."

"Well, he can't see you if he's in Columbus. Set down and take a rest from pickin'. Ain't healthy to pick all day in this heat."

"I dunno." The girl shifted restlessly around the cluttered deck and the River Man's eyes followed her hungrily. She wore faded blue shorts and a pink cotton blouse with the sleeves cut out. For all her work in the tomato fields only her arms were stained with sunburn. Her legs gleamed pale and dewy, and the downy golden fuzz on her calves seemed to the River Man like the pelt of a small defenseless animal. Her face was shaded by a wide straw hat.

"Come on, Elva honey. Set down and relax." He patted the aluminum folding chair beside his own invitingly. "Will you have a beer?"

Elva sighed and sat down. "Don't mind if I do. Thank you, Mr. Heskill."

"How many times I got to tell you. Don't call me Mister. I'm Woody to my friends. You *are* my friend, ain't you, Elva?"

"Yessir."

"Good. And I'm your friend. Now drink up."

Side by side they sat on the deck of the

houseboat. Elva guiltily watching the tomato fields and Woody Heskill, the River Man, watching Elva. He watched her as she took a bite out of the ripe tomato in one hand and noisily sucked the juice. He watched as she sipped from the frosty wet beer can in her other hand and belched softly after each sip.

He breathed in the sharp green tang that flowed from her body. All summer she carried the bitter pungent odor of tomato vines heated in the sun. It was in her hair and on her hands and in the shallow bony place between her small white breasts. The River Man stirred uneasily and marveled at how he'd never noticed Alva until this summer and now he couldn't seem to stop wanting more of her.

"Gettin' pretty warm out here, ain't it?"

"Mmm." Pale juice, and a few tomato seeds ran down Elva's chin. She wiped it away with the back of her hand.

"Might be a tad cooler inside. Would you like to go inside, Elva honey?"

"Don't mind if I do."

Elva ripened out of season. It was almost Christmas before the Tomato Man noticed that some stray seedling had taken root in his daughter's body.

"Who done it to you, Elva?"

"Who done what, Pa?"

"Judas Priest, girl! If you're old enough to swell up like a prize pumpkin, you're old enough to know what's been done to you. Who you been sleepin' with?"

"Nobody, Pa. I always sleep alone. You know that." Elva was mystified.

Earl Mildrum, tomato grower and lay preacher, accustomed to tidy platitude and comfortable euphemism in public and private utterance, was forced to be explicit. At the end of his embarrassed monologue Elva was enlightened.

"Oh, that," she said. "That was Mr. Heskill."

"Anybody else?" demanded her father.

"No. I don't think so," said Elva, trying to look thoughtful.

"You don't think so! Don't you know?"

Earl Mildrum launched into a jaw-breaking sermon, dwelling at length on the fiery torments reserved for wayward daughters and the shame they brought on the heads of their hardworking, respectable fathers striving only to raise them up clean and pure without the guiding hand of a mother who'd had the temerity to die of a ruptured appendix when Elva was a baby.

Elva, as always, listened rapt and uncomprehending to the words that tumbled

484

from her father's mouth. They were fine words, words of biblical certainty; damnation and abomination, fornication and harlotry. Elva loved the strong ringing sound of the words and thought that when her father spoke them he must be like the prophets of old telling the people how bad they were.

But she didn't really understand the words or their connection with events in the River Man's houseboat way last August. Hellfire couldn't be hotter than the tomato fields in August, and surely if she had to burn, as her father said she must, surely there would be a river nearby with a houseboat and a cooler full of beer. Elva waited, open-mouthed and vacant-eyed for him to finish.

"So he'll have to marry you, girl! That's all there is to it!"

Elva smiled, much taken with the notion of getting married, and said, "Can I have a puppy for a wedding present?"

After bashing Elva a few satisfying whacks with a handy tomato stake, Earl Mildrum left her howling in her room and marched across his winter-stiffened fields to the River Man's domain.

In addition to the houseboat Woody Heskill's armada included several rowboats and canoes, a perpetually deflated rubber

485

raft, a fiberglass fishing skiff, and the flagship of his fleet, an ancient PT-boat said to have seen action in the South Pacific. This relic perched on the slope overlooking the river well out of reach of high water.

The River Man had grandiose plans for scraping its rust and recaulking its seams, with the objective of a voyage downriver to Cincinnati. But year after year the old Navy veteran sat high and dry, manned by snakes and spiders and occasional children playing war games.

Earl Mildrum scowled as he left his own neat fields and stepped into alien country. Behind him his acres stretched brown and clean, waiting only for spring and the burgeoning of the queenly tomato. Four-foot tomato stakes lay bundled in military ranks and covered with plastic sheeting at precise intervals along the edges of the fields. Order prevailed in the Tomato Man's territory.

Before him sprawled chaos. Long yellow grass flattened by winter rains and shriveled by frost was studded with bits and pieces of broken-down machinery. Lengths of rusty chain lay in wait to trip him. The PT-boat loomed gray and menacing to his left, a haven for hibernating rattlesnakes. Across the fallow cluttered field to his right the

River Man's house strewed itself along a short rise overlooking the river.

Whenever Woody Heskill felt the need for more room in his house, he simply tacked on an addition and cut a doorway through to the adjacent room. The basic house was a square green shingled affair, but fore and aft, port and starboard, the house sailed off in all directions in a maze of salvaged brick and aluminum siding, fiberglass awnings, and the gray rotting timbers of an unfinished addition.

The River Man was not content with water transport as a way of life. His dooryard was littered with cannibalized cars, crippled motorcycles, disabled tractors, and a large shiny new camper, wheelless and foundered on four cinder blocks. It was the River Man's dream to construct for himself an amphibious craft in which he could sweep down the highways of southern Ohio, dipping into the river when it pleased him, emerging on the West Virginia or the Kentucky side, astounding both sides of the river with his marvelous machine. He tinkered on his dream in a weatherbeaten shack to one side of the house.

Earl Mildrum had difficulty finding the front door. There were doors aplenty, but none revealed a doorbell. He couldn't tell which door was intended to receive guests, especially a guest on such a diplomatic mission as his. In all the years the Tomato Man and the River Man had lived side by side in the valley, they had never been on visiting terms.

The Tomato Man rapped loudly on a door that had three small rectangular windows set diagonally into peeling veneer. There was no answer. He squinted off into the pale lemony winter sunlight that defined the River Man's property.

Acres of junk, he thought. It's a crying shame. Acres of junk and not a single thing growing on it ever. Except only weeds. He envisioned the field cleared of debris, tilled and tamed into fruitfulness. He could grow a lot of tomatoes on that idle field. He rapped again.

"You lookin' for me?"

The voice came from behind. Earl Mildrum turned slowly, searching the cluttered yard for a sign of the speaker.

"Over here," came the voice again. "In the camper. Hurry up, man. It's cold outside."

The Tomato Man spotted the close-cropped gray head protruding from the half opened door of the camper. He trotted over, picking his way carefully through scattered wheel rims and dead batteries. He stopped

488

at the narrow steps of the camper and called through the door.

"Woody Heskill! Come on out of there! I got to talk to you!"

"Can't talk outside," the voice replied. "It's too cold. Come on in, Earl. I seen you comin' across the field. Says to myself, 'I ain't seen old Earl Mildrum since the Lion's Club carnival last summer. Wonder what he's comin' here for.' Come on in, man. Don't stand there with the door open."

The Tomato Man hoisted himself reluctantly onto the narrow steps and entered the camper. He would have preferred to conduct this discussion outdoors in the neutral air, or at the very least in a large room where he could pace judiciously, gesture and declaim and maintain the advantage by weight of oratory. Inside the cramped space of the camper he would be at a disadvantage both by being well within enemy territory and by having his words and motions confined to fit the boxlike interior.

The inside of the camper was hot and fuggy with the smell of coal oil and stale food. A small heater spewed warmth and fumes into the atmosphere. The tiny sink was stacked full of used TV-dinner trays and a grocery sack on the floor bulged with empty beer cans. At the rear of the camper both bunks were a tumble of heaped bedding and musty pillows. Earl Mildrum eyed them speculatively.

Woody Heskill buttoned a plaid shirt over his thermal underwear and tucked the tails into his green workpants.

"Costs too much to heat that big old house," he said. "I been winterin' out here. Set you down, Earl. Bet I know what you come for. Time you got a new truck, ain't it? I got just the thing for you. It's down at bud Wither's garage. Ain't exactly new, but it's only got six thousand miles on her. Clean as a whistle and –"

"Hold on, Woody. I didn't come here to talk about no truck."

The Tomato Man slid onto the vinyl-covered bench behind the small pedestal table. Although he was short and compact, his bulky mackinaw jacket made it a tight squeeze. He was hot and uncomfortable, but felt that removing his jacket would lend the proceedings an unwelcome air of informality. Bad enough that Woody Heskill was perched on the rim of the sink with his feet swinging inches above the floor.

"You and me, we got to come to a little understanding."

"Yeah? What about? Care for a beer?" Woody reached down and unlatched the tiny

490

refrigerator. Earl could see that there was nothing in it but rows of pop-top cans. Woody gathered up two cans, but put one back when Earl said stiffly, "No, thanks. No beer."

"What do we got to understand? You got some gripe about my property being an eyesore? 'Member what happened last time?"

"No, it ain't that. I still think it's a shameful waste of good land. But that ain't what I come to talk about."

The River Man threw back his head and laughed. "I do believe you had your way, you'd plant the whole world in tomatoes."

"What's wrong with tomatoes?"

"Nothin'. Nothin' atall." Woody emptied half his beer can at one pull. "Well, what *is* on your mind? You got a face on you like a hangin' judge, and I can't wait to hear the bad news."

"Well. It's about Elva."

"Oh, it is."

"Ah – Elva is – Um, Elva's going to – well, she says you're the daddy."

"Oh, she does."

"Well? Is that all you got to say?"

"Where's your shotgun, Earl?' The River Man chuckled. "Suppose I say I never laid a finger on that girl!"

"Elva don't tell lies."

"No. Elva don't. Would you say she's just a tad too dumb to go tellin' lies?"

"Now, look here, Woody," Earl blustered. "She maybe ain't the brightest thing in creation, but you got no call to insult her. If she was smart she never would of took up with you. She's a good cook and does what you tell her to do. She'll give you no trouble. And besides, she's kinda pretty, even if I say so myself."

"She got all her teeth?"

"'Course she does. Wisdom teeth and all. And she don't smoke."

Woody shook his head and finished off his beer. "Anybody ever tell you you're a filthy mean old horse-trader? Suppose I say I already got a wife?"

"Now you're the one tellin' lies. Everybody knows you got no wife. Never had. Never would have if I don't make you do the right thing by Elva."

"Suppose I say I just won't do it." Woody aimed his empty beer can at the grocery sack and missed. "I'm too old a dog to get housebroke at this stage of the game. Why, Earl, I'd just make her miserable."

Earl Mildrum reared back and planted his forearms squarely on the little table. His chin jutted forward and his eyes narrowed craftily.

"Suppose I tell you that Elva's only seventeen. And suppose I tell you that unless you're prepared to walk nice and gentlemanly into church next Sunday afternoon, I am prepared to march that little lady right down to the police station where she will tell the whole story. Everybody knows that Elva don't tell lies."

"Like that, is it?" The River Man snaked another beer out of the refrigerator. "Well, well. I hear that old man Lutz wants to sell his houseboat. It's a lot bigger than mine, more suited to a family man, if you know what I mean. Elva sure does like livin' on a houseboat in the summer."

"I'll go see him about it."

"Why, thank you kindly. That's a fine weddin' present you're offerin'."

"If you'll agree to clear all that junk off of your big field and let me plant tomatoes."

"Share the profit? Half and half?"

"Sixty forty. Unless you're willin' to pitch in on the work."

"Sixty forty." The River Man laughed. "I'm a lover, not a field hand."

"It's a deal, then?"

"It's a deal. Care for a beer?"

493

"Don't mind if I do."

The Tomato Man's daughter became the River Man's wife with scarcely any change in the quality of her life. There was just more of it. She still kept house in her father's neat white cottage and cooked his meals for him. Then she would scurry across the fields to the sprawling heap on the river bank where she would chip away at the year's accumulation of rubbish and dirt, and cook meals for her husband and herself. Neither her father nor her husband suggested that they take meals together and thus ease Elva's chores, and Elva didn't think of it herself.

Once in a while Woody Heskill would look up from his tinkering and say, "Hey, Elva honey, don't bother cleanin' up. Place gets too messy. I'll just bulldoze the whole thing into the river and let it float away. Come sit beside me and have a beer."

And Elva would say, "Just a minute. Soon's I finish scrubbin' this wall" – or hauling this trash or washing this window or whatever she happened to be doing.

If there was one thing in this world that Elva understood, it was work. When her hands were busy she felt good. There was only one thing that made her feel better, and she yearned for summer when the new houseboat would float on the river and she and Woody could sit on the deck with the beer cooler between them, and then go inside when the heat got too much for them. Drinking beer in the house and then going off to the cold dark bedroom wasn't the same. It didn't have the same delicious feeling of playing hooky, of running off to sea and spiting in the eye of all the rules.

In late April, Elva bore fruit, a red-faced wrinkled girl-baby with a thatch of red-gold fuzz on its head.

"Looks like a little old shriveled-up tomato," said her father. "Elva, you gonna be able to help with wettin' out the weedlings? It's getting close to time."

"Sure, Pa. I'll be there."

Her husband said, "Now you just take it easy, Elva honey. Your daddy can afford to get himself a hired hand to help out this year. You're gonna have plenty to do takin' care of this little monkey. What you want to call her?"

Earl Mildrum spoke up first. "I think you should call her Amelia, after your mother."

"I think you should call her Earleen, after your mean old daddy," said the River Man.

The two men glared at each other across Elva's hospital bed.

"I'm gonna call her Dandy, 'cause that's

what she is. Just plain Dandy." Elva felt important with the baby cradled in the crook of her arm, and both her husband and her father waiting on her decision. "Dandy June Heskill, that's her name."

Dandy June lived in a laundry basket on the deck of the new houseboat. Woody brought an old rocking chair down from the house and placed it beside the laundry basket. For a week Elva did nothing but rock Dandy June and feed her, while Woody beamed proudly and poked at the baby's tiny clenched fists.

"Ain't she somethin' else?" he said. "You done real good, Elva."

The weather was mild and clear for May, promising a long hot summer. Good tomato weather.

Each evening the Tomato Man would trot across his fields and down to the houseboat.

"How you doin' there, Elva? Gotta get those tomatoes in next week."

"Doin' fine, Pa. Just fine. Me and Dandy June'll get those seedlin's in. Don't you worry."

And Woody Heskill would mutter, "Don't have to do it if you don't want to, Elva honey."

On the Saturday evening, in addition to

his reminder about planting time, Earl Mildrum said wistfully, "Elva, I ain't had a clean shirt to put on my back for three days. You gonna do some washin' pretty soon?"

Elva stirred in her rocking chair. "Guess I will, Pa. Guess I'll do that right now." She put Dandy June in her basket and took the basket by its two handles and drifted off up the fields behind her sternly marching father. Woody Heskill glowered after them and opened another beer.

By Monday when the truck arrived bearing the seedlings in long wooden flats, Elva was back on course cooking and cleaning, washing and polishing, swinging like a pendulum between the houseboat and her father's cottage. Wherever she went, Dandy June and the laundry basket went too. While Elva set out tomato seedlings in neat rows, Dandy June slept in the basket in the shade of a tall old elm.

When Dandy June cried, Elva sat under the tree with her, fed her and played with her, and dearly loved her fat red baby. Elva worked harder than she ever had in her seventeen years, and was happier than she could ever remember being. She felt she could go on tending tomatoes and Dandy June and the chores of two households forever. She felt important.

One morning, when the tomato vines were knee-high and the yellow blossoms and the green horny worms had both put in their appearances, her father said to her, "Elva, I seen some mole holes round and about. There's some mole bait down in the cellar. You put it out today."

Dutifully Elva went to the cellar and got the can of mole bait. She spelled out the label to herself. *Chopped Poison Peanut Pellets.* And tried to read the instructions. CAUTION, it said. LEAD ARSENATE. But the fine print defeated her, and she decided that the best thing would be to put a handful or so into each mole hole that she could find.

She deposited Dandy June under her tree and spent the morning searching out mole holes and dropping the poison in. The mole bait was a funny color for peanuts, sort of a pinkish gray, but it smelled like peanuts and Elva guessed that moles couldn't see very well anyway. Once in a while she thought of the little furry star-nosed creatures deep in the earth coming up to nibble at the poisoned peanuts. She didn't like to think what would happen to them after they nibbled. But Pa said to put out the mole bait, so she had to do it. And anyway they ate the roots of the tomato plants.

When Dandy June cried her lunch cry, Elva put the lid on the can of mole bait and put it back in the cellar. She picked up the laundry basket and carried it across the fields toward the houseboat. She was thirsty and thought a beer would taste awful good. She would sit in the rocking chair and sip a beer and feed Dandy June. Woody was out on the river somewhere trying out a new second-hand outboard motor.

As Elva crossed the fields, knee-deep in tomato vines, she saw someone sitting on the porch of the River Man's house. It wasn't Woody. Even at this distance she could see it was a woman. The woman just sat there on the top step with her elbows on her knees and her head in her hands. She looked tired. Elva decided to see who it was.

"Hi," she called out. "Hey, hi. You waitin' for somebody?"

The woman looked up, shading her eyes against the noon sun, but said nothing. As Elva drew closer, she saw that there was a small battered suitcase beside the woman on the porch.

"Hi, there," Elva said as she came up to the porch. She set the laundry basket down and Dandy June, who had been soothed by the motion, began crying again. "Nice day, ain't it?"

The woman looked at her with tired, aching eyes. "Woodrow Heskill live here?"

"Uh-huh. But he ain't here now. He mostly lives down on the houseboat." Elva pointed. "But he ain't there neither."

"Where is he?" The woman sighed.

"Oh, I dunno. Out on the river someplace. He comes and goes."

"Same old Woody." The woman sighed again. "Well, I guess I'll have to wait for him. Got noplace else left to go."

Elva picked up Dandy June to stop her crying and looked closely at the woman. She looked to be about forty years old, but it was hard to tell because of the dark circles under her eyes and the heavy makeup that couldn't conceal the tired lines of her face. The dark roots of her hair turned suddenly to dry brassy yellow about two inches from her scalp. She wore a sagging orange jersey dress meant for a bigger woman and high-heeled pointy-toed black patent-leather shoes. The leather was cracked and bulged over large bunions.

"Well," said Elva. "I got to go feed the baby. Are you hungry, Ma'am?"

"That your baby?"

"Uh-huh. Her name's Dandy June. Mine's Elva."

"You're pretty young to be mother of a

baby. I never had a kid. If I had he might be looking after me now, instead of me having to look up old Woody."

"Is Woody your brother?"

"No."

"Cousin?"

" No."

"Any kind of kin?"

"For what it's worth, he's my husband. though I ain't set eyes on him for fifteen, sixteen years. Did you say something about food?"

"Well, yes. Would you care for some lunch?"

"You're a good kid. Yeah, I could use some lunch. I ain't had anything to eat since yesterday afternoon. Used my last money for a bus ticket to get here. What did you say your name was? Mine's Lauretta."

"Elva. My daddy grows all those tomatoes over there."

"Yeah? And I bet you got a handsome young hubby who works in the fields and takes you to the drive-in movies on Saturday nights."

"No."

The woman looked sharply at Elva.

"You got a husband?"

"Oh, yes." Elva grinned proudly.

"Woody's not *your* brother?"

501

"No, Ma'am."

"And he's not your cousin?"

"No, Ma'am."

"Oh, my god. this is too good." The woman hooted. "Don't tell me. Let me guess."

Elva giggled. It was kind of funny, come to think of it.

"You mean to tell me that sweet little lump you're holding was fathered by that shiftless old river rat?"

Elva giggled and nodded.

"And you actually married him?"

"Pa made me. But it's okay. I don't mind."

"You don't mind!" The woman shook with laughter. "Oh, this is too much." She gasped and shuddered and her laughter turned suddenly to a fit of coughing that racked her frail body.

"Oh, Ma'am. Lauretta. Mrs. Heskill. Can I get you somethin'?"

The woman choked and put her head down onto her knees. Her answer was muffled in the skirt of her orange jersey dress.

"Got any whiskey?"

"Oh, yes, Ma'am. I believe Woody has some down on the houseboat. Can you make it that far?"

The woman raised her head and smiled. "Little girl, for a glass of sipping whiskey, I could make it to the moon."

When the River Man came in off the river, he found a party in progress on the deck of the houseboat.

"Hey, now, it's Woody himself," cried Lauretta, limp and feverishly animated in the rocking chair. She held the whiskey bottle straight-armed toward him. "Have a drink, Woody. Have a drink with Number One wife. And with wifey Number Two." She nodded and bowed elaborately to Elva.

Elva sat giggling on the deck. Dandy June in her laundry basket on one side, a neat pile of hard-boiled eggshells and empty beer cans on the other. "Havanegg, havanegg," she chanted. "Eatanegg, you old river rat. Whoops! Guess I ate 'em all."

Woody Heskill mopped sweat off the back of his neck with a blue bandanna. "Sweet dear Jesus! Never thought to see you again, Lauretta. What brings you here?"

Lauretta shrieked with high shrill laughter. "Smelled your whiskey clear in Dayton. Said to myself, 'The old river rat won't let you down, Lauretta. Might's well go see if he's still alive and kicking.'" She widened her heavily mascaraed eyes in a maudlin parody of sentiment. "Remember those good old days in Dayton, Woody? Me waiting table all day, and you sleeping? You never did like Dayton much. Dayton made you mean and sleepy." Lauretta subsided into sullen memories.

The River Man turned to his young wife. "You okay, Elva honey?"

"Havanegg. Havabeer. Havababy. Don't cry." Elva giggled.

"Is there any beer left?" Woody asked.

"Don't mind if I do." Elva sighed and fell asleep on the deck.

Woody Heskill reached into the cooler and pulled out the last can of beer.

"I'm sending Elva away. Should of done that in the first place. It's bigamy. That what it is. You should of told me you already had a wife."

"I did, Earl. I told you. You didn't believe me."

"You didn't say it so's I could believe you. I thought you was just tryin' to squirm out of your duty to Elva."

"Look here, Earl. Lauretta'll go away. She hates it here. She never did like the country life. That's why we split up in the first place. I'll give her a little money and she'll go away. Elva don't have to leave. It's only that

504

Lauretta's sick and tired and had a dust-up with her present boy friend. Just give her a few days to pull herself together and I'll give her bus fare back to Dayton. And she'll go. She don't want to stay with me. She don't even like me. She just needs a little vacation."

The two men stood in the dim cool camper, the Tomato Man short and square and angry, the River Man bemused by his need to hang onto Elva. Lauretta was in the River Man's house sleeping off the effects of the previous afternoon and evening, while a white-faced and repentant Elva, under instructions from her father, was removing all her belongings from the houseboat.

"Where are you gonna send her, Earl?"

"Where you can't find her. You ain't ever gonna see her again, Woody. And you ain't ever gonna see Dandy June neither. My daughter and my grandbaby are too proud to live sinfully with another woman's husband."

"Oh, stop shouting, Earl. That's my baby as much as it is your grandbaby. And Elva don't mind about Lauretta."

"No. Elva don't mind. Elva never minds. that's why I got to mind for her. and I mind a lot. She's goin'. Today."

Earl Mildrum stomped out of the camper

505

and marched away across the deep green tomato fields. Woody Heskill stood in the doorway and thought about how Elva had come to him. He hadn't really wanted her except as a pretty playtoy through the hot summer days. He hadn't courted her or paid much attention to her. He'd let old Earl bulldoze him into marrying her, and she fitted easily into his ways.

That was the thing about Elva. She was an easy person to have around. He'd grown used to the green tomato smell of her, to the warmth of her kitten-soft body in his bed. And then there was Dandy June. Woody tried to puzzle out how he felt about them, about losing both of them. He never thought or spoke of love, but it pained him to think of sitting on the deck of the houseboat with only the beer cooler for company.

Elva cried in the kitchen. Her clothes were all packed and ready for the trip. She was going to her mother's sister's place in Indiana. She didn't want to go. She rubbed the welts on her legs where the peach-tree switch had stung and burned. They only itched now, but Elva still cried.

The real hard pain was inside her. When Earl Mildrum had told her that morning that he wanted her to leave, that she must clear all her things out of the houseboat and that she and Dandy June would have to go and live with Aunt Millie, she had defied him.

"No," she said. "I ain't goin'."

"You're goin'," he said. "Nobody will known you there. You can keep your shame to yourself. Anybody asks, you can tell them your husband died in a car wreck."

"I ain't ashamed, and I ain't goin'. I got a husband. You made me get married. It's all your doin'."

That was when he'd cut the peach-tree switch and whipped her just as if she was a little kid and not a married woman with a baby. She had cried at first from the cutting pain of the switch on her bare legs, but she kept on crying long after that pain had turned numb.

Even as she wept, Elva's idle hands caused her misgivings. The kitchen was swept and clean; Dandy June was taking her afternoon nap. There would be no more meals to cook in this house. Or on the houseboat. Elva was waiting for her father to finish irrigating the long tomato rows. Then they would be off in the car on the long drive to Indiana. At the thought of the drive a new freshet of tears fell down Elva's cheeks.

"Got to find somethin' to do," she muttered.

She got out the big old kettle and a jug of syrup.

"I'll make somethin' for his sweet tooth," she said to herself. "I'll make somethin' sweet and leave it for him and he'll find it when he comes back from takin' me to Aunt Millie's. I'll be in Indiana and he'll be here and he'll have somethin' sweet to eat to remember me by."

She poured syrup and sugar into the kettle and added a tad of water. She put the kettle on the stove and stirred it a bit. While it was heating, she ran down to the cellar. When she came back the syrup was bubbling. She stirred and stirred and when the syrup was sticky and thick she poured in the contents of the can she'd brought from the cellar. It was a funny color, but after the sugar syrup turned brown no one would be able to tell the difference.

Elva stirred the mixture in the big iron kettle and her tears stopped flowing. What was it Pa always said? "The Devil makes work for idle hands." Yes. Well, it was true.

She smiled as she thought of coming back from Indiana after Pa ate the peanut brittle. Would they call her on the phone? Or send a telegram? Either way would be just as good. "Your Pa's dead," they would say. "Come home." And she would come back home and live on the houseboat and work in the tomato fields. Woody would still be there, but she didn't mind about that.

The sryup bubbled and thickened. When it was brown and so thick she could hardly stir it any more, she slicked it down with a gob of butter and threw in a spoonful of soda. The syrup foamed up and turned butter-scotch yellow. She poured the sticky yellow mess onto a cookie sheet and smoothed it out. All the lumps and bumps were covered with yellow candy. It looked real good. And it smelled real good. She set the cookie sheet on the window sill to cool.

Elva put the kettle in the sink to soak the sticky candy off. While she was scrubbing the stove clean, she heard a sound at the window.

"Psst. Elva. Elva, honey."

"Oh, Woody. You better go away. Pa sees you here, he'll whip me again."

"Elva. Come away with me. We'll get on the houseboat and float downriver. We'll go as far as we want to and then we'll stop a while. Just you and me. And Dandy June."

"Pa told me not to set foot out of the house until he's ready to go."

"You always gonna do what he tells you to do?"

"I guess so. I guess I just don't know what

else to do." Elva felt the tears starting up again, and scrubbed hard at the sticky kettle.

"What's this here?" Woody was poking at the hardened sheet of candy on the window sill. "It sure smells good."

"Oh, it's just some peanut brittle. I made it for Pa."

"Elva, I just don't understand you. He treats you like a dumb little puppy dog and you go makin' peanut brittle for him." Woody poked at the candy again. "It's hard enough to crack. Elva, break me off a little piece of peanut brittle. I just love homemade peanut brittle."

"Woody, get your hands off that. That's for Pa. Nobody else."

"If you want it, come and get it." Woody snatched up the tray of candy and backed off from the window. "This looks too good for your mean old daddy. If you don't come and get it, Elva, I'm gonna eat it all up."

Elva stood at the window. "Woody, put it back. Please, Woody. I can't come out there. Pa said not."

"Elva, you got to make up your mind. Either you're gonna go all your life doin' what he tells you or you're gonna come with me on the houseboat. I'm gonna set right here and eat this peanut brittle till you make up your mind which one it is."

Woody sat down on a stump in the yard and picked up a rock to crack the hard sheet of candy. Elva stood in the window and watched him.

"Please don't break it!" she cried. "Please don't eat it! It's for Pa!"

"Make up your mind, little lady. It's either him or me."

"Woody, I can't. I just plain can't. I don't know what to do." Her voice trailed off in a plaintive moan. She stood in the window and watched him raise the heavy rock and bring it down on the shiny surface of the peanut brittle.

"No! Oh, no!" she cried. "It was for Pa! I only meant it for Pa!"

"Well, Devil take your mean old daddy. He ain't gettin' none of this."

Elva watched as Woody lifted a jagged chunk of candy and put it into his mouth. His hard square teeth chomped up and down and he licked his lips.

"This is real good, Elva. You ought to come on out and have some." Woody ate another piece of candy.

Elva, in the window, shivered. Woody was right. It was either him or Pa. One or the other. Dimly she realized that if Woody wasn't there, she wouldn't have to make up her mind. She wouldn't have to go away. Pa would always be there to tell her what to do, and she could just go on tending to Dandy June, tending tomatoes, cooking and cleaning. She could be happy and busy and work hard without all this having to make up her mind between them. It would be better that way. Without Woody.

"Come on out, Elva honey. Come out and have a bit of this peanut brittle. It's real good. Come on down to the houseboat and we'll eat it all up and have a beer."

"I'm sorry, Woody. I really meant it for Pa. But you can have it if you want it. It's all the same to me. I don't mind."

Elva closed the window. She put the lid back on the empty can of mole bait and threw it in the trash. The kitchen was neat and clean. She sat down to wait for her father to come in from irrigating the tomato fields. He would tell her what to do next.